Things My MotherS Never Told Me

Things My MotherS Never Told Me

Yvonne Craig Inskip

AuthorHouse™ UK Ltd.
1663 Liberty Drive
Bloomington, IN 47403 USA
www.authorhouse.co.uk
Phone: 0800.197.4150

Published by AuthorHouse 07/02/2013

ISBN: 978-1-4817-9648-4 (sc)
ISBN: 978-1-4817-9649-1 (e)

Contents

About the Author

Since studying social anthropology at Cambridge University, Yvonne Craig Inskip has been a campaigner, a TV presenter, a magistrate, a City Councillor, journalist, student counsellor, university lecturer and an obituary editor. She was President of Newnham College Cambridge Alumnae and has written three books including *Learning for Life,* designed to help you find your personal learning style as an adult. She has an M.A. in Creative and Life Writing from Goldsmiths College, London University. And is a wife, a mother and grand-mother.

In the optimistic 1960s she fought for free contraceptive advice at a time when campaigners thought that if every child was wanted, there'd be no more abortions and child poverty She started life in war—torn London and is back again near Westminster Bridge, where she writes a blog on art by living artists on show in central London and freely available for the public to enjoy. **walktofreeartlondon.blogspot.uk.**

1

THE NUN'S LETTER

My ambitions start the day I discover I have one mother too many. And no father. At nine, I set my mind on being a nun; at thirteen a missionary. If I'm lucky I might even end up as a Christian martyr snapped up by a passing South American crocodile.

That would teach them a lesson.

One October Monday I slide out of bed feet first onto a rag-rug pegged out of scraps of orange and green, then cross cold brown lino to my school uniform. It lies on a dressing table with a heart—shaped mirror: a creamy Chilprufe vest, baggy navy winceyette knickers, and a navy dress with a red sash. And two pieces of linen, white as Communion wafers. The first is a piqué collar which I clip to my dress with a ring of snap fasteners. The second is a diamond lozenge to line those terrible knickers. Washing, then drying them every day on the wooden airing rack in front of the fire, is too much like hard work.

I've just turned six and school is still a novelty. I love it. I snuggle under the routine—prayers, lessons, playtime—as if it were a patchwork quilt. But this morning after our last hymn in Assembly, Reverend Mother holds up an envelope.

'I want every girl to take a letter home to her parents'.

I don't like the sound of this. What are 'parents'? Her accent makes 'parents' rhyme with 'ants', which get everywhere, live in colonies, make routine tracks, pass secret messages. I'm not sure what parents are but somehow I know there has to be a man in it somewhere. Many things I have at home—an upright piano and our tortoiseshell cat Tommy—but there's not a daddy in sight. Already I've heard of other girls' mysterious midnight epiphanies when fathers come home from the War and astonishing baby brothers and sisters appear out of thin air. No such excitements at the house where I live.

Tyna is standing in the scullery beside a copper where white sheets are being boiled.

'I've got a letter from Reverend Mother. It's for my parents.'

'It'll be the bill for your fees for this term,' she says quickly without looking up. How do grownups know what's inside an envelope without even opening it? I watch her wipe her hands on her cotton pinafore—a tiny pattern of faded tangerines and pale green leaves and as she does so she jags her gold signet ring on the olive green bias binding round the edge of the apron. She puts the letter on a dry bit of the wooden draining board.

'What are parents?' I ask.

Silence. She turns and wrings the rinsed sheets so tightly they squeak. It's as if she hasn't heard. She's made a bit of a mess by splashing soap suds on the flagged floor and I dip the toe of my shiny Start Rite lace-ups into the puddle and drag it round to make a proper circle. Tyna doesn't tell me off. I walk out of the scullery through the kitchen into the living room. I curl up on a rug in front of the fire and our patriotically-misnamed tabby cat, Tommy, climbs into my lap. Her tummy is swollen and knobbly. Some mornings I wake up to find kittens which I treat as tiny dolls and put to bed in a small hand-carved box from Switzerland. I keep them warm with bright blankets knitted by Tyna from scraps of wool. The kittens, like me, appear to come from nowhere.

As I sit by the fire I can hear the bell ring as customers walk in and out of our shop, called *The Corner Handy Stores.* Customers stand sedately in front of the counter to ask for packets of Persil, Typhoo tea and Bisto gravy powder, or, on Friday nights, a bottle of Amami shampoo, all stacked on shelves out of reach behind Bigga. Inside glass cabinets standing on the counter are the small things of life: drums of bicarbonate of soda—good for the digestion as well as cooking—strips of Aspro, boxes of Swan Vesta matches. The Rifle-the Shelves-Yourself-Shop has not yet been invented.

There's a bigger more up-market grocery store nearby with marble counters and girls in white overalls and caps. Bigga can remember how before the war they cut your butter off a huge slab and knocked it into pretty shapes with wooden ridged pats. She says it's on the up and up. It's called Sainsbury's.

Picture the three of us like dolls in a doll's house. The front's been taken off and there we are strung out along the ground floor. Tyna is standing in a steamy scullery at one end, in front of a big rectangular Belfast sink, sheets twisted like giant skeins of wool piled up on the wooden draining board beside her. She has a Craven A cigarette between her lips and is probably coughing but that sound is so familiar no one hears it. She's 37 years old, 5ft 2ins, with delicate bones, hazel eyes and pretty but wispy hair. She doesn't rate her looks. 'If someone picked me up they'd drop me at the first lamp post,' she'd say when warned about walking down a dark street in the black-out. Her hands are scaly and roughened by the hard work she has done since a child. The nail on the index finger of her right hand is permanently deformed and corrugated. She tells me often that it's her fault: as a child she'd disobeyed and kept taking the bandage off. I take note.

Bigga is at the other end of the house, at the front, serving customers. She is taller than Tyna and older, with thick black wavy hair and a body sheathed in a Spirella corset. The Spirella lady comes to the house for a fitting and I watch her kneeling beside Bigga and lacing up her tummy. Once the lady joked, 'If you have corsets which lace up at the back you need a maid or an understanding husband.' Bigga doesn't have either of those. When we shop at the big Boots the Chemist in Bedford, I'm the one who carries home the huge box of Energen bread rolls with its promise of getting slim. The rolls are as light as air and feel like paper in your mouth but don't seem to work any miracles.

I'm in the middle of the house, kneeling in front of the fire. I lift a sleepy Tommy off my lap and, with the fire tongs, build precarious castles and caverns out of glowing coals. I crash them all down with the poker and start again. Tommy sleeps through it all. I'm bored. I wander into the shop and slide behind Bigga to get to the cabinets.

'Please, can I play?' Sometimes if she's not busy, she lets me make pyramids and towers inside the cabinets, using the packets and boxes as if they were building bricks. But this time on the other side of the counter is Mr Blunt, a very deaf widower, comfortably settled on the wooden chair ready for customers with a long list. His string shopping bag is down on the ground among crates of soda water with silvery siphon tops and bottles of Tizer the Appetizer, a florid glowing fizzy drink with a sweet and slightly fruity taste. Next to them is a small sack of potatoes and one of carrots.

'I want half a pound of digestives,' he bellows. In a military row stand tins of biscuits like silver cubes, each with their own flip-up glass lid through which you can see digestives, custard creams, gingernuts, Marie, Bourbons and Cream Crackers. Bigga lifts the counter flap and slips through the gap to the customer side. She'll weigh whichever you choose—half a pound, two pounds or even a quarter of mixed—and you take them home in a white paper bag.

'Why haven't you got any cheap ones?' The broken biscuits left at the bottom of the tin are sold off at bargain prices.

'Because I didn't sit up all night breaking them into pieces. I went to bed instead, you silly old bat,' she says out loud and laughs. She catches the eye of the only other customer, tiny Miss Goodacre, always dressed in black, who tries to manage a tiny smile. It's only a joke but I hate it. What if Mr Blunt heard what Bigga was saying? What if Jesus and his angels came down and made the deaf man hear? They could if they wanted. The nuns said so. Jesus often did. Whenever he felt like it. I feel hot and red. I want to wee. I hide under the counter where the shelves are half empty because everyone says food is scarce when there's a war on. I push aside some old Oxo tins where Bigga puts the coupons cut out of ration books. On Saturdays we'll sort them out into different colours and then count them. That's how I learned my colours and numbers. I climb onto the broadest shelf. Inches away from my face I can see Bigga's apron with its tiny pattern of bluebells and purple violets.

'I'm a poor devil who's only got one person's coupons,' Mr Blunt is not happy, 'At least with a family you can get a bit of cheese big enough to see. Even a mouse would walk past what I get. The perisher wouldn't notice it was there. And you promised me a tin of salmon the next time I came in.'

'You haven't got enough points,' she roars, then hands him the smallest size across the counter. Bigga feels sorry for

Mr Blunt. He's the only one of our registered customers who lives alone and she says it must be hard being by yourself.

I lie there curled up and I stuff my fingers in my ears. If you close your ears no one's talking. If you close your eyes no one's there. Anyhow it'll soon be time for tea. I hope it'll be kippers.

That night I have one of many similar dreams. Tommy the cat sends me on an errand, first giving me a piece of paper folded in half. I run to the house of a friendly customer, Mrs Richardson, who opens the door beaming at me, wipes her hands on her apron, adjusts her glasses, and tries to take the message from me. But I know it's not for her. She mustn't see it. I know I'm at the wrong door of the wrong house and start to cry as I wake up. The door to Tyna and Bigga's bedroom is never shut and I can always go along the corridor to see them if I have a nightmare or ear-ache or there's a thunder storm. I climb carefully over Bigga as she is the nearest to the door, snuggle down in the crack between them and pull the cerise satin eiderdown over my head. The only time they tell me I'm a nuisance is on Sunday mornings when they want a lie in. I have to keep quiet and look at the pictures on the wall which are lakes and sunsets which they say is Scotland. I like the crinkly gold frames best. I mustn't play with the long cord which dangles from the ceiling above our heads and switches on the light because it might bang on the headboard and make a noise. If I'm too early and wake them up, 'No peace for the wicked' Bigga says, quoting the Book of Isaiah and giving me a hug, and

Tyna murmurs, 'And not much for the righteous either' then turns over to go back to sleep.

I love their bed. It's the place for sorting important things out.

'Why are you called Tyna?' I prop myself up on one elbow and stroke her hair.

'Because when you were little you tried to say 'Tiny Mummy' and 'Big Mummy' but you couldn't do it. So you said 'Tyna' to rhyme with 'finer' instead.'

'What were you called when you were a baby?'

'I was christened Doris Ivy Nellie,' says Tyna 'but I've dropped the 'Nellie'. It's such a mouthful. My father called all his children by three names. He was a stickler for getting things right.'

'Have I got three names?'

'No, just two. You're called Doris after me. That's enough for anyone.'

I turn over to ask 'Is that why you're called Bigga, because you're bigger than Tyna?' I prod her arm.

'Yes, that's it.'

'What's your real name then?'

'My Mummy and Daddy called me Gertie but I was christened Gertrude Annie when I was a baby.'

Their bed on Christmas morning is the best place in the world. I tip toe on the icy cold lino along the landing in the dark and slip into the space between them. I can see a lumpy white pillowcase at the end of the bed. I don't want to spoil it by letting my cold feet touch them, waking them up too early when they might be cross, so I keep very still. When they stir I crawl to the end of the bed and pick up the pillow case by the two corners at the bottom and everything tumbles out all over everywhere. Their bed is covered with parcels wrapped in crepe paper or tissue paper: could be hand knitted dolls' clothes, Glitterwax, Snakes and Ladders, Diary Box chocolates, a magic painting book where coloured pictures appear when you brush the page with water, fat wax crayons, a tin box of paints ('be careful not to cut your finger on the sharp edges'), a fine lawn hankie edged with handmade lace, and Enid Blyton's *Nature Lover's Book*.

An Aladdin's cave.

2

THREE'S COMPANY

Bigga was born in 1897, the year of *What Maisie Knew* and *Liza of Lambeth.* She lived at a time when artists painted ethereal girls in a golden glow, draped in loose sensuous robes, with pure hearts and ravishing hair. This photograph shows her at a Fancy Dress Ball where she won First Prize dressed as an advertisement for a shampoo she'd never used. I think Bigga looks just as romantic as any of the painted girls, with her circlet of ribbon rose buds and her voluptuous black cloud of hair, 'long enough to sit on' she told me. There the likeness ends. She was born into a railwayman's family in a small cottage at Clapham, a village three miles from Bedford, far away from artists' studios and bookshops.

I wonder when she realised she was ambitious for a life outside the village where she was born? Clapham was simply a string of cottages either side of a quiet village road pointing north west. In her mid-20s the person she called 'my angel mother' died of breast cancer one Good Friday. She was distraught. Her vicar sent her a sweet letter of condolence, describing the virtues of a woman of whom he was 'very fond', and reminding Bigga how much must now be expected of her. Bigga did her duty. As the remaining spinster daughter she kept house for her widowed father and her brother Percy, who'd been a prisoner in France during World War 1. But she continued to work and be promoted at a local firm, Marion and Foulger's, manufacturers of photographic mounts, frames and albums. When she was appointed Manager she was, she once proudly told me, the highest paid woman in Bedford. It was to her family cottage that she invited Tyna to join the household. Why? Because Tyna, a work colleague and a friend, was homeless. She'd been thrown out by her step mother. Where can she go? No single woman without family money can rent a flat on the unequal pay of the 1920s. So who is Tyna?

Here Tyna and I are walking towards one of our favourite places, Kew Gardens, where I might be taken as a treat after a bout of ear ache. Ear infections are a problem.

A few years later I'm lying on my side on the couch while Tyna pours olive oil from a warm teaspoon into my ear, which, yet again, is stabbing with pain.

'I won't have to have my tonsils and adenoids out, will I?' I once heard my mothers talking softly about a boy who had to have his out lying on the kitchen table and there was blood all over the doctor's hands.

'I don't think so. Now keep still. Shall I read you something?'

'No, I don't want a story. I want to see what it was it like when you were a little girl. Let me see your photograph album'.

'Say 'please''.

'Please, Tyna'.

When she comes back I'm allowed to sit up provided I hold my head on one side. I loosen the cord which holds together the stiff black pages of the album; nestle up to her, tickling her hand with the black tassel.

'That's my brother John sitting next to me in the boat. We're going for a trip on the Ouse'.

'People don't go on the river nowadays. It's empty—except for some silly schoolboys practising their rowing'.

'The Ouse used to be packed with punts and skiffs and canoes in those days. You took your picnic with you, moored up and had your sandwiches and ginger beer under the weeping willows. They used to say that on Bedford Regatta Day you could walk from one bank to the other stepping from boat to boat'.

'What happened if you couldn't row?'

'You could go for a trip in a motor launch, or walk up and down the Embankment showing off your pretty dress and meeting friends'.

I peer more closely at the photo. 'You've got your best clothes on. You might get them splashed and dirty'.

'Yes, in those days you always dressed up in your best to go out. A nice girl like me wouldn't be seen dead without a hat and gloves'.

'John's got a fountain pen and handkerchief in his top pocket. What colour's your necklace?'

'I can't remember—perhaps they were coral beads'.

'I think you're both trying very hard not to smile. Who was rowing the boat?'

'It would have been my father'.

'Tell me about him'. I know she loves to do that. He's dead of course, like her mummy and Bigga's mummy and daddy so I don't have any grannies and grandpas.

'He worked in an insurance firm. He was a proud man. Never left home of a morning without his kid leather gloves'.

'Did you love him?'

'Of course I did', she says quickly.

'Did he love you?'

'Go and look in the sideboard drawer'. By now the olive oil must have reached its healing destination. I'm allowed to jump up and rummage among Tyna's things: bundles of knitting needles of every size and colour clasped in thick rubber bands, and skeins of wool piled on top of knitting and crochet patterns. 'What can you see in the corner?'

There it is, a small black leather-bound prayer book.

'Look what he gave me when I was 19', she turns to the inside cover and reads, '*To my dear daughter Doris from her affectionate Father Christmas 1923. May God bless and keep you always*'.

Tyna's father had three wives, fortunately for her one at a time. Of her own mother, Laura, the second wife, she never spoke and I didn't ask. The third wife brought a double tragedy into the family. The birth of her only child, Annie Mary Florence, when Tyna was twelve, triggered off what was then diagnosed as milk fever and mother (and the baby?) were sent to an Asylum for a time. Perhaps Tyna's step mother never really recovered. Tyna told me she had to take over the role of maid-of-all-work running errands, fetching coal, scrubbing the pine kitchen table until it was white, and polishing lead grates until they were black. She left school that year, worked an apprenticeship in haberdashery shops and then moved on to Marion and Foulger's where she met Bigga. Several years later her step mother threw her out and Tyna moved into Bigga's family home in Clapham.

The best record of Bigga and Tyna's time together in the 1920s and 1930s is a bundle of black and white snaps, thanks to some genius in the late 19th century who hit on the idea of a cardboard box with a basic shutter area, a viewfinder you could hardly see though and a handle to wind on. The Box Brownie camera launched a new generation of photographers: Bigga and Tyna and their friends could for the first time take spontaneous candid pictures, as and when and where they liked. A camera, which cost a month's salary at the turn of the century, was now within their reach, and they made the most of it. They say that even Queen Alexandra's portable box of watercolour paints gathered dust.

So you can see Tyna and Bigga now as wedding guests, in cloche hats, high heels and patterned silks; or draped casually across a motor bike; in evening dress at a works' dance; lying on a grassy bank by the Ouse. In one picture five 'girls' in bathing costumes have made a human pyramid in the sea which is about to collapse as they're laughing so much. Bigga and Tyna looked forward to their seaside holiday for a whole year. Before 1939 you didn't get paid holiday leave, so they saved a small sum each week to pay a landlady for an annual treat at a Skegness or Cromer or Hunstanton boarding house.

I have two untitled and anonymous holiday photographs dated within a year of each other in the 1930s: 'girls' being eyed by 'boys' while walking along the prom.

This was taken at Deauville, France, photographer unknown. I like the wide empty sky taking up half the picture, and the men being playfully 'inferior', on the floor, submissive, casually dressed, captivated by beauty and slim elegance. The girls are pressed together, their arms twined round each other. The man at the front has his toes off the floor, like a dancer ready to spring into action. An astute dog, looking the other way, is bored to death. It's seen it all before.

It contrasts sharply with this snap by a friend at Skegness in Lincolnshire, with a Box Brownie camera. Here is the mundane, the plebeian—hair tousled, hands full of clutter, and crumpled frocks. But they also are pressed close, their arms linked; and judging from Ethel's smile (she's on the left) and the modest downcast eyes of Bigga (next to her) and then Tyna, these girls are enjoying a spot of appreciation every bit as much as the Deauville belles.

Saucy Ethel, on holiday at Margate, sends a Donald McGill postcard to Tyna. A plain, stout woman, her tiny black hat tied with a ribbon under her many chins and wearing a red and white striped blouse, stands amid a couple of Gladstone bags and some scattered suitcases on the station platform. Umbrella in one hand, she's lifting up her blue ankle-length skirt a few inches to show her voluminous frilly bloomers. A diminutive porter scuttles away, taking his trolley with him. *'I wish a porter would come and take my bags'* is the caption. Frustrated women are endlessly funny in the postcard world of the 20s—is it an expression of the unease felt in a country which had lost nearly a million men in the First World War? Bigga and Tyna loved these cards, selecting them from among the stock jokes of the time: naive vicars, poorly endowed men, adultery, nudity and honeymoon couples. On the back Ethel writes: *I am having a jolly good time. Plenty of boys to say nothing of a widower I've met.*

We hear no more of the widower. Instead Ethel gets engaged to a local boy, Ted, marries him and as far as I know, lives happily ever after. On their wedding night they find a bell tied underneath their bedsprings by 'the girls'. Tyna told me that she, being the smallest, was the one who first climbed through the cottage window the night before the wedding, after crawling along the branch of a pear tree in the garden.

But Bigga and Tyna do not marry, although Bigga got engaged to a Bertie Maxie. When he died of TB she cycled from Marion and Foulger's to Bedford cemetery to tend his grave each lunch hour.

They live happily in the Inskip family cottage at Clapham for several years. Perhaps they would have gone on doing so if Bigga's brother had not fallen in love. Percy is a hero. His picture is propped up on their mantelpiece—one of eight soldiers in uniform standing, squatting or lolling on the ground around a notice propped against a tin kettle: *Somewhere in France*. But World War 1 is over now and Percy is a grounds-man at Bradgate Road Tennis Club. His wages are low but he wants to bring home his sweetheart. She will only consent to marry him if her widowed mother comes too. She'll need her own bedroom. He wants 'the girls' out of the family house. Stalemate. Then uproar. Bigga's sister Amy pleads on their behalf, as do Arthur and Fred, their other brothers. Percy wins, but no one goes to the wedding. Tyna and Bigga move out to share a flat in Bedford and the following year they leave for London after finding *The Corner Handy Stores,* a shop they could run together in Hammersmith.

It's Christmas Eve 1936 and Bigga and Tyna are not tempted to stay in London for the festivities. I can imagine Tyna locking up the shop, Bigga tying up the laces of her Spirella corsets a little more tightly and setting off for St Pancras station to catch a London, Midland and Scottish train to Bedford. Never be a loose woman—better to be strait-laced. The bus then takes them to the end of Green Lane in Clapham where it's a short walk to Amy's house. They pass the lilac tree and the honesty plants by the garden gate and at the front door Eddie, Amy's husband, stands in the lighted hall strung with paper chains to welcome them. On Christmas morning the ladies go to church while the men have a tiny tot of whisky to keep the cold out.

Then there's nothing to beat Amy's cooking: a turkey with carrots, Brussel sprouts and roast potatoes grown by Eddie, followed by her flaming pudding, dowsed in brandy which she allows—despite its alcohol content—because, after all, it's Christmas.

But what about me? Where do I come in?

I'm eight weeks old and am probably being looked after by the kindly couple who have just moved in to the basement flat of our Hammersmith house, which is over the shop. I'm sure I come complete with tins of Cow and Gate milk powder, plenty of feeding bottles, talcum powder, safety pins, muslin squares and terry towelling nappies. You could say it's a good time to leave a baby with a stranger. She won't be upset because she's too young to know what's what. No harm in that, is there?

But the following Easter I too am on the train going to Amy's house at Clapham with Bigga and Tyna. Everyone loves the new baby. Or that's what I was told much later, because it was possible—just—to talk about those days after both my mothers were dead. I suspect that Amy and the rest of the family who had gathered for the Bank Holiday would have been surprised, but not astonished, when they saw me. Adoption and fostering were much less regulated then. And much less talked about. The visionary Dorothy Kerin, a single woman who founded the remarkable Burrswood hospital as a Christian centre of healing in Kent, adopted nine children—including two pairs of twins—in one year (1941), all of roughly the same age. It was generally believed that anything which took a child out of an institution and away from the stigma of being 'an orphan' was a good thing. Passing a child from someone who had too many to someone who didn't have enough seemed like a good idea. Think of Fanny at Mansfield Park, think of Dickens' child characters who ricochet round the text from person to person. Think of Silas Marner, the half-blind recluse who thought baby Eppie's curls were a heap of gold coins when he first saw them. No one put him on the child protection register, and Eppie was the making of him.

On Easter Monday, I imagine, the three of us caught the train back to Hammersmith because customers expect the shop to be open six days a week except for Bank holidays. Bigga and Tyna are making a go of it: I have the first page of a tall ledger recording the takings for the week when they took over the shop: £10 19s 3d, which contrasts well with the £16.5s 1d appearing by the time they reach the bottom of the page.

It looks (again, from the photographs) as if the three of us enjoyed those brief pre-war years: there are snaps of us on the Thames in a rowing boat, taking tea at Kew Gardens or walking in Ravenscourt Park, where fresh air was said to blow into city lungs from seven winds. Expensive walks too when my mothers pushed my pram into Kensington to get my hair cut in the hope that Harrods could save my precious baby curls. And trips several times a year to a photographer's studio in Beadon Road, Hammersmith.

Why so many photos? Who wanted them? I don't recall seeing them framed and standing on anybody's mantelpiece or sideboard and I never found an album. In one I'm gripping a replica of the full-sized Gold Cross pram I'd been pushed around in as a baby. A large baby doll beams back at me wearing tiny mittens knitted by Tyna and a poke bonnet edged with angora wool. An enormous white ribbon tied in a bow settles on my head like a toy helicopter. In another I'm standing by a mock Grecian pillar hugging a black toy Scottie dog, in a third I face the camera, arms crossed to show off my wrist watch. Do the camera, the clothes, haircuts, props and settings hint at my mothers' hope of a more prosperous future? Do they just want to record a few luxury goods and services which for the first time are within their reach? Or were they posted off to an Interested Party?

When I was two someone sent me a postcard of a Chapman's Zebra and her foal, from Whipsnade Zoo. It's a strange photograph because the mare is turned modestly away and her hind quarters fill half the picture. On the back it simply says: *I may show you this one day! The best to all of you, R.* When I read the card decades later I saw for the first time its bleak, cautious, promise. I did indeed go to Whipsnade Zoo and may even have seen those very zebras, but I was on a Sunday School outing, not with 'R'. 'R' turns up again in 1938. Now that Bigga and Tyna have a family of their own—as do most of their friends—their carefree summer holidays at a sea side boarding house are a thing of the past. My mothers rent a bungalow in Norfolk called The Fo'c'sle, with steps down to Snettisham's bare stony beach. Among their papers, which I read decades later, I found a letter from a considerate owner. There's no opening greeting and this is what it says:

> *Included please find the key to the Fo'c'sle which is yours from Sunday the 19th for four weeks up to Saturday July 16th. Should you like to have it a little longer let me know. I was out at Whitsun and I made a good clothes line arrangement as requested . . . . The bungalow is in good working order. The boat is outside and you can ask the neighbours and Leslie Parsons to launch it for you, only it must be brought up on the beach after every tide. You will find oars and rudder in the garage (key hanging in kitchen) and the rowlocks in the living room.*
>
> *The only thing is that the tank in the lavvy is not functioning properly so that you will have to chuck pails of water down the doings. Otherwise you will find a number of improvements, amongst others a much better and quicker paraffin stove for cooking*
>
> *All the best to all of you, R.*

And that's the last we hear of him.

Snettisham must have been quite a shock for my mothers. 'Skeggy', as Skegness was known to its friends, was a Purveyor of Fun, with tea shops, a concert party, dances and the luxury of a landlady who waited on you with your bacon and egg breakfast and perhaps your evening meal. If you were bored with the sea you could go to the flicks or walk among the neat Municipal Gardens with beds of sparky scarlet salvia and pink geraniums ablaze on the picture postcards you'd send home to your less fortunate friends. All Snettisham could offer was shingle, sea and sky.

But the holidays were a great success if the snaps are to be trusted. We're always with friends. There's one photo of Bigga standing by an open door of the bungalow looking radiantly happy with a shy little girl in a white frilly frock standing beside her. On the back it says her name is Betty. Bigga has me in her arms. In another I'm standing triumphant waist-deep in the sea with several people holding me upright, then we're on the beach, the grownups in deck chairs while I'm sitting wound up tightly in towels, almost mummified, my tin Mickey Mouse bucket and spade and a Brownie camera case at my feet. There's a strange spoof photograph too, which looks as though Tyna and Bigga are on the sea in a rowing boat with Betty and me. If you look closely you see that the boat is lightly beached on the shingle and what is angled to look like an oar is Betty's wooden spade. I look in vain for a photo of the three of us as a family or of my mothers as a couple.

War breaks out the following year and there are no more seaside holidays. The East Coast in particular has its shores wrapped in barbed wire, its sandy and stony beaches laced with explosives. By the mid-1940s, when the war had ended, Tyna has moved to Lowestoft and that becomes the place where Bigga and I make our annual trips. In 1953 a devastating flood rages down from Scotland along the whole of the east coast and The Fo'c'sle is just one of thousands of buildings swept away or irreparably damaged by the sea. 30,000 people have to be evacuated from their homes and 307 people die. It's the worst natural disaster of the twentieth century in the UK.

I go back to Snettisham once, in the 90s, and trace the spot where the Foc's'le stood. No children kicking a rainbow ball around, no teenagers messing about with a rowing boat, no woman hanging the nappies on the line. I take out of my bag a postcard sent in 1938 on that same holiday to a Mrs Maund. The card is from the owner's wife, who has a problem. She's forgotten her golden tie pin, the one with a pearl, because she left in a rush. She's coming up on Saturday morning, but if they don't meet, would Mrs Maund give the pin (and the key) to Mr Les Parsons, the trusty handyman / caretaker/ boatman. Overleaf she reminds Mrs Maund that the rent is 5 guineas a week like last year.

I read the card again. There's no such person as 'Mrs Maund'. 'Maund' is Tyna's surname but she's unmarried. Perhaps you need a story about an absent husband in days when letting a property to two spinsters and a baby would invite curiosity.

All the owner's wife wants back is her golden tie pin—the one with the pearl. Does she know she has already lost much more? As I stand on the beach Snettisham looks cold and hard, I feel the damp restless shingle under my feet and listen to the shuffling waves. The sky is grey, the sea is grey. I remember playing on a sunny Lowestoft beach with my children and my son Aidan's graceful movement when he leans back and hurls flat pebbles over the sea so that they bounce and dance and sparkle far out of sight. I pick up a small rock. Today I want to smash the sea, I want to hurt the smooth, complacent skin of the sea, scratch it and tear at its face.

3

HITLER'S BARMY, SO'S HIS ARMY

At first the blitz is fun. Tyna scoops me up and carries me down three flights of stairs. The house is very, very black. She doesn't dare to put the light on, but feels her way by pressing her shoulder against the wall. Everyone wants to do their bit so there are shiny black roller blinds at the windows to stop the Germans from peeping in. I find myself in a makeshift bed in the bath in the basement, the safest place when the Air Raid siren sounds. She's leaning over me singing the same lullaby again and again. Angels, I gather, are on sharp-eyed duty each night watching over me. Other times I'm carried downstairs to play Bigga's game. We creep under a wooden table covered with rough hairy blankets which hang low enough to touch the floor. It's like a little cave. Bigga is already there. 'Look' she says, 'We're trying to catch a mouse'. Tyna shines a torch where Bigga is poised with an upturned Bakelite beaker in her hand. We never catch one. Indeed I never even see one. I fall asleep in someone's arms while the bombs keep dropping. The All

Clear Siren doesn't always wake me but I sometimes know when I'm slipped back between the cold sheets of my bed upstairs.

When I'm a bit older Bigga says something to reassure me but it's a puzzle, 'In any case the aeroplane won't hurt you unless it's got your name on it'. I think about this. I imagine that Bigga knows all about bombs. Before the plane sets out someone has painted the names of all the people the bomb is going to kill in big white letters on the side. I worry about it at first but then comfort myself: how could anyone in Germany know our names anyhow, because we didn't know theirs?

But one day Mr Hitler finds us out. I'm standing in the doorway of the shop. When Tyna calls me in for a cup of Ovaltine, I turn and run inside. A lump of shrapnel hits the kerb. 'Missed her by seconds' the customers say. My mothers decide that enough is enough. Like many children I'm evacuated. To Clapham.

"You'll be alright with me, won't you, Yvonne?' I look up from where I'm sitting on the rug in front of the fire. Aunt Amy expects me to nod and I do so. She is monumental with indivisible bosoms sloping down to her waist at the angle of a church lectern. She makes all her own dresses—beautifully—to the same pattern, with tiny pin tucks running up and down her chest: fine grey wool crepe in the winter, fine ecru linen when it's hot. Since their parents died, she's the head of the Inskips. 'You can always rely on Amy to do the right thing', everyone says. Bigga and Tyna say they think the world of her but her straight black hair is drawn off her face and fits like a helmet. She's married to Uncle Eddie from Yorkshire. I love it when he lifts me up and swings me round and then I snuggle into his Harris Tweed jacket and breathe in his sweet-smelling pipe. One day even the Queen will say he's magic. She gives him a medal for all the wonderful things he's done to help win the war at his factory in Peterborough, but sends him a letter saying she's very sorry—she can't pin it on his jacket herself at Buckingham Palace because we're getting over the war and things are tricky.

I cry on Sunday nights when Bigga and Tyna climb into the bus to catch the London train without me, but walk back up Green Lane hand in hand with Uncle Eddie. He pretends he can't remember the way home so I skip ahead and show him how high I can jump until we get there.

Aunt Amy has always longed for a daughter. When a brother was born for Clarence, she scandalised the village by pushing Kenneth out in his pram in the layette she had been sewing and knitting for months. Every single garment was pink. Seven years later, when a miscarriage meant the doctor rode out on horseback from Bedford to tend her, he said, 'Don't worry, it would only have been another boy, Mrs Wilson'. I wonder what she felt when her younger sister turned up with a surprise baby girl. Amy had the proper home and family any little girl would be proud of, but she'd been passed over. As I grew up I saw Amy's eyes as dark and small, like berries which could give you stomach ache. It wasn't until Bigga died that I discovered I was a cause of her misery, but not for envy's sake, not for that reason at all.

Aunt Amy knows what girls are there for. to get married, and to do that you have to be pretty. I'm sitting sideways on a brown leather pouffe in front of her log fire, stroking the side of my leg where it itches, scorched by the flames.

'Careful, don't let your dress go too near the fire'. I'm wearing a frilly flouncy Shirley Temple dress with a high yoke and puffed sleeves. Aunt Amy made it for me and covered it in embroidery silks.

Shirley was the most popular child film star ever. She casts a big shadow over us girls who are neither cute nor pretty. In *Curly Top,* she's a sweetly precocious orphan. In real life she's six at the time. The plot is kicked along by her sparkling toes sometimes tap dancing on top of a white piano, sometimes leading her fellow orphans in a sing-a-long. Wherever she goes, everyone lives happily ever after. A shining example to small girls everywhere.

But she's a hard act to follow. I'm sitting on the pouffe because my hair needs remedial treatment. The delightful baby curls I once had are just a memory. They slipped through my mothers' fingers. The fortune they spent on Harrods' haircuts and on a daily anointing with a lotion—called *Curly Top* of course, and guaranteed to do the trick—is money down the drain. By the time I'm three I'm already past my best. The newspapers say that 55 golden ringlets are tossed every time Shirley Temple shakes her pretty little head, but without the curling tongs I can't manage one ringlet of any colour. My hair has made a life-long commitment to be dark, heavy and straight.

'Nearly done now, sit still. You'll be such a pretty girl'.

I don't like the sound of it. What would happen to me if I didn't turn into a pretty girl? I might not. Then what? She takes a pair of tongs—which look like huge blunt scissors—out of the fire, wraps a thick lock of my hair round one blade, clamps the prongs together and winds it close to my ear. She hums her favourite hymn under her breath:

There is a green hill far away/ Without a city wall.

I wonder where the hill is and why it's lost its wall. And why did it need it in the first place? After a couple of minutes she slides the tongs out and a long ringlet slips down on my shoulders. I poke my finger up it and can smell my hair singeing. Perhaps I can be a bride after all.

Despite much kindness I do not take to country life. I pine for my mothers. They come for visits at the weekend and keep catching the cream Birch bus back to London without me. I howl. To cheer me up my aunt takes me to the Cadena café for a glass of milk. When I sick it up all over the smooth damask table cloth, I'm fascinated by the white on white pattern. (Now when I see Robert Ryman's paintings, I'm back at the Cadena). Why have they left me behind? Will they ever come back to collect me?

In London the blitz doesn't go away. Aunt Amy reckons that she can only save her sister's life by threatening to return me to the bombs. She issues an ultimatum: sell up and all three of you come back to Bedford or else I'll put Yvonne on the train. They got out just in time. Records show that a high explosive bomb fell near our Hammersmith shop killing three people. Our shop and house were destroyed and haven't been rebuilt. Much later I visited Holy Innocents' Church where I was christened and met a man in his sixties, one of a gang of boys who had golden memories of a childhood making dens in our wrecked and abandoned corner site.

Bigga and Tyna had to get out quickly. Most of their capital disappeared. For a long time afterwards they gave filmic accounts of selling tins of Coleman's Vitacup, bottles of HP sauce, packets of washing powder called Rinso—a magic washing powder where *No Boiling Needed, Makes Clothes Last Longer, Does Your Washing Up Too*—at rock-bottom prices. Things which should have been eleven pence went for four, soap and bacon sold at half price. At the end things went for whatever anyone would give for them. But, safe and sound, the three of us move to another corner shop, this time in Bedford, and start again.

What's the first thing they do when they get there? Find a school for me. Where should I go? No, the local elementary school won't do. I must cross the town to the convent, a small private school run by nuns, Daughters of the Holy Spirit, who sailed over from France at the turn of the century on a campaign to evangelise Protestant England. Why am I enrolled at a convent since my mothers are not Roman Catholics, nor do they want to be evangelised? Religion has little to do with it. All many convent school parents want at the end of the day is a nicely turned out young lady. With minimum expense.

My mothers are probably encouraged by the example of Eleanor, the nicely turned out convent girl who lives in a pleasant house across the road. Eleanor is older than me, and she lives with six ladies: one mother, three aunts, one stooping, white-haired grandmother and a great aunt, Miss Goodacre. The house is full of cleanliness and kindness. When the door opens and you walk in there's a tangy smell of Ronuk polish. We're invited to tea: I remember home-made strawberry jam glistening in dishes with silver spoons dangling from the handles, iced cakes piled up on tiered plates, crocheted doilies, damask napkins, anchovy paste sandwiches, weak tea in egg shell china cups, sugar plopping in them from silver tongs. But food was rationed so though they might have grown strawberries in their garden, where did the icing sugar come from? Did Bigga slip an extra bag of something into their shopping basket even when they'd run out of coupons?

So that autumn I set off each day on the bus in my navy velour hat and navy mackintosh which nearly reaches my ankles 'to make it last, because money doesn't grow on trees'. My mothers ask their good friends across the road for help. Would Eleanor be my guardian angel and take me to and from school? They will pay her some pocket money. She agrees, but it turns out that she's no angel.

4

BIGGA TELLS A FAIRY TALE

WELL TRIED

I see in the van.
Dan has put his cap on
the peg. Nan is a nice girl
I am a good boy. Daddy
was good to me. We have

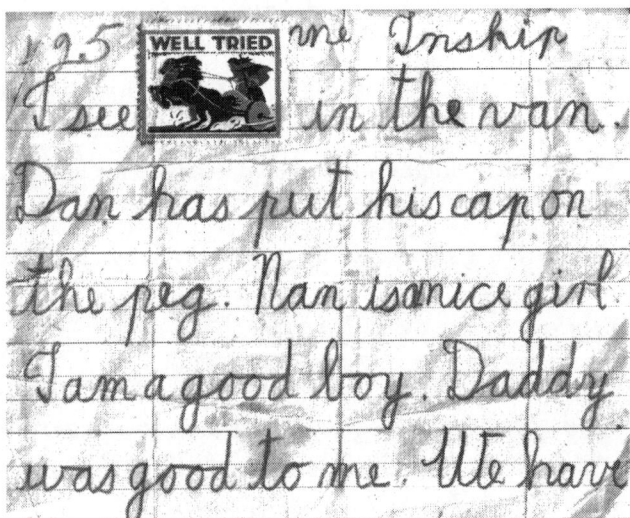

I never think about my Daddy. In my writing book at school I copy out sentences, taking each letter of the alphabet up or down so as to touch the pale magenta guidelines. I like it when Sister Madeleine sticks a coloured stamp on my page saying 'WELL TRIED'. Like the other 29 girls in the class I copy '*Daddy was good to me*'. and think nothing of it. It's just letters of the alphabet which need to be tall or short, curly or straight and it doesn't matter what they mean. 'Daddy' is an imaginary thing which only exists on a page and I don't care tuppence about him. His only usefulness is to help me get that stamp—especially the one with two horses rearing up. I'd like to stand at the back of the cart too. It looks windy and you might fall off. I think that's a knife coming out of the wheel. Sister Madeleine said there once was a Queen of England who had a knife just like that.

But things change about a week after I brought home the letter to my 'parents'. Bigga decides to deliver the cheque for the school fees in person. After school she's there, wearing her lovely musquash coat, the thing she likes best in the world. It's warm and silky and I love stroking it. In spring it goes to the cleaners and comes back in a special brown paper bag which hangs in the wardrobe until the grand opening next autumn. (Once, years later, I buy my own musquash coat from Oxfam in memory of her, rip out the lining, find a tiny maggot which I keep quiet about, wipe and reline the coat and wear it with pride until the animal rights movement makes it unsafe).

'Wait for me here, Yvonne', Bigga says as Sister Madeleine holds the classroom door open for her, 'I'll only be a few minutes'. I stand in the corridor outside and trace with my finger a snaky path along the thin black painted line which divides the green bottom half of the wall from the cream above. The paint is glossy and brittle like nail varnish, chipped too, but nobody's got any paint to fill in the holes 'because there's a war on'. There are one or two hard bubbles and I'd like to press them until I could pick them off like I do to the scabs on my knees when I fall down, but I daren't. At last the door opens and Sister Madeleine comes out beaming at me.

Overnight I become her favourite. I wonder what I've done.

'Yvonne, what colour do you prefer? You can choose first', she says holding out the box of crayons. I take the purple before anyone else gets a look in. Then I forget my hankie, leaving it in my coat pocket in the cloakroom when I need it in class and I'm allowed to fetch it without being scolded. I don't know why. Why did Bigga go to see Sister Madeleine? Is there something wrong with me? The two of them were talking about something that really happened, something so bad that they can't tell me.

At home I'm happy enough. Our corner shop has lots of friendly neighbours and I call them all 'Aunt' or 'Uncle', because it would be rude to say 'Gwen' or 'Tom' as they're grown-ups; and 'Mrs Jones' or 'Mr Dawson' would be rude too, because it would sound as if they were strangers. Sister Madeleine asks us to draw the house where we live.

'But all the doors and windows are open' she says, leaning over my shoulder. I wonder what all the fuss is about. We don't have rules like the convent at our house. Friends are always streaming in. My favourite is Aunt Mary who used to work for Bigga at Marion and Foulger's. She's an important lady now because she keeps getting in the local papers. Bigga reads out loud things she says like,

'Children are not bags of buns to be passed from person to person'. For my birthday she gives me a real leather satchel from Walsall and *Aesop's Fables,* full of beautiful and scary pictures. The customers are nice too, though Tyna says some are 'a perishing nuisance'. They keep coming to the back door in the evening when the shop is closed and we're having cheese on toast, because they've forgotten to buy something important like bread or a rasher of bacon or matches to light the coal fire.

Sometimes friends don't just pop in but they come to stay for weeks. The telegram boy comes on his bike with a golden envelope one morning and that very afternoon Baby Roger arrives from London with his mummy Esme, who used to live in Clapham.

'Don't touch!' Tyna calls out to me quickly, 'You'll cut yourself!' Roger's Carri-cot blanket still has tiny prickles of glass from the air raid last night.

Bigga went to Esme's wedding at the Park Lane Hotel in London and I've seen the photo but she's not wearing a lovely white wedding dress 'because there's a war on'. She even has a hat instead of a veil and I don't think that counts. I like his mummy and daddy but Roger is my favourite. He's supposed to sit up nicely in his high chair and eat his spinach. I don't think he likes it but he can't talk and everyone says it's good for him.

'Do you want to help, Yvonne?'

I have a lovely time swinging his daddy's watch-on-a-chain in front of him until a grownup can ease a spoonful into his mouth. The best bit is when he blows it out again over everything including my frock. I really like babies and want to have a lot of my own. I'm sorry when it's safe enough for them to go back to London.

But at school I begin to do silly things. We're standing in rows round the grand piano in the Assembly Hall with its beautiful parquet floor polished until it shines like an ice rink. We're learning to sing *Frère Jacques.* I want to wee. Badly. This is not good news.

'Open your mouths wide to sing a big 'Ding, Dang, Dong'', says Sister Cecile, the music teacher. I clench everything I've got as tight as I can. If it comes to the worst, I must put my hand up and wait until she sees me and say what I want out loud in front of everybody, 'Please Sister may I be excused?'. Then she'll say 'What's this I hear? I can't believe it. Why didn't you go before the lesson? Why can't you wait like all the other girls?' There'll be silence and then I'll have to walk alone the length of the Hall to the exit with everyone watching me.

I can't do it. My eyes fill with tears. At last I feel a warm trickle down my legs which dampens my Oxydol-bright snowy socks and dulls my shiny brown indoor sandals. Between my legs first my white liners, then my navy knickers turn wet and warm, then wet and cold. The bell rings, the lesson ends and I have to move.

'Choose your partner in silence and walk slowly and quietly hand in hand back to your class room', says Sister Cecile. No one wants to be my partner. As we move away I turn round and look back. I can see that the rows of gleaming wooden tiles, identical and spotless, now have one ugly pale stain. Sister Cecile doesn't say a word. There's no fuss. I am not scolded. Later an Irish maid in green overalls will come with a pail and mop and make it better. Tyna scolds me about my wet knickers and calls me a baby but she soon forgets. It is as if it didn't happen, but I know it did.

Eleanor from across the road takes me to and from school and sometimes we're best friends. At the weekend we climb the ladder at the end of her garden to drop down onto the banks of the Ouse. She teaches me to weave mats out of bull rushes to carpet the dens we make under the willows. We even light a bonfire and try to roast potatoes but they always burn. When we have something to eat I want to be first and Eleanor says I can be first but she must taste it first because of 'cook's privilege' so I'm always second. It's not fair.

But on bad days she strides ahead along the pavement on the way to school with legs that have had more time to grow. That's not fair either. I can't keep up. I'm out of breath and tearful, scared of being left behind in an unknown town, scared of being late for school, worst of all scared of being called a cry baby. Her voice streams behind her in the wind, coloured balloons of speech, acid green, bitter lemon.

'When we get to number 55 I'm going to put you inside the garden gate. It's the dentist's'.

I've seen the brass plaque on the fence so that bit is true.

'He will come out and drag you inside to his dentist's chair and pull one of your teeth out. It will hurt and there'll be all blood in your mouth'.

Eleanor does what she said she'd do. But the dentist doesn't. Of course he might have done—or he might tomorrow. But far, far worse than the prospect of a bloody mouth is being dragged into a place where I have no right to be, outside the wrong door of the wrong house, just like in my nightmares. Blind with tears I scrabble at the latch of the garden gate, get free and run the last hundred yards or so into school.

But at least that terror has a beginning, middle and an end. Much worse are Eleanor's tales of mad people. They don't live in a specific house, like number 55, but roam the streets having 'escaped'. I've no idea where they have escaped from but that's not as important as another question I hardly dare ask: what will they do to me if they find me?

'It's too terrible to talk about', she says.

Eleanor's stories make my heart knock on my ribs whenever I hear the voice of one particular lady who wanders about the streets of Bedford and Kempston. Some say that her son has just died in the war but others say it was her husband who was killed in another war long ago. Whoever it was she's trying to find out when he's coming back. On bad days she roams the streets shouting out 'June, January, August, February . . . I think she's mixed up because she doesn't know what happened and I wish someone would tell her. I never hear the end. I run home and hide under the bed with my hands over my ears, but I can't stop the voices inside my head telling me one day I'll be mad like the woman. Sometimes grownups say about someone they know that 'he's having a Nervous Breakdown'. Perhaps I'll have one. I daren't ask what you do if your Nerves break down and how everyone knows that they're broken when you can't see them because they're inside you. Tyna sometimes says I get on her Nerves, but they don't break down. She also says very loudly 'What a Nerve!' when someone does something naughty like telling her that her rose pink cardigan doesn't suit her.

I'm getting more and more confused. Before I'd heard about parents, I used to be alright. If anyone had said 'Who's your Mummy?' I'd have said 'I've got two Mummies, and one's called Bigga and the other's called Tyna because she's tinier'. Now I sense that having two mothers isn't quite the thing.

Why don't I simply go up to Bigga—or Tyna—while they are sitting at the table eating raspberry jam on toast and say, 'Are you my real Mummy?'

Because I don't want an answer. Because if one says 'Yes', the other will have to say "No" and I can't imagine either of them not being my Mummy. It'll never be the same and I like the same. Or they might both say, 'No, neither of us is your real Mummy'. Where is she then? Why isn't my Mummy with me? Babies are sweet and everyone makes a fuss of them and presses a silver sixpence into their tiny fists when they're born. What was so horrible about me that she went away? Is she in heaven? Did Jesus take her? Perhaps he's looking after her somewhere far away. Will he ever give her back?

Since the day when Bigga came to see Sister Madeleine, I'm getting more and more certain that I'm different but I don't know why. I think they're talking about me. I'm sure they're talking about me. Well, I must make sure they say something nice. The rich pickings at the convent, as far as I can tell, lie in being Obedient All the Time. That might do the trick. 'Look at her,' they'll say, 'what a lovely, obedient little girl. She always does what she's told'. That'll make me better than everybody else. It sounds like a tall order but I reckon it's worth a try.

I'm surprised to find that obedience turns out to be child's play. It's easy because the nuns, as God's messengers, have kindly set out the rules. It is as if, barely visible inside navy and cream habits, square faces peeping out of starched white coifs, they had once ascended up to heaven, had a good look round, ran their fingers along the shelves for dust and sailed down again—like the rain of bowler-hatted men in Magritte's painting—to make a little heaven of their own. Everything is as spotless as the Immaculate Conception and the nuns have rules to keep it that way. Dirt of all kinds is an offence. Matter out of place.

Not a dropped bus-ticket, apple core or toffee paper in sight.

'More elbow grease' urges Sister Madeleine as we scour our desk tops to get rid of ink blots and dribbles at a time when I was young enough to wonder in which cupboard tins of elbow grease were kept.

What else does an obedient girl have to remember?

Thou shalt not laugh nor cry out loud.
Thou shalt never, ever tell a lie.
Thou shalt not eat in the street, no, not even a wine gum.
Thou shalt never touch any other girl's clothes or body unless walking hand in hand in procession in church or in a crocodile outside school.
Thou shalt have a Cash's name tape sewn into every stitch of clothing.
Thou shalt pray without ceasing.
Thou shalt walk along the corridors between lessons in total silence it goes without saying.
Thou shalt never drop litter, nay not a crumb.
Thou shalt not run anywhere unless playing hockey or netball and even then only after the whistle has blown.
Thou shalt never wear Indoor Shoes outdoors, nor Outdoor Shoes indoors.

I am so fastidious about the last two Commandments that one day they nearly kill me.

WHAT DO I DO

when I hear guns, explosions, air-raid warnings?

I keep a cool head. I take cover.

I gather my family, with gas masks, and go quietly to my shelter or refuge room.

I do NOT try to "have a look."

I do NOT rush about alarming people.

I remember that a lot of the noise is GOOD noise — our guns firing at the enemy.

And I remember the odds are thousands to one against my being hurt.

Issued by the Ministry of Information

The kind government has put up this helpful poster telling us what to do when we hear guns and explosions, such as keep a cool head, don't rush about alarming people and put your gas mask on. I clearly hadn't read or understood them. My head is not cool and there are no people about for me to alarm. I don't even have my gas mask with me, which is a trifle injudicious on the morning when, as I'm walking to school, the Germans try to blow up the nearby railway station. I hear the bang, guess it's a bomb and give myself permission to move to a fast walk. A Sixth Former flies past on a bike in a flash of silver and blue.

'For heaven's sake run! There's been a bomb on the County Theatre and there's one on the railway line that might go off! Hurry up!'

I begin to walk very fast indeed, but keep it decent because not only do nice girls refuse to eat wine gums in the street but they never ever run in the street either. The nuns know what well-bred girls do and don't do, and I really want to be well-bred. Then I hear another bang even closer and run until I can't get my breath and my throat hurts and my heart is very noisy. At the school entrance I push open the heavy metal and glass door. I can hardly find my peg because my eyes are bleary with tears. I want to go to the toilet.

In the cloakroom I untie my tan Start Rite lace-ups (Outdoor Shoes) and fish around in my shoe bag for my brown Clark's sandals (Indoor Shoes). A nun bursts in and sees me fumbling. A stream of French fills every corner of the cloakroom. She grabs my hand and drags me off to a corridor which has been lined with bare bricks to reinforce it against the bombs. She pushes me down on the narrow bench and I sit squeezed up tight in a row of girls chanting Hail Marys and Our Fathers until the All Clear sounds. I'm not afraid, just cross. No-one has told me that in God's scheme of things escaping from a bomb is more important than the rule about Never Wearing Outdoor Shoes Inside. It's enough to make a girl despair. How am I ever going to be able to second-guess His mind if He's so fickle and unpredictable?

But it's not God's capricious nature which finally convinces me that being Obedient isn't getting me anywhere. In a world where everyone obeys, it lacks star quality. For in the convent we can't stop ourselves being good. The nuns care about us, they know our names; they don't go home to their families in the evening and talk about the football results or the price of coal. If anything goes wrong, they're always there, our Personal Safety Zone, a giant net ready to catch the wounded and fallen as we wobble towards adolescence. Who can argue with that? I've got to branch out into something new. I'll try to be Very Clever, and see where that gets me.

'Sums today' says Sister Madeleine, handing out small sheets of card wrapped in cellophane paper, each with simple sums written on it in a beautiful French hand. I copy it carefully on to the pale turquoise grid of my squared arithmetic exercise book and work it out. Each sum has one perfect answer and all I have to do is to find it. I'm good at that. When I was little I hurried up to learn my numbers quickly because I was bored watching the grownups having fun playing cards. They said I made myself a perishing nuisance. It came to a head one Christmas Day.

'Each and every one of them is someone's son', says Aunt Amy of the German prisoners-of-war housed in a camp by the golf links at the end of Green Lane, 'I'd like to think someone would look after my boys if they got captured'.

So an extra leaf is put in the pale oak table and two of them sit down with us to dinner. It means that the back of my favourite cousin Lance is scorched by the fire and I am squashed against the wall in a space so small that when the plates are cleared away my only escape is to slip down under the table and find my way out through grown ups' legs past the overhanging white lace tablecloth. I'm careful not to drop the sticky lucky sixpence which I, as the only child present, always find in my slice of Christmas pudding.

The men settle for whist while the women wash up. After the King's Speech on the wireless the cards are shuffled again. The Germans have picked up the rules by watching the men play and Uncle Eddie gives them a heap of coins so they can join in. The kitty in the middle is mostly half pennies but sometimes someone puts a shiny three-penny bit in to spice things up. I make such a fuss at being left out—after all the Germans are playing and they can't even talk English—they have to promise to teach me Sevens, then Chase The Ace, then Newmarket, then Rummy, then Whist just to keep me quiet.

Although I love patterns and sums and am good at them, it's a sad and private game I'm playing because I'm not clever enough to understand that the nuns are massively unimpressed by cleverness. They give us medals at the end of the week but it's almost a case of false pretences. 'Pray, girls, that Our Lady helps you with your lessons today'. Well, I think Our Lady, Mary the Mother of God, ought to get the medal herself. Perhaps she ought to have all the medals in the world across her chest. Actually I don't like getting something wrong so, when stuck, I cheat a bit by trying to get a bit of help by praying to the Holy Spirit. After all, He's really part of God and Mary is only God's mother. Also the nuns are members of the Community of Daughters of the Holy Spirit so they must have a hot line to Him. They say He's inclined to pour down grace on you if He gets half a chance. It says in the Bible that He has the spirit of wisdom, which is handy in a test. His Feast Day is Pentecost and we all get a chocolate biscuit to celebrate, which must prove something.

But I gradually have to face the fact that Being Clever is not working either. The nuns think that trying to be top of the class is not very lady-like. A bit pushy, like jostling to get to the head of the queue and I don't think well-bred girls do it. Better to stand quietly in line. At our school no one minds if you're not much good at lessons. Two girls' schools nearby take the rich or clever ones but anyone can come to us. It doesn't cost much because the nuns don't get paid. We're not very ambitious. We sit most of the day wearing identical uniforms, in rows, each with our own desk. When lessons end, and a nun leaves or enters the room, we stand up and chant 'Thank you Sister Odile' or 'Good morning

Sister Madeleine' and that's the exercise for the day. The ability to sew a fine seam, speak a little French, and behave like a lady is top of the agenda. Exam results are a bit of a distraction. Think instead of your immortal soul. One girl has beautiful red hair, another comes top of the class, and the third is a twin. Watch out! Red hair means you have to guard against vanity, a twin could be jealous; cleverness will probably end up in the sin of pride. What matters is being good and that is inside you. You can't bring it out and show off like you can with sums and the alphabet.

Bigga and Tyna think that too. They say 'Just do your best, that's all anyone can do'. They like it when I bring home good reports from school but then they tuck them in their envelopes behind the mantelpiece clock and forget about them. And in my bedroom they've put the best picture in the world; a girl in a snow-white frilly organdie and lace frock standing ankle-deep in a flowery meadow. She's got curls, golden curls—perhaps as many as Shirley Temple—mostly tucked inside a lacy bonnet trimmed with flowers. She's picked a bunch of white daisies, blue forget-me-nots, purple thrift and pink harebells and is gazing dreamily at something or someone I can't see. I wonder if it's her Daddy. Underneath it says *Be good sweet maid and let who will be clever.*

I decide to give up cleverness for ever. Instead I'll be spectacularly good. You never know. Suddenly I have a great stroke of luck. A saint walks into my life and things look up.

'Today I'm going to tell you about Blessed Rose of Lima', says Sister Vincent. Can she give me some clues? Sister Vincent gives us a holy picture of her. Her eyes are looking down. She looks very sad, perhaps because she's thinking of all the naughty things that people do. She's crossed her arms over her chest. I think the wooden crucifix in her right hand is too heavy. You can only see her face because her neck and hair are all wrapped up. I know I don't look like that and I don't have a light shining round my head like she does but you never know, I might one day.

Sister Vincent says 'She was a beautiful girl and devoted daughter who lived and meditated in a garden, embroidering things to sell for her family and help the poor'. Beauty, I know, is not my strong point but I did hem a lovely hankie for Aunt Amy last Christmas and she's my family.

'Lima is in Peru, a very hot country but Rose always chose to drink tepid stale water so as to mortify the flesh'. Bedford is not known for its tropical climate. Indeed at this moment the chilblains inside my socks are prickling despite being smothered in bright pink Germolene ointment, so I don't see much of a future in the water-drinking department.

'She was very patient and docile'. It's good that God doesn't only notice the noisy ones. I want him to notice me being patient. I can see him folding his arms and leaning down from Heaven to say 'What a lovely, docile little girl'.

'She never complained, just ate and drank lots of things she didn't like'. Excellent news. I'm good at that. Bigga and Tyne often produce horrid meals because there's a war on, food is rationed and they're bad cooks. I know that's true because Aunt Amy cooks lovely cakes and stews. She doesn't do what Bigga does, sprinkle powder and a few dry currants over the mince when it's cooked and call it curry, curry which looks (and tastes) not altogether different from her chocolate blancmange, though not so sweet. Aunt Amy makes jam tarts that melt in your mouth, while Tyna turns out any amount of brittle pastry, burnt bacon, tough dumplings and sloppy cabbage. But it's wartime and everyone makes allowances. I can be even better at making allowances than everyone else. And I have another idea. When I look at a statue of Jesus suffering on the cross, I screw up my eyes and try to squeeze real tears when someone is passing by, in case they notice them trickling down my cheeks and think how pious I am. I give up after a few tries.

A few weeks later Sister tells us, 'When Rose was a little girl someone carelessly clamped her thumb in the lid of a heavy box. Instead of crying out she hid the pain. It grew worse and part of her nail came off. A surgeon was called because a bit of nail was still there and festering. He had to pull it out and he was astonished at the way that she didn't scream. Afterwards he said her calm and sweet manner was 'truly miraculous'.

I think of the story of Tyna's horrid crinkled finger nail and wonder if she might be a saint one day, though it seems unlikely the way she shouted at me when I lost my fountain pen—and it was only down the back of the sofa. But if Rose of Lima says that sweet suffering is just the ticket, that's good enough for me. What's more, suffering means getting souls out of the torment of Purgatory, so I'm all for giving them a helping hand. After that it becomes second nature to bite back the tears when one or other of my mothers tugs my dark tangled hair until the knots come out in the comb. Just think of Jesus and his crown of thorns. Not that Tyna and Bigga are cruel. They are the kindest people you could hope to meet. But my hair is thick, they say, and you can't have me running around looking like a scarecrow, can you?

But being holy is not always easy. Sometimes I'm tempted to be wicked. Sister Madeleine cuts out black paper Mission babies going up to Heaven, each with its own little ladder made of thread, one for each girl in the class. I know what I want—to get my baby to the top first.

I call her Serena, which is Aunt Amy's second name and I think I do like Aunt Amy after all. She makes me a beautiful birthday cake with candles every year. Whenever I bring a penny to school Serena climbs one rung up her delicate thread. To get to Heaven costs half-a-crown, or thirty pennies. The race is on—and I lose.

'Well done, Patricia', says Sister Madeleine, as she pushes my best friend's fat curly cardboard baby called Odette into heaven. Serena only manages fourth place a few days later but I know I mustn't hate Odette or my friend Patricia. That would be wicked. To make matters worse, the nuns say that I must feel sorry for those little ones who live in foreign lands and have no clothes and no faith, and help them share in the good fortune of those of us who have plenty of both. I don't think that's fair. We don't have a lot of clothes 'because there's a war on'. I'd like a party dress with lots of pale green silky net frills but I can't have one.

'Once you've spent the coupons in your ration book', Bigga says, 'That's it. And there's nothing in the shops anyway'. I'm wearing Eleanor's old gymslip she's grown out of and it's got a horrible line where her aunt let it down when she grew too tall. So how can I possibly feel sorry for children in other countries whose mummies let them walk around barefoot? Imagine feeling cool grass between your toes—it must be lovely. And I'd like to try splashing in water with nothing on instead of the woollen bathing costumes Tyna knits for me, which as soon as they are soaked become stiff and cold and heavy, slapping round your tummy.

But I must persist if I'm going to be a saint like Rose. I need to do some serious thinking about God's plan for my life. He's top of everything of course. The rest of us come in a neat row working downwards: the Blessed Virgin, angels, saints, bishops, priests, monks, nuns, men, married ladies with children, married ladies without children, and spinsters. It looks as though girls can't get very far up the ladder and are certainly not fit to make it as priest or monk. I don't want to be a spinster but I'm a bit worried by the thought of trying to be a married lady because you need a husband for that and what if no one wants me? I could be Christ's bride of course, that's what the nuns say they are. Then I might leap-frog over the monks and priests and get to be a saint. It's not something you talk about of course.

At night I comfort myself that, thank God, He's not very choosy. Sister Vincent is bad-tempered enough to throw a book at Patricia because she's a chatterbox. Sister Joseph is tiny and old and can't speak English very well but she's useful because she can teach piano. You can be an eccentric nun too: Sister Vincent sends a girl to spy on a girl who has already been sent to find a girl who might have been loitering on her way back from an elocution lesson. Nuns that excite us most are Old Girls. We find out their real names by looking in old School Magazines and imagine how they once had hair and spots and bicycles.

In particular there's a nun, Sister Odile, who has the face of an angel and who rules her admirers like an Ice Queen. She moves elegantly and swiftly through the silent corridors of school, her long skirts making only the tiniest rustle. Oh joy, her 'real' name is Yvonne—if only I could be like her. She's French and when she speaks it sounds magical even before I understand a word. 'Parapluie" she breathes. A word which begins with a tiny explosion of sound and ends in a sigh. Like when somebody blows you a kiss. Today she wants me to draw lots of umbrellas, then colour them in poupre, bleu, orange, rouge, brun, violet, blanc. I pick up my crayon.

Meanwhile God sounds more and more interesting.

'Who made you?' Sister Vincent asks, catechism in hand.

'God made me', we chant back sitting in still rows at our desks.

'Stop fidgeting, girls!' Sister Vincent is getting irritable. Fidgeting appears to be high on the list of things God doesn't like. I take note.

'Why did God make you?'

'God made me to know him, love him and serve him in this life (pause) and to be happy with him forever in the next'.

It gets even better. Sister Vincent explains, 'Just the fact that you were born means that there is already something new in the world, for there is nobody and nothing like you. There never has been before and there never will be again when you are dead'.

It's just what I need to know, it's beautiful and it makes me feel better. She goes on, 'But just you remember God made every other single person in the whole world and he loves us all equally. Everyone is precious to him'. That's a bit of a surprise. Does he really love Hitler, really truly? I bet he doesn't. Not if he's really honest.

But even Sister Vincent's good news can't blot out the secrets in our house. Sometimes funny things are said or happen which I can't explain. From time to time I'm dropped in the busy, dirty, scary side of life and those closest to me are part of the problem.

5

RADIO ACTIVE MOMENTS

On the first Sunday after Christmas we go to a special tea party with Eleanor's family across the road. It's special because there's a cut glass decanter of sweet sherry. Bigga lets me have a sip of hers and it's lovely and syrupy. If you don't like sherry you can have a port and lemon. I think Bigga's had one of each. I drink a huge glass of Tizer not because I like the taste but because I love the colour: orangey red with silver bubbles. If I were the Queen I'd ask a footman in a powder blue jacket with a white wig to pour out for me fizzy water of a different colour every day for as long as I liked, probably from bottles not jugs, because I like the glug glug sound too.

All ten of us sit round a polished table covered with a dazzling white tablecloth edged in white lace, which Eleanor's Aunt Elsie made. This year we can hear rain beating on the window pane, the lights are low 'because there's a war on' and the flames from the coal fire make shadows which dance round the room. I'm eating a gentle, tasty, ham sandwich when a sudden blob of Coleman's mustard stings my tongue. It prickles my nose too and I sneeze.

'Oh, don't you like mustard, Yvonne?' The ladies are both amused and concerned. I feel silly and babyish and my face is hot. I want to change the subject. The word 'mustard' reminds me of a word I've got stored away which is a bit of a puzzle. There's something funny about it.

'What's a bastard?' I ask. Silence. All eyes on Bigga and Tyna.

'Big girls like you don't ask silly questions like that', is the best Tyna can do.

'Who would like another cup of tea?' says Miss Goodacre to no one in particular.

'Yes please'. Cups and saucers fill the air.

'I heard someone say Mrs Oliver has two,'. Eleanor is sitting next to me and she kicks my leg, 'Some Yankee soldiers gave them to her but she shouldn't have them, she was old enough to know better. Why not?'

'I expect she said 'baskets', says Eleanor's grandmother in a quiet voice.

'That's enough of that talk, Yvonne', Tina drops her napkin on the floor and dives to pick it up.

I know they didn't say 'baskets' and won't give up. Eleanor's eyes are shining. 'They said she was no better than she ought to be. What does that mean?'

'Oh well, you know the old saying', Bigga's cheeks look a little pink, '*Be good, sweet maid'*. That's the first bit written under my picture in the bedroom, but then she goes on, '*If you can't be good, be careful, if you can't be careful, remember the date*'. I think she's making that bit up because that's not under my picture. I have no idea what she's talking about. She thinks it's a joke but no one is smiling.

'It feels chilly in here now. I'll go and get another shovel of coal', says Eleanor's mother.

Words like bastard are confusing things until you get the hang of them. And here comes another. One sunny afternoon half a dozen of us children walk up the main road to the playground at Addison Park, Kempston. It's a big day because I've just graduated to the tallest slide. I climb to the top and am struggling to sit down in the small cage and stick my legs out in front when a small boy, younger than me, clambers up behind me and leans over my shoulder. He whispers 'I bet you don't even know what 'fuck' means, you silly little girl'. I whizz out of earshot, jump off the end of the slide and run across to the corner of the park to my friends.

'Guess what, do you know what a boy said to me?'

They're impressed: 'I don't know what it means either but I know you mustn't say it'.

'My mother said she'd wash my mouth out with soap if I ever said it, but I know she wouldn't'.

We make a pact to tell each other if one of us finds out, but we soon forget. A month or two later a girl at school who lives in the country—where anything can happen apparently—gathers us up in the corner of the playground to whisper so the nuns won't hear, of a strange sighting of a man and a woman wriggling around and about, under a hedge. It'd been raining.

'They'd even put some of their clothes on the grass without worrying that they'd get soaking wet'.

We don't believe her. Nobody would be that silly.

But in families sometimes it's ordinary words which have been flying around your head since you were born which congeal into a sentence, rise up when you least expect it, and sock you on the jaw. You just don't understand, so you pick those words up and store them away. At least you think they're safe there because you can't see them, but it's as if they're radioactive and one day they could heal or burn you, you don't know which.

The Renaissance artist Simone Martini has got the hang of what words can do to families. This picture is a bit of a shock. Sizzling with gold leaf in the background and Mary in lapis lazuli blue, Jesus is resplendent in red on the right. The last time the Holy Family got some family portraits done it was the Nativity when everything was hunky-dory and the angels were whooping with joy. And then came Epiphany when the Three Wise Men turned up with splendid gifts for a grand celebration. Not any longer.

Jesus, Mary and Joseph are gathered together and even their encrusted golden halos can't hide the fact that something is seriously wrong. We might even call it a dysfunctional family. It's the story in St Luke's Gospel of parents discovering that they've accidentally left their twelve-year-old son behind in the Temple at Jerusalem, each thinking he was with the other. No media frenzy, no police hunt, no child protection list but it takes three days to track him down and when they do they are 'amazed', St Luke says, because Jesus is sitting in the Temple questioning the religious experts and discussing things with them way beyond his years.

There might be trouble ahead. Joseph in the centre is leaning anxiously over his son, one arm round his shoulder. Jesus, to the right, arms folded across his chest, looks like any teenager who, when found out, is unapologetic and resigned—but sad to think how stupid grownups can be. The saintly Joseph, his robe a subdued brownish mauve, looks more like a badly-stuffed doll than a father. He's caught on the wrong foot, literally. You can feel the awkwardness of the moment in the crazy angles of his head and limbs, and know that you could push him over with one finger. He looks pretty useless. No one's going to listen to him. What is it with fathers, or rather, with the man standing there who may or may not be the real father?

But Mary, unflappable as usual, is stretching out her hand towards Jesus as if to say, 'Let's be sensible about this, shall we? There's been a misunderstanding. I'm sure we can talk things through'. Time and again in his Gospel St Luke understands women. He knows what they have to put up with, including ones like Mary Magdalene who, Aunt Amy always said, 'are no better than they should be'. The mother of Jesus doesn't understand why he has put them through three days and nights of misery, then justified himself. St Luke gives her the last word: she 'kept all these sayings in her heart'. She knew she'd just have to wait and one day she'd understand.

I too get the knack of hiding words away. Around VE day I'm standing at my bedroom window looking out at the street below. Britain is celebrating the end of the war and Bedford's joined the party. I'm looking at the bunting stretched across the road between our houses. First I try to fit some of the fluttering triangular flags together to make a pattern—a sort of virtual jigsaw. Then I choose my favourite colours. I like the plain white one because it's like a cotton sail on a yacht set in a clear blue sky. But it can only come third because it's a bit dirty. Next comes the triangle split down the middle, orange one side and green the other, looking just like the colour of real oranges and their leaves if picture books are anything to go by. Best of all is the one which is half the purple of lilac and half the gold of crocuses. I'm trying to fathom out why it's best when Bigga interrupts me by coming into the room to make the bed.

'It's a beautiful sunny day', she says, smoothing the cotton twill under sheet.

'Yes'. What more is there to say?

'In Switzerland you can have sun and snow together at the same time'.

'I know'.

Of course I know no such thing. I only know I want to stop this conversation as quickly as possible. I do not want talk of Switzerland and I have no idea why. Bigga leaves the room, the sheets and blankets crumpled. When she's gone, I'm in two minds about believing her. What a strange thing to say. How does she know? She's never been there. Abroad is where rich people go or people in books or our brave boys across the sea. If true, Switzerland must be the most beautiful place in the world. Snow and sunshine. My two favourites. In real life you have to put up with so much boring weather to get to them: days and days of grey skies snapped like a lid over the world, like having to eat piles of bread and butter before you can come to the cake. And then one day snowflakes settle like jewels on the sleeves of your navy overcoat or touch the ground when they make a smooth white matting which covers cigarette ends, dog dirt, weeds and bus tickets. When you look at new snow close up it's like seeing the inside of an apple. No one has seen it before. Imagine all this together with the sun which races down and prickles your skin and makes you happy. Is it possible?

'Uncle Ro is dead', Bigga says out of the blue another day while I'm concentrating hard on drawing some ladies in crinoline dresses.

'I know', I reply again. I have no idea who Uncle Ro is, dead or alive. Nor do I want to know. What would happen if I said in a bright tone, 'Who's Uncle Ro, Mummy? I don't remember him'. Would she have said, 'He's a kind man whom we used to know and we went on holiday in his bungalow by the sea and he was very fond of you when you were little?' Or 'He's someone we used to know and love but he let us down very badly and I'm glad he's dead'.

Of course I don't think clearly like this but I seem to sense the sadness behind her words and don't want to be drawn into her grown up world. Perhaps I fear I'll discover she and Tyna have lied to me. We don't do lies in our house. Once when I was very little some big girls pushed me into a neighbour's front garden and made me pick some of her flowers.

'Did you pick those daffodils out of Mrs Raker's front garden?' Tyna was by the gas stove pouring milk into a pan and stirring briskly so that the custard didn't burn or get lumpy. I'm crying, 'I didn't do it. Some big girls made me do it'.

'Tell the truth and shame the devil, Yvonne, 'I'm disgusted with you,' she said, and I was so young I heard her say 'I'm dis-custard with you'.

Since then Tyna has told me dozens of times, 'If you tell a lie, Yvonne, no one will ever be able to believe you again for the rest of your life'. She makes it sound awful. In my mind she makes me see a cloud of innocent new-born babies floating down from heaven, trailing clouds of glory. One lie and they'll be struck dumb. It would be like being in a dream when you scream but no one can hear you.

I put my crayon down and snatch up my crinoline ladies' picture which looks stupid anyway as I can't draw faces. Three of them have their backs to me, so that I can concentrate on what they're wearing, frilled dresses with shawls and trains, plus plaits and curls and ribbons and sashes. I've drawn one, my favourite whom I call Meg, side on, but she has a big nose and looks ugly. I run upstairs to my bedroom, the place to sort life out. I curl up on my cosy bed which has a slightly scary oval walnut headboard. Scary because if you turn your head fast you can see your reflection in it and I don't like the thought of a face behind me, it might be watching me. Instead I turn my head so that I can see myself in the round bevel-edged mirror on my dressing table, which grownups call kidney-shaped. I stick my tongue out. I'm not a pretty girl. The drawers and the wardrobe have a green trim, with shiny metal keys poking out which are never used but look important. And you never know when they might come in handy. The walls are lined with creamy paper scattered with tiny green balloons. Beside my bed is my rag rug made by Aunt Amy out of scraps of material left over from her dressmaking.

To stop myself from thinking about dead Uncle Ro I make up a list of all the friends I'll invite to my birthday party in five months' time and then a list of all my friends whom I hate and won't invite so that they'll be sorry. I start to feel better. I always feel better in my bedroom. I can't help it. Even when I'm ill. Mumps, chicken pox, measles and German measles are what all we children get. Whooping cough and scarlet fever are rarer and more exciting. Our family doctor, Dr Leahy, comes to see me and is very kind. His son Dominic used to be in my class because boys can go to our school until they are seven. We played Airmen and Nurses so that he can fly round the playground arms outstretched while I, the nurse, patiently wait for him to crash. Bigga and Tyna like our doctor because when I had scarlet fever I didn't have to go into the Isolation Hospital. They told all our neighbours that he'd said I'd be so well looked after at home.

Illnesses are not all bad anyway. I should know because I have more than my fair share of ear infections and although they hurt a lot and make you deaf, they're a break from needing to be top in everything. And it means Bigga or Tyna spend more time with me. They have to give me Aspro regularly and I like being the only one to have small enough fingers to poke down the neck of the brown bottle to hook out the cotton wool plug which always falls to the bottom. Then sometimes one of them stays to help me with jigsaws lent by friends or to play cards on a tray across my legs. Tyna teaches me to make tiny dolls' books out of magazine pictures, and dolls' house furniture by gluing match boxes together. Aunt Mary lends me books from the library like *Dr Doolittle* and *Gulliver's Travels* and *Treasure Island* but their covers are dull brown leatherette and they don't have any pictures and there aren't many girls in them so I don't read them but I remember to say 'thank you' politely. By beautiful chance Aunt Ethel sends me a book of paper cut-out dolls exactly like one I already had so I have twins to play with, each with her own name and clothes and I dress them every morning so they're ready for adventures and quarrels and making it up. Once I was so ill the District Nurse had to come round on her bike and inject my bottom with a new miracle drug called penicillin. She tells Tyna that without it I might have got meningitis and died. I feel excited that I'm important enough to have a miracle drug sent round specially.

I take yet another long hard look at the best picture in the world, that pretty little girl knee deep in a flowery meadow, a little girl who, unlike me, has curls. Underneath are the four words Bigga used at the tea party. *Be good, sweet maid* . . .'Be good', that's what everyone says. It doesn't matter who Uncle Ro is, I must be good. I must hang on to that. I turn over on the bed and with my finger trace patterns in the wallpaper which feels knobbly to touch. If only I had some parents. Other people have one of everything: one ration book, one identity card, one gas mask, one father, one mother. I wonder if the little girl in the picture had a Daddy? Perhaps they walked in the meadow together and he helped her pick the flowers and then painted her picture. Perhaps she's looking at him. I shiver. I should have put my Liberty bodice on over my Chilprufe vest this morning but I'm always in a hurry when I get out of bed as it's so cold. The fire is downstairs in the kitchen. Why did Bigga talk about Uncle Ro and not about my Daddy? What happened to him? If I had curls and was as pretty as that little girl in the picture he might have loved me, and remembered my birthday and given me a Christmas present. Perhaps it was my fault. Had I been rude and answered back or been dirty and lazy so he'd turned away in disgust? Babies are lovely and cuddly and strangers smile at them and laugh when they snatch their hair or necklace. What's wrong with me? I try to work it out but this time there are no nuns with cellophane-wrapped cards with the one correct answer. Perhaps it's his stupid fault. If he didn't like me then, why didn't he wait and see? Perhaps I could have shown him how clever I was at sums? He didn't give me a chance. I thump the pillow until my arm's tired. I won't cry. Instead I run downstairs.

'I'm cold'.

'Don't put your feet too near the fire, Yvonne'. My chilblains are hurting but as it's the only heat in the house you make the most of it. Anyway I like the winter, I like the way fire burns things up until you can't see them anymore ever and I like Jack Frost's icy patterns inside the bedroom windows which you can scrape with your nail. You don't often see them in the bathroom as they melt when the gas geyser is lit.

'Please can I have a spoonful of dried egg powder?' First I draw the devil on some scrap paper, a small spidery shape in thick black wax crayon huddled in the corner, his arms shielding his eyes from the shocking orange yellow powder which covers the rest of the page. I love watching the silver water drops perch over the yolky powder grains which want to stay separate, too grand to mix with the others.

That night I have the nightmare which often visits me. It's about Rin Tin Tin, a huge German Shepherd dog I'd once seen in a film shown by the nuns on a Saturday morning as a special treat. The original Rin Tin Tin started life as a shell-shocked French pup found in Lorraine by an American serviceman at the end of World War One and was taken home to Los Angeles. The film producer, Charles Jones, discovered him and made him a star. On good days they say he could leap nearly 12 feet high. He certainly needed everything he'd got to outwit the goodies let alone the baddies. The humans never learned. They couldn't see looming danger which was screamingly obvious to us sitting safely in the cinema seats. Everyone always misunderstood the dog's intentions. So Rin Tin Tin has a hard life in each of Warner's 26 films, always in trouble, constantly being thwarted, chained up or transported across the prairies in the back of a lorry just at the moment he's about to miraculously rescue someone from a horrible fate.

What haunts my sleep is the sound of Rin Tin Tin barking furiously and scratching and clawing at a high wooden fence while an innocent baby on the other side is crawling over a dusty yard. A gigantic vulture is perched on the roof. It has eyes which never leave you and a sharp beak which could tear you to pieces. While the bird swoops down to snatch the child and carry her off in its evil, gristly claws, the mother's locked inside the ranch, hammering at the door, tearing her nails, splintering the wood, screaming, out of control.

'Where was the father?' a therapist asked me years later.

'I didn't ask'.

6

GOOD SEX, BAD NEWS

At school I'm learning a lot about Good Sex and Bad Sex. I'm quite an expert. The nuns explain that God has prepared some wonderful things for Mummies and Daddies to do together. Sex is one of God's best ideas, a garden of delights which takes a lifetime to explore. But it only works like that if the man and the woman are married to each other. And that means the baby has someone who always loves it right up until the mummies and daddies die. But beware Bad Sex, which means crying babies with no one to go on loving them when their mummies and daddies don't love each other. How do I know all this? Nuns do not trivialise sex. They say if you don't take it seriously you don't just hurt other people, you hurt yourself too.

'Girls, we all live in houses and can go where we like in our own homes, can't we?'

'Yes', we chorus. But I wonder what she's going to say next? Sister Madeleine thought it was funny when I drew our house with open doors and windows.

'When you invite them, your aunts and uncles can come to your house too, can't they? Who else?'

'Grannies and grandpas . . . And friends . . . And neighbours . . . they can come in'.

I probably added 'and customers'.

'But not into your bedroom', Sister is nothing if not persistent.

'Father Michael can go there if he's bringing the Blessed Sacrament'.

'And the doctor if you're poorly'. We wait for the punch line.

'Postmen come to the door and the boy delivering the papers, but there are rules about who can come in and where they can go. Perhaps just to the kitchen—or to the front room. If you don't let strangers into your house, how can you possibly let them into your body? Your body is the temple of the Holy Spirit. It's a precious gift, look after it. There are parts of you which are private and special and you look after them very carefully'.

This is very bad news. By making me, had two people risked everything simply so that they could be very rude with each other? But in the next few weeks I discover it's worse than that. The real culprit is Eve, a woman.

'Women are more spiritual than men', say the nuns. Yippee! But the bad news is that it means ladies always have to be on the watch and set the limits. Boys and men appear to be pretty hopeless when it comes to sex. I can't help feeling God's a bit unfair on them in that case. Does he make allowances at Judgement Day?

As I write this I can see Sister sitting there in front of the class, frail as a bird, and I owe her so much. I love her. But why didn't she leave sex alone? Sister, couldn't you work out a child's logic? You opened the door to bad theology, a real bully who marched in and began throwing its weight about, reckless or careless about who got hurt. God apparently says that fornication and adultery are mortal sins and you go to hell if you commit mortal sins. Perhaps not one but both my real parents are wicked. If two people had not committed one or both of those sins, I would not have been born. God could not have wanted anyone to commit sin. Therefore I should never have been born. If I'm not adopted, I have no right to breathe the air of this planet, to share its food, to stand on its ground. It's as simple as that. I don't know where to turn. I'm nobody's daughter. My cutlery of words and ideas cannot help me digest this meal on my own and the people closest to me are the very ones who make me fearful. These classes fracture my world beyond repair.

At first I make up stories and each one helps for a time. I tell myself I'm dying of an incurable (and unspecified) disease and that would explain all the secrecy and why everyone is nice to me. But after a few weeks or months I'm as healthy as ever and lose interest in that idea. Then I have an even more florid fantasy in the bitter winter of 1946/7, when roads and rail are blocked by snowdrifts and England's run out of coal. Pubs, shops, offices and banks are lit by candlelight. It's not a good time to be a cyclist either—nice girls don't wear trousers, even to cycle to school, so the frost and snow play havoc with skin. As well as chilblains burning my feet, I get chapped and sore legs if I forget to plaster them with Pond's cold cream. Then something called lip salve appears, like a fat white worm of lipstick, and I suspect someone has poisoned mine. I refuse to use it and refuse to explain why. I'd rather be alive with sore cracked lips than dead with lovely ones.

The good news is that as long as I don't know who my parents are I can make it up. What's the best I can hope for? Dead parents. That would nail them down. You can't blame anyone for being dead. And you can't be blamed for having dead parents. Dead would be good. I'm hoping that Bigga and Tyna adopted me, which wouldn't end the mystery but I could carry it around in a more comfortable pocket.

Supposing I'm their adopted daughter, would I want to find out who my real parents were? No way! Nor why I'd been given away. I want a blank sheet. On that I can write anything: imagine any parents, grieve for their loss, feel kindly towards them . . . It's nothing personal. I want them to have had a lovely wedding with a lacy dress with a train, a bouquet of white lilies and six bridesmaids, probably in lilac. And a page boy in blue. Afterwards they had this beautiful baby girl which they loved to bits. And then it happened. A crash of some sort but no pain. It didn't hurt even for a minute. Could have been train or car—I can't be bothered with that sort of detail. I know Tyna and Bigga are lovely. But I don't want to find out that one of my mothers—it doesn't matter which—has had Bad Sex with a man who had made wedding promises to another lady. Tyna and Bigga say you can't trust anyone who breaks a promise because next time they'll do it to you.

Then one tiny incident gives me hope. No, it's certainty.

'I remember you—you used to live at The Warren, next to Daisy Taylor. How are you? Haven't seen you for years'.

It's a dark rainy evening in Clapham and a lady who's just joined the queue for the bus back to Bedford is talking to Bigga. Tyna and I watch them greet each other but soon they lower their voices—a sure sign of trouble—and I try to listen. I do not trust quiet words. They are much worse than shouting. They can hurt and sting you inside. Bigga glances back at me and I pull the belt of my navy mac so tight I can hardly breathe. Then I tuck the end inside my belt instead of putting it through the loop.

'Tuck your belt in properly', Tyna barks, 'You look like a scarecrow'.

In a flash, Tyna opens her hand bag and scrabbles around for her knitting. She pulls out a ball of yellow wool.

'Come over here, Yvonne', she moves away from Bigga and towards the light of the lamppost. She breaks off a piece of wool, makes a long loop with a knot and threads it over her fingers. She starts to play a version of 'cat's cradle' called *The Bed*, by picking up and threading the wool under and over her fingers and thumbs. She weaves what could—with a very vivid imagination—look like a bed with a man lying on it. If I sing 'Sam on a bed, Sleepy head, Bed breaks, Sam wakes' she'll release the wool on her little fingers and it all collapses. Does she think I'm a baby? She knows I'm trying to listen to Bigga. I shiver with excitement. Tyna talks louder but she can't stop me catching the word 'adopt'. It's just what I want to hear.

Then things get even better. I'm left alone in the house because Bigga and Tyna nip across the road to say hello to baby Valerie. Mrs Smith, one of our registered customers, brought her home from hospital yesterday and I've already been to see her and tried to slip a silver sixpenny piece in her tiny clenched hand to bring her luck and make sure she'll never be in need of money. The fist remains tightly closed. Baby Valerie at seven days old is impervious to concupiscence. Now it's my mothers' turn to go across to see her. It's Thursday, the shop's closed for the half-day and I know they'll be ages because they love babies. I've never been told not to look in Bigga's bureau and now's my chance. I pull down the flap and rifle through the inner compartments. Bigga is very proud of her bureau—it was hand-made for her as a farewell gift by craftsmen at Marion and Foulger's. I find a small round Quality Street tin stuffed with folded bills and receipts and tip them out on the desk flap. At the bottom is one sweet wrapper of silver paper with fuchsia cellophane on top. Beneath the wrapper is a letter. I take a long time smoothing out the foil with my finger nail until it's flat as a mirror because I'm afraid to look at what the typewritten words might say.

The London address is embossed but there's a fold and a little tear—maybe it's 16 Park Avenue South, N8. I must be careful not to make the tear any bigger or Bigga might find out what I'd done. The letter starts off pleasantly enough:

> *It is wonderful that you are making it such a success (of your business) . . . I am glad you find*

> *London agrees with you. It is very nice air in the part where you live, and I think you would like it where I live, but I should not like to be on the South side of London nor of course in the East End . . .*

She asks if she and her Father could drop in one day when they're visiting Hampton Court but the last paragraph is what matters:

> *Thank you for telling us about the baby; it is indeed very pleasant for you and Miss Maund to have this great joy of taking care of the little girl, and more so, seeing that she is so sweet. Her father must be very glad to think that he can go and leave her, knowing that she is in such good hands. You are quite right to do this and I know how very fond you are of children from all you told us from time to time of your sister's little ones. Good luck to you both . . .*
>
> *All good thoughts and best wishes to you; and best regards to Miss Maund (and Baby!)*
>
> *Yours affectionately,*
> *D. Squire*

Wonderful, wonderful letter! Here's a friend, someone they worked with at Marion and Foulger's, congratulating Tyna and Bigga on their kindness in 'taking care of' a little girl, who they said was 'sweet'—perhaps I had curls in those days. The baby's mother must be dead and she has a sorrowing father, no doubt a distraught widower. Widowers I'm not interested in, distraught or otherwise, and I don't care where he's gone. I hope he doesn't come back. I've found the right answer. Bliss and rapture! Adoption means I'm all right after all. Now I'm free to spend a life being grateful to both my mothers for looking after me so well.

And I don't have to be a nun if I don't want to.

7

UNCLE JACK

I'm 10 years old and I have known more successful picnics. The War is over and Tyna and I are sitting on a knobbly bit of Worthing beach on holiday together, while Bigga is home at Bedford minding the shop. Gritty wind is prickling my skin. I am eating a Shipham's salmon and shrimp paste sandwich and, half buried in the sand, is a bottle of diluted Kia Ora orange squash. Tyna is lying face downwards, the straps of her wet blue woollen bathing costume sagging awkwardly across her back. She lifts her head and turns towards me. She's crying. I have never seen a real grown up cry before, nor a picture of one because you only take photos of smiling people at weddings or parties, not when they've got tears running down their cheeks at funerals. I remember the mother screaming for her baby in the film I once saw because she didn't know that the wonder dog Rin Tin Tin would come to the rescue. But she sobbed all over the place, she didn't cry like Tyna, quietly, gently, as if nothing would staunch the flow. I hold my breath. I sense this is important, it's as if she's taken me by the hand and led me backstage, behind everyday things like homework and chilblains. She's hurting, raw as an unwrapped wound, and she's letting me see it.

'Uncle Jack wants to marry me'. I feel cold and pull a towel over my shoulders. No wonder she's crying. So would anybody. How dare he? Tyna is ours. Who does he think he is? He's nobody, just a tall soldier with black curly hair and dark eyes, who used to come to our shop because he lived at Grange Camp Barracks nearby. I'd hardly noticed him. I can remember lots of people billeted on us during the war: they were usually strangers sharing our front bedroom overlooking the lime tree. Sometimes two men, sometimes two women. Victor played the saxophone, Dennis drew me lovely pictures, Joni and Kaye were two ladies who cracked codes at Bletchley Park and after they left they sent us their picture and it said 'To three lovely people' on it and that meant me too. Everyone hated Edna, a blonde with lipstick, because she smuggled goods into her room which you couldn't buy in shops—chocolate, bananas and nylons from the Yanks. She never shared. When she left Bigga found a big bleach mark where she'd spilled nail varnish remover on our beautiful navy blue leather Put-U-Up, ruining it for life. She'd hidden the stain under a cushion. Now that's someone I remember. But Uncle Jack?

Tyna, tears in her eyes, hands me a letter on scrawny, cheap paper. Why should I bother with stupid Uncle Jack? I stuff my toes into the dry, powdery sand, scoop up a heap and let it float away in the wind. Then I take one look. 'It's a mess'. I feel better as I say that. 'The nuns wouldn't like his silly, blotchy writing'. Silence.

'Just read it'. Tyna's voice brings me back to the beach and the awful thing in my hand. I do as I'm told.

> *Just a line to let you now i got home all right as promised i got into oulton broad at ten past five so i didn't do Bad i didn't have to wait at Norwich as the train was waittin in the station for Lowestoft i thought a lot about you on the way home I have told you our parting days will finnish one day and thats soon I hope still dear keep smiling this war won't go on for Ever. I will right again tomorrow Thurs for now all the best*
>
> *Yours for Ever Jack'*

For something to do I count the row of 'Xs'. Seventeen kisses.

'It's all blotchy. He's done some crossings out'.

Surely Tyna can't marry someone who can't spell 'finish?' It's easy peasy. And he says he'll 'right' again and he means 'write' again'.

'Sister Vincent would have drawn red rings round them and made him write them out three times'.

I'm baffled. Tyna's very proud of her own spelling and minds about mine, asking how many marks out of ten I've got in the latest test. I'll think about that, not about Uncle Jack wanting to have Tyna when she's ours.

'He's been asking me to marry him for a long time'. Again she interrupts my thoughts, 'He's very lonely'.

'Is that why you're crying? Because he's lonely? Why doesn't anyone want to live with him anyway?'

'Yvonne, he grew up in the house at Lowestoft, his father died at sea when he was a boy and his mother died last year. And then you know what happened to his sister . . .'

Of course I know, but I say, 'Tell me again. I've forgotten'. I haven't really forgotten but any story will do to stop me thinking about Tyna getting married. And a bit of me wants to hear about Uncle Jack suffering.

'He was especially fond of Vera and he was her favourite brother'. I can't imagine what having a brother would be like, let alone having enough to choose a favourite, but let it pass. 'When the war started she had to go away to work at a munitions factory'. I've seen pictures of cheerful ladies in rows, each with a flowery headscarf, knotted at the top, to keep their hair safe from being caught up in their machines which are turning out guns to kill the Germans with. 'One lunch break there was an air raid warning siren and all the girls ran to the shelter. Vera nipped back to her workbench to get her cardigan. She was the only one killed, blown to smithereens. When they found her the factory radio was still playing her favourite song '*You are My Sunshine*".

"I know. I know all about *You Are My Sunshine*. You told me Uncle Jack can't bear to hear it. I'm a good girl, Tyna. I always switch it off if it comes on the wireless. Don't marry him, Tyna, please . . . you've got a signet ring, you don't need another one'.

We walk back in silence, Tyna pushing her big sit-up-and-beg bicycle by my side, the Kia Ora bottle sticking out of the square wicker basket. I don't cry until we get back, when I fling myself on the floor.

'Don't upset yourself, Yvonne, it's not worth it', she kneels down and tries to put her arms round me.

'Don't come near me. Don't touch me. He's only a customer. I know what you're going to do. You're going to marry him and . . .' I suddenly stop crying and sit up, 'Where would you live?' I look her straight in the eye.

'Lowestoft, in his house by the seaside. You could come for lots of holidays. It would be lovely!'

'No it wouldn't be lovely. I love you, Tyna. I don't want you to go. We need you more than he does'. How could he write like that and ask her to leave us behind? He's being selfish. 'It's not fair. I love you'.

'Uncle Jack says I've got to make up my mind. He says I'm his Sunshine'.

I do not want to hear another word about Uncle Jack.

'I think Vera was stupid. Why did she go back? She probably only wanted her hankie in the pocket. And she was a baby. If she was cold why didn't she put up with it? Didn't she know there's a war on?'.

'Yvonne, listen to me. Forget about Vera. Uncle Jack wrote that letter nearly five years ago, do you hear? He wants to get married and he won't wait forever'. She's almost shouting.

'Whom do you love best?' I turn and face her. This time it's Tyna who is silent. Why doesn't she say 'You, of course. What a silly question. Why do you bother to ask? I love you more than anyone in the world. I always have and always will'.

When we get back to Bedford I throw myself in Bigga's arms. While I've been thinking about Uncle Jack I haven't given her a thought. It's been just me against him.

'Cheer up, you'll still have me', she strokes my hair.

'You don't understand anything. If you had two little girls and someone took one away from you, you wouldn't like it if someone said to you, 'Cheer up, you've still got one left'.

'Don't you speak like that to me, Yvonne, after all I've done for you'. Surprised I look up and see her eyes full of tears too. I pull myself away and go up to my bedroom. She must have known all along about Uncle Jack writing letters about love to Tyna. It was their secret. They all knew and were plotting against me. For once even my bedroom can't help.

There's no tug of war. Tyna has a few weeks in which to say good byes and prepare for her new life. She chooses some of our furniture to take to Lowestoft.

'Are you sure you can spare it?' she asks Bigga.

'Go on, take whatever you want'.

They never argue.

'Uncle Jack said you could come with me when I go'. Tyna explains one day just before she leaves, 'but Bigga wants you'. So Bigga and Tyna get one each. Better than three against one. I'm glad they don't tell me to choose between them but I weep because Tyna means the world to me. She'll be so far away she might as well be dead.

One bitter October day Tyna piles her belongings into a taxi and leaves. She'll catch the Cambridge train at St John's station Bedford on her way to Lowestoft where she's going to marry Jack Mullender, the man in the picture at the beginning of this chapter. Bigga and I wave her good bye until she is out of sight and then I run into the kitchen and fling my head down on the green and white chequered tablecloth. Its oil cloth and the tears stand like jewels until I smash them into the shiny surface. Bigga puts her arms round me and we cry together.

'I'll buy you a new frock for the wedding. What colour would you like?'

'I don't care. What will you wear?'

'My musquash coat', she says, 'for comfort'.

Neither of us can think of anything else to say about the wedding.

On a chill November Saturday Bigga closes the shop early and we catch the train to Lowestoft. Tyna lives in a long street of tidy semi-detached houses, pebble dash, with two bay windows, three bedrooms and French windows at the back. For the last time I lie between my mothers, in the centre of a double bed in the spare room. We sleep in snatches, listening to Jack coughing his way through the night on the other side of the wall. I don't think he'll ever stop.

'That's his nerves' says Tyna, 'He's a bundle of nerves. He's been smoking like a chimney all day. Mind you I don't think being a docker helps. All that dust from the sacks of coal he has to carry down, and the chemicals—you never know what's in them'.

They get to the church for a quiet wedding on the morning on Sunday, Armistice Day 1947. The service is at eight o'clock as if they're ashamed that they are getting married when they are so old and don't want anyone to see them at it. The wedding service itself in the 1662 Prayer Book is bad enough with its talk of procreation and fornication and man's carnal lusts and appetites. I don't yet know what all these words mean but I've heard them at school and get the gist. It's as if the nuns had left labelled suitcases around, empty of meaning for the time being but probably full of explosives. I also know that real brides always wear white but Tyna wears a lime green woollen suit, the most expensive thing she's ever bought in her life, which is not saying much. She has brown shoes and gloves and a small perky hat with a tiny veil. There are no bridesmaids or photographs or flowers or kisses or confetti. Back home Tyna cooks us all an egg and bacon breakfast and afterwards we are driven down to the Esplanade. It's too cold to linger and we shelter on the leeward side of an ornate statue of Triton, son of Neptune who, glad of his trusty trident, is struggling with a frisky upside-down sea serpent and it's by no means certain who is going to get the upper hand.

Bigga and I catch the train home alone to manage as best we can without her. For a treat she sometimes takes me on the 5.30 am workman's train to London (3s 6d return) and we walk round Kew Gardens or Ravenscourt Park or along the Thames by Hammersmith Bridge. It's almost as if she's looking for something. She likes Kew Gardens especially. In the winter she brings a Thermos flask of Camp coffee laced with a dash of brandy. When we find a big spreading tree we stand beneath it and take sips to warm us up. Looking back, I wish I could say we faced the future without Tyna together, drew closer, that I became her trusty little helper. Instead she gradually bent under the weight of running a house, a shop, lodgers and a child and became increasingly tired, irritable and distraught.

Later that year I take my 11+ exam and learn something new. Some men are clever enough to be teachers. I take the exam in a primary school in the north of the town and find to my surprise that men are in charge of us and hand out the papers and walk up and down the aisles coming quite close, almost close enough to touch us. All the boys and girls call them 'Sir,' but I've never called anyone 'Sir' in my life and don't intend to start now. The morning begins well but when, after a break in the playground, a bell rings for the second lot of papers I can't find my way back to the cloakroom so stick a half-eaten Kit Kat back in my pocket. What have I done? The nuns say food is OK in its place at meal times sitting at a table. Just. But to bring food into the classroom would be as disgusting as bringing it into church. 'Sir' walks up and down. What would a man think about my secret? What if he makes me stand in front of the class and says, 'This girl is a glutton. You can see it in her eyes. She can't manage a few hours without chocolate.' Or: This girl is a cheat. If she smuggles chocolate biscuits in to help her pass the exam what other things are hidden so deceitfully about her person?'

My white Aertex gym blouse is damp on my back. The chocolate melts out of the silver paper and onto my hand and gymslip. Whenever he comes near I stop writing and crouch over the sordid sticky secret I've brought into the room. Both hands get more and more stained and guilty.

Nothing happens. I walk home free and undisturbed. An envelope arrives a few weeks later to say I've passed the 11+. The convent doesn't take scholarship girls so I'll have to move to another school. Money is tight now there's only one wage-earner. Before Bigga has time to write a letter about it, we get a message from Reverend Mother to say the convent will make an exception to their rule and waive my fees from now on. She doesn't say why. Bigga is grateful but I'm uneasy as to why I've been treated differently. What have I not been told? Perhaps they know I'm going to die very soon so I won't cost very much—but I don't feel very dead, so I soon forget about that.

'I have to do everything', Bigga moans, 'even fill the cruets'. I don't know why pepper and salt and vinegar are so often mentioned. She never criticizes Tyna or says she misses her. I on the other hand miss her every day, and probably say so. Twice a year I mark off the days on a calendar. Every Easter and summer I go to see her and Uncle Jack at Lowestoft. No one thinks it remarkable that a twelve year old travels by herself. When I change trains at Norwich Station I am suffused with joy. Nothing, but nothing, is between me and Tyna's smile and her wide open arms on Lowestoft platform—except for Brundall, Cantley, Reedham, Haddiscoe, Somerleyton and Oulton Broad North, stations which stretch across the fens, 'like a string of pearls' I say to myself and wonder if the nuns would give me an extra mark for thinking of that. Tyna will be waiting on the platform with her sit-up-and beg bicycle. We'll loop my bag on the handlebars and pile books in the basket and as we walk to Kimberley Road my feet hardly touch the pavement. Each time I'm happier than I've ever been. Each time I spoil it all by quarrelling with Uncle Jack. I want all of Tyna while I'm there. In real life he's won hands down. He's got her day in, day out, what more does he want?

I hate Uncle Jack. I hate him. He's gone too far this time. Only a few minutes ago he was out there in the garden putting paper bags over the heads of his precious prize chrysanthemums in a battle against earwigs. When he came in he had found me sitting on Tyna's lap, my arms round her neck.

'You're too old and too heavy to be sitting on her lap'.

'It's only puppy fat'. This is as far as Tyna will ever go in disagreeing with him.

'If she goes on like she is, you know what we'll have to do? You know that old weighbridge by Jewson's timber yard? Where they take the fishing lorries to weigh their catch? Soon we'll have to take her there to be weighed. No good doing it at Boots the Chemist. She'd break the scales'.

I'll never, ever forgive him for being so rude. I wish he were dead. I run upstairs two at a time, slam the bedroom door and lie on the bed face down, rigid as a plank of wood. I'm not going to cry. Bigga says I'm not fat. I've just got big bones. I'm well built. He can't make me cry. I slide off the bed, fling open the bay window and breathe deeply. Below is a long, quiet, narrow road, not a soul in sight, just a faint smell of sea in the air. I turn towards the end of the bed and start to unscrew one of the big brass globes decorating each of the four bedposts. It's hard to get it started but gets easier until suddenly it slips off and up and I nearly drop it. I wave it around in triumph. 'I've decapitated the bed.' I say out loud. I'm pleased I've just learned that word. I know it means having your head cut off.

Then I creep into the next bedroom, which is Tyna's and Uncle Jack's, and quietly open the window which looks out on to Uncle Jack's garden with its rows of prize chrysanthemums and a grimy neglected greenhouse with a vine that never bears anything except tiny green pebbles. The globe could sail through the air and slay those flowers with their vacuous faces and stiff stems. The glass would shatter and get into everything. Then I imagine Tyna's distraught face, her tears, the way she would clean up every crumb of glass, bind up every stem, re-arrange every petal of every flower which had had its face put out of joint, make everything better for Jack. Only Tyna would suffer—and me. I don't care what happens to me but I can't bear to see Tyna crying again

I close the window and go back to my room. One black bedpost is now a stump. What have I done? I try to fix the globe back in place before I'm found out. It's tricky finding the screw thread but once there it spins round smoothly. When it stops I force it tighter and tighter with my teeth clenched. By the time I'm satisfied that I can do no more, my knuckles and finger pads are white and my wrists stiff.

'Are you coming down, Yvonne? It's supper time'. Tyna calls. I close the window. Of course I'm coming. I'm not going to let that man see me cry. And I can smell the fish.

'It's nearly ready. I've cooked you a lovely plaice. Just out of the sea'.

'I know'. I'm running down the stairs. 'I heard the gate bang. It woke me up'. I'd got out of bed at dawn to see who it was. Our next door neighbour was walking up his path with a huge canvas bag which meant his trawler had docked in the night and he was bringing home a feast. In our road there are plenty of fishermen but few fridges and no freezers. We share each other's spoils. A bundle of fish appears over the fence. In return neighbours like Tyna water their garden, mind the baby, feed the cat, and collect a knitting pattern from a faraway shop.

'Would you mind laying the table, love?'

I set two places complete with the blue linen napkins I'd embroidered with black cross-stitch as a wedding present. Jack sits in his arm chair and stubs out his Woodbine on the hearth. Tyna brings in our supper and as she puts the plates down I watch her eyes meet Jack's and they smile. He gets up to sit at the table. He doesn't need a napkin or knives and forks, because he dissects skate with delicate surgeon's fingers, then wipes his hands on small squares of tissue paper Tyna has saved from wrapped oranges. He throws the paper in the fire. Tyna told me that's what Lowestoft people do. But Tyna and I have napkins and knives and forks.

I don't want to talk to Uncle Jack. Instead I read labels. They are always good to read. I especially like the one on Daddies' Sauce because it has a perky little girl on it. Finally I ask a question Uncle Jack knows nothing about. 'Where did these fish knives come from?' I like their bone handles and the curly pattern on the blunt blade.

'They're a bit of a nuisance because you mustn't put them in water when you're washing up. I don't know if it's because water will spoil the bone or if the glue they use to stick the handles on will melt. Aunt Amy and Uncle Eddie gave them to us'. I know that already—Aunt Amy often says no wedding is complete without a set nesting in white satin in a cutlery box among the presents. I just want to hear her talk.

A huge crack of thunder makes me jump. Lightning floods the room. Uncle Jack has told me about these east coast electric storms with waves at sea as high as houses. His father was a fisherman who drowned in a storm so he should know. I seize my chance.

'I'm scared there'll be a real thunderstorm to-night. Promise me you'll come to my bed if it's really bad'. I beg Tyna, glancing at Jack and silently daring him to object.

'We'll see'

He says nothing. Fifteen all.

The journey home at the end of a fortnight's holiday is very different. The first thing I do when the train comes in to Lowestoft station is find an empty compartment and let the window down by its thick leather strap. I poke my head out of the window, kiss Tyna good-bye and keep my arms round her neck until the train steams away pulling us apart. I sob out loud leaning out of the window. The fenland cows and windmills don't take a bit of notice.

By the time I get out at Norwich to change trains, the worst is over. For the rest of the year I move myself into a less painful world, a soothing rhythm of homework and books, church and prayer. I help a little in the shop when I feel like it, but take every opportunity to escape to my bedroom, folding up inside myself to get on with polishing my soul, which is a never-ending source of fascination.

8

MIRROR IMAGE

It's Speech Day and the Upper Fourth is standing on the platform in tiered rows of navy and silver uniform, utterly still, poised and ready. We're waiting for the applause to die away. Our teacher, Eva Fovargue, arranged the music which has just been played and the audience is enthusiastic. Now, we've got to sing *Rose Among the Heather.* I'm hopeless at singing. I hate having to do things I can't do. Worse still, it's the only day of the year we have to wear stockings at school and they're killing me. The tops cut into my skin and my suspender belt feels loose. Perhaps the hook's come undone and it'll all fall down.

I scan the room for Bigga who will be looking resplendent in her musquash coat. No Tyna to look out for now. I wonder if she's shopping for a nice piece of skate for Uncle Jack's supper. I catch sight of Bigga looking pleased and proud three or four rows from the front. Of course I've been looking at her every day since I was born—but this time it's different. I look away quickly, then glance back. It's like looking into a mirror.

I look exactly like her.

And if I can see it, surely everyone else can? Here am I standing in front of the whole school as a living monument to something which should never have happened. Everyone must be staring at me knowing she's my mother, a woman who's had Bad Sex. If they don't see it now, they will soon. I dread what their lips will make of it. I feel dizzy and sick. My heart stops, there's a long pause and then it rushes into a new deranged rhythm. I'm gasping for breath, shoulders heaving. The walls of the assembly hall bend and melt. I would look ridiculous if I fell off the stage. The prospect of crashing down, of having everyone's eyes on me, of being the talking point, then the laughing stock of the whole school for 'showing off', for drawing attention to myself, is more effective than a pail of cold water. I open my mouth and mime the words so that I look like everyone else.

I don't have a picture of how alike we looked that afternoon. Instead the triptych at the head of this chapter show three generations: Bigga to the left in her fancy dress costume, Claire, her granddaughter in the centre on her eighteenth birthday and me to the right in a photograph taken by HarlechTV when I did some freelance interviewing in my mid-30s. What strikes me now is that when Claire was growing up hardly a week passed without someone noting our likeness to each other, but no one ever mentioned that I looked like Bigga. Did everyone believe I was adopted and therefore couldn't see it?

Speech Day is over at last, parents have gone home and I'm in the school Library. I've got to talk to someone. Not Bigga. Supposing she cries and hugs me and says, 'Yes, my darling, I'm your real mother', and expects me to say 'Oh, that's alright then, we needn't think about Tyna or the lies you told me or the man who walked out on us . . .' Out of her mouth might spill some terrible story of lust and betrayal, and once uncorked, black filthy words cannot be poured back.

But I must talk to someone and cannot decide to whom. I pull back the lace curtain a crack. Below on the tarmac I see Sister Odile and Sister Brigid, my science teacher, wrap their robes round their ankles, climb into a car and drive off (always in pairs). Not many women drive in the 1950s. The nuns run everything themselves—teaching, finance, cleaning, administration, cooking. As for poverty, chastity and obedience, a girl could do worse. All my mothers' friends, married or single, live quiet lives at home except for one summer holiday a year by the seaside. But nuns travel abroad to other parts of their community in Africa and Europe and Australia; they live in a spacious mansion with grounds; some are sent to university to get degrees. They have books and time for thought and contemplation.

I don't want Sister Odile to know my secret in case she'll think less of me. I ask if I can see Sister Brigid after school the next day. Before we meet I brace myself by taking four Aspro tablets which seems to me to be a dramatic gesture, though I'm not clear why. We meet in the labs and perch on high wooden stools. I rest my satchel on the work bench and stroke the stem of the Bunsen burner which is bent.

'My dear', says Sister Brigid, after listening to the story of my perfidious origin and Bigga's future career in hell, 'I cannot possibly impress upon you enough that, whatever you do, you must not speak of this to anyone'. She goes on to explain with great delicacy that the discovery of someone with an unusual background like mine might upset some of the parents. They might even be moved to take their daughters away from the convent. 'And you wouldn't want to be responsible for that, would you?'

'No, Sister'. I shake my head.

I'm astonished. Why isn't she worried that my mother is damned and the gates of hell are wide open for her? She's talking is if I'd described an infelicity, a peccadillo. On the other hand, she's saying I'm a walking, talking source of something bad, even polluting. But I feel strangely comforted. She's saying that what's real is what you see. People are what they appear to be. Sister Brigid has tidied everything away, out of sight, out of mind. And I'm good at secrets.

When she's gone I realise that now my secret's inside her too. It feels rather exciting. No nun has ever spoken to me—nor I to her—about anything as personal as that. I wouldn't dream of saying 'What part of France do you come from?' or 'What's your real name? Do you have any brothers and sisters? Do you miss them?' It would be like stripping off their veil. I'm glad Sister Brigid and I are in this together. I could hide—as well as confide—in a convent.

I mean to start my homework but instead take out of my satchel a pencil and a scrap of paper and cover every inch with an intricate repetitive doodle. I can't stop. I search a thesaurus and find what I'm doing is called perseveration. The dictionary doesn't say why you can't stop doing it. Is it the first sign of going mad?

I think I'll be a nun. Aunt Amy asked me one day when I was very young 'What are you going to be, Yvonne, when you're a big girl, when you grow up?'

'A widower', I replied.

The grownups thought this was funny and Aunt Amy kept telling this story and I was so ashamed I used to run out of the room—but I was on to something. I didn't know what a widower was but I was in the right area: marriage. That's why Aunt Amy curled my hair and made my pretty Shirley Temple dresses, and why now I'm older she and Bigga keep telling me I ought to get my hair permed. Weddings are what girls do. They don't have real jobs like boys. But what if no one wanted me? Not even with a perm. No one wanted Bigga, and I hadn't come up to scratch as far as my father was concerned or he'd be here with me now. He put me in the Left Luggage department for life. I'd be safe in a convent—no man could ever do that to me again. I like the nun's recklessness too. They don't even think about perms. They have to cut all their hair off and there it is on the floor. They know they can't put it back on again.

But where would my children come from? I want them so badly. And there's another snag. Things haven't been working out between God and me recently. He and I have known each other for as far back as I can remember and I talk to him in prayer every day but I don't think he'd want me as a bride. I've taken him for granted and you can't call that love. You'd have to love properly to become a bride of Christ, which is what nuns are. The trouble is I'm never good enough at anything. At what? It doesn't matter. I try hard to make a go of it but before I get up in the morning I've had it. I look out of the window and wish it was fine. Wham, I'm doubting God's loving providence in sending the rain. I sigh because I can smell Bigga burning the toast again. Gluttony. I wish my school uniform didn't make me look so fat. Pride. Would being a nun cure all that? I'm not at all sure it would. It's asking a lot.

Bigga doesn't like the way things are turning out either. Perhaps I talk too much about the nuns. We're sitting on a green Eastern National bus going to Clapham and it's Sunday morning. Aunt Amy's mouth-watering Yorkshire pudding is at this moment being beaten to within an inch of its life in her kitchen. Soon it will rise in crisp golden downy undulations and appear on the table as Uncle Eddie likes it, as a first course served in a dark rich gravy before the roast is put on the table.

What are you reading now?' asks Bigga.

'*Little Women*'. I don't bother to look up.

'Not again, you'll wear the book out'.

'Tyna used to say I'd wear my eyes out'. I like bringing Tyna into the conversation but I'm a bit fed up with all this argument when I'm not a great reader anyway. I only like safe books. I like *Silas Marner* because Eppie didn't have proper parents and it turned out alright, but it's a huge let down when she only wears a sprigged muslin gown at her wedding. *Little Women* is my favourite because there's an almost total lack of fathers and that suits me very well. Someone told me their father was a clergyman, a chaplain with the soldiers fighting to stop slavery in America. Anyway he's never there, which is all that matters. He's just a hazy hovering benign presence, a fantasy, no more real than my father. Of course his family pine for him, as is right and proper and so they should. But no matter, Meg, Jo and Amy are formidable: cheerful, rigidly honest, self-critical and passionate. The only one I can't take to is Beth who is a saintly invalid making people feel better just by seeing her, like Rose of Lima. They would get on well together. I think Beth's unfair on the reader because she keeps getting ill and then rallying round and raising your hopes, but eventually you get to the chapter called *The Valley of the Shadow of Death* and you know that's the end of that.

'And what's that bookmark?' Bigga calls me back from the page to the present. 'It's a Holy Picture'. Reluctantly I hand it to her. 'We've got a new American nun at school called Sister Regina. Americans are rich. They can give things away and she gave me this for Easter'.

'Let me see'. I pass it over and she reads aloud what's written on the back, 'God bless you, Sister Regina'. She turns it over, 'Who's it supposed to be?'

'It's St Joseph holding Jesus in his arms when he was a little boy. You can tell because they've both got golden halos looped round their heads'. I like the bearded man with long fair curly hair and wrapped in a voluminous russet robe, who's tenderly holding the little boy clothed in white. Their faces are so close I can almost feel his cheek. I know that St Joseph is only sort of Jesus' father but I don't expect Jesus worried too much about it because he had a real one already: God.

'And what about the white lilies? They look as though they're growing out of the man's staff. What are they there for?'

'I don't know'. I do know that every Easter Bigga takes white lilies to decorate Clapham church in memory of her Angel Mother who died years ago. She has to take them straight there from the shop because Aunt Amy won't have them in her house. She says they bring bad luck.

'Please can I have it back? It's very special'. The card came all the way from America and it's exciting to have a present from a nun, even though she didn't write my name on it.

'It's only a bit of card. I think nuns should have better things to do than talk about Holy Pictures'. I bite my lip.

I wish she wouldn't say that. Why is she talking like that about the nuns? Doesn't she want them to be nice to me?'

The sweet pungent smell of horseradish sauce makes my mouth water. By the time the Yorkshire pudding plates had been emptied and filled again with roast beef, potatoes, onions and carrots from the garden, I've gathered that Catholics and Holy Pictures are not altogether popular.

'What are you going to be when you grow up, Yvonne?'

'I don't know'. Same question but a more prudent answer.

'I hope you're not thinking of becoming a nun?' laughs Aunt Amy. I blush. At school we don't say things like that. No one is good enough to be a nun anyway, so we don't joke about it. 'I think you are getting a bit too religious for your own good. I don't hold with all this Catholic nonsense'.

'The trouble with Catholics', Bigga joins in, 'is that they sin on Thursday, go to Confession on Friday and do exactly the same sins on Saturday'.

'No they don't. For the Confession to be any good they have to promise not to do it again. It's called a Firm Purpose of Amendment'. I try to put them right but they don't listen.

'It's about time you went to the village church here in Clapham, that's a proper church'. I hear in her voice that Bigga is not going to put up with a Catholic—let alone a nun—for a daughter after all she's been through.

I like the idea of Clapham church, which stands at the end of the garden. They say the huge tower was built a thousand years ago for fighting the enemy. The only doorway then was more than twenty feet above the ground so you had to put a ladder down to let your friends in. Every week someone in the family walks down the cool tunnel of beech trees skirting the churchyard to put fresh flowers on the Inskip family graves. All the ladies go to church at Harvest Festival, Christmas and Easter but Aunt Amy goes every week. She's the one to ask the vicar what to do with her over-zealous niece.

9

ENTER, ENTER AND NEVER LEAVE ME EVERMORE

Mr Skinner, the vicar, stands in the church porch shaking hands with the congregation after Morning Prayer. He is a petite, dark, serious man with eyes for which the word penetrating could have been invented. And a family man. I'm interested in families. What exactly do they do? I haven't much to go on. I've noticed that the nuns are deferential to fathers on Speech Day, and fathers make the big decisions like whether or not to pay for violin lessons or a school trip to France. Apart from that they don't seem to do much except go to work and remember their daughters' birthdays.

'Would you like to come up to the vicarage this afternoon, Yvonne? About three o'clock'. Mr Skinner has a welcoming smile, 'My wife is just starting a Bible Class for your age group'.

After lunch I walk up the hill to the vicarage at the top of Green Lane and sit in a sunny lounge with a big bay window overlooking the lilacs in the garden. Mrs Skinner fills and refills my glass with homemade lemonade. She is a sweet lady with pale wavy hair, a constant smile and two lovely little girls.

'I'm sorry but it doesn't look as though anyone else is turning up today'. I'm glad. I'm hungry for information about proper families. I cast my eyes slyly around the room like a would-be artist in a studio for the first time. I file away in my head new information: 'so this is what you do to comfort a child who's fallen down . . . this is how you get obstinate sandals on to hot, sticky feet'.

'I don't think we've met before today', Mrs Skinner says when the vicar takes the children for a walk. 'Now tell me something about yourself'.

Over the weeks and months she puts me right on all manner of things. Poor Rose of Lima bites the dust.

'All those good works you are trying to store up count as nothing, my dear. God doesn't need any human help. He accepts you as you are. We can't work our way into the presence of God, because we're already there. When we rest in God we find the safety and the space to be who we are.'

Hooray! I'm fed up with battling with a world which is one large market place of opportunities to sin, each saying 'grab me, you know you want me!' So I escape each Sunday afternoon to wholesome family life at the vicarage where they say grace at meals and always use a butter knife. Time not spent there is wasted time. I long for their calm and joy. I slip into their family routine, especially at Christmas and school holidays, and love being a sort of au pair, paid richly in friendship rather than money. When I grow up I'm going marry someone like Mr Skinner and have a vicarage just like his. And Mrs Skinner tells me all sorts of things that women need to know including what it's like having a baby.

'Not too bad at all. I sat on the edge of the bed chatting to the nurse until I was nearly ready. Nothing to be scared of'.

Up in the pulpit one Sunday morning Mr Skinner announces that the good people of Clapham need converting. Not that there's been much pillaging or plundering in the village recently—not many naughty deeds at all as far as I know—but there's going to be a Campaign to Save Clapham. It will start with a Sausage Sizzle for young people in the Vicarage garden. I go round the village putting leaflets through letterboxes.

I'm kneeling back on my heels in front of the bonfire, slicing open white bread rolls with a group of girls, my circular turquoise gingham skirt spread out on the damp grass. Drizzle is turning into something more serious. The boys, a couple of shy Clapham lads—plus three keen members of University Christian Unions home for the vacation—are cooking sausages in crooked blackened frying pans. One, who has clearly cooked at least once before, handles a pan of golden, sweet-smelling sliced onions.

'Welcome to you all. I hope this will be the first of many happy evenings together'. Something wrapped in brown paper is in a small carrier bag at Mr Skinner's feet.

'To night—and every night—I want to start with the Bible. In a few minutes our supper will be ready and we'll talk together round the fire as we eat. But before that I have a brief message for you. My text tonight is the Book of Revelation, chapter 3, verse 20. If you've brought your Bibles with you, turn to it now'.

Of course I have my Bible with me. I rarely step outside the house without it these days. It's less a story book, more something which is changing my life. I've been reading John Bunyan's Pilgrim Progress too. I love the way he says that bits of the Bible 'dart', 'rowl', boult' and 'fall' upon his soul without him expecting them. I'm on the lookout for some rowling and boulting myself. I turn over the pages of my Bible and feel the silky gilt-edged leaves of paper as thin as dragonfly wings. I'm trying to learn the order in which the 66 books of the Bible come, so I'll never be caught out fumbling through an index and looking like someone who doesn't take the Bible seriously. The Book of Revelation is what I'm looking for now and it's easy—there it is at the very end.

'Would you read it for me please, Malcolm?'

The strong steady voice of someone training to be a vicar flies through the air and the lilac bushes.

> *'Behold I stand at the door and knock. If any man hear my voice, and open the door, I will come in to him and will sup with him, and he with me'.*

Mr Skinner dips into his carrier bag. He pulls out a parcel, unwraps it and drops the brown paper on the floor. His wife picks it up and folds it carefully. He holds up a framed print of *The Light of the World,* by Holman Hunt, a picture which I already know and love as it's at the front of my prayer book. Jesus is looking out at me, standing in princely robes by a closed door. The light is velvety green and he's in a bosky clearing amid shiny plush leaves, yellow and gold. Plump apples lie on the grass, heavy and relaxed as if asleep.

'What's strange about this door?' Mr Skinner stabs at the dark surface. I sense that the students know but are holding back. Even if I knew I'd be too shy to say but I've no idea what he's talking about.

'It has no key'. Silence. 'No one can open it from the outside. It's the door to your heart. Jesus is helpless, waiting for you to open it from the inside. There's a lantern in his hand but nothing else. No scroll with a list of sins you've committed, no tally of all the good things you've done in your lives—and I expect you've done a few of each'. We smile at his little joke. 'Grace is free', he says as he places the picture on the grass.

He flings open his arms wide as if to embrace us all. For one curious moment it's as if he himself is on the Cross, 'Open your heart's door to a gracious Saviour and Lord. You and he will meet in wondrous union'.

The flames from the bonfire are winning over the drizzle. I can feel my face glow in the reflected light and heat. Mr Skinner's words are passionate and his energy is contagious. I want to escape an all-seeing and all-measuring God and my heart is strangely warmed by this novel approach. Jesus is someone who'd take care of me and has a plan for my life.

It's what Sister Vincent used to say about a God who created and loved absolutely every single person in the world.

But is it too good to be true? When I get home I pick up my prayer book and look again at *The Light of the World*. Yes, Jesus is dressed like a Lord and looks like the sort of person who wants decisions. He comes mysteriously in the night. I don't understand all this but meanwhile I'm rooting for him. He has my vote any day.

'How can I say 'No?', I think to myself.

But I keep him waiting.

Meanwhile Bigga comes off rather badly from all the time I spend at the vicarage.

'You're never here when I want you and we don't see friends like we used to. I want a bit of company', she complains, 'And get that cat off your lap, it's moulting hairs'.

When Tommy the tortoiseshell died, a Blue Persian cat was given to us by some customers who became friends, Louis Stevens and his Burmese wife Margaret. Louis was the leader of the BBC Symphony Orchestra which came in 1941 to Bedford by special train from Bristol to escape the bombs. They played at concerts at the Corn Exchange and Bedford School but we never went to one. We called the cat Scheherazade (Uncle Louis' suggestion) though we'd never heard of Rimsky-Korsakov or any ladies with a gift for story-telling.

'Do you remember when Uncle Louis used to come round before he went back to London? He was good company if anyone was. If only they still lived round the corner'.

With a push from me Scheherazade (Sherry for short) flicks out her legs and jumps delicately down.

'I can't remember when I last played a game of cards', Bigga moans.

The Skinners don't approve of cards and nor do I. I know a good Christian would care about Bigga more than I do. The shop is only just making a living, and she's taken in lodgers who need feeding.

'Boiled kipper and boiled potatoes or a slice of ham with cabbage. What do you call that?' asks a young Swiss engineering apprentice lodging with us. They complain about the food to me because they like Bigga and don't want to hurt her feelings.

'Shall I do some cooking? Would that help?' I ask Bigga.

She gives me a free Be Ro flour cookery book with a cute Mother and Daughter in frilly aprons on the cover. I really want to learn so that I can be a good wife. I'm happily standing in the kitchen slipping an omelette made out of dried egg powder onto a warmed plate, thinking of Mrs Skinner and how I want a husband like hers to cook for, when Bigga interrupts with an SOS. I can't believe that again she's promised more than she can deliver and I've got to rescue her. I snatch up my bike. My foot slips on the pedal and it crashes into my shin. Serves me right. I cycle to a nearby bakery to buy bread because we've sold out. Customers who've ordered bread from us must not be let down but Bigga forgets more these days and the number of people registered with the shop is dropping.

The Bishop of St Albans is coming to lunch with the Skinners tomorrow, so Mrs Skinner and I take the children for a walk to gather blackberries. A pie is planned. That evening when the children are in bed the two of us wait to have supper whenever Mr Skinner comes back from a funeral visit. Mrs Skinner picks up a book and opens it at the bookmark. 'Yvonne, I looked up what John Ruskin said about the picture you love. I'll read it to you'. I've never heard of John Ruskin but who cares? Anyone who likes my picture is a friend of mine.

> *The door of the soul is fast barred, bars and nails rusty . . . creeping tendrils of ivy showing that it has never been opened . . . . Christ approaches it in the night*

I think I hear Mr Skinner come home, hesitate at the door and turn away again. My skin prickles with excitement.

'You have suffered so much from your conscience. Remember this: God made you. He has a plan for you. He maintains you with every breath you take. It means that God is choosing your existence now . . . and now . . . and now. There is nothing more beautiful than experiencing your life as a slow unfolding celebration of joy and of thankfulness'. She pauses. 'Are you ready, my dear?'

I know this is it.

'I think this hymn will help. I'll read the first two verses'.

> *'O Jesu, thou art standing/Outside the fast closed door/In lowly patience waiting/To pass the threshold o'er.*
>
> *O Jesu thou art knocking/and lo thy hand is scarred/and thorns thy brow encircle/and tears thy face hath marred*

'Yvonne, when you get home tonight will you read aloud the last verse and ask Jesus into your heart? I'm not going to read it now'.

'I will', I whisper.

I say good night to them both. I walk out into the dark and down Green Lane to Aunt Amy's house in a daze of delight. I say nothing to anyone about what has happened.

The bus journey home has never taken so long.

'Oh, I'm glad of my rest on Sundays'. I know Bigga's facing another hard week's work in the shop but I suddenly feel irritable with her. She doesn't understand anything. She sits swaying on the seat opposite me, wearing a tight red crepe de chine dress. I wish it wasn't so tight. Once she went to the races at Ascot with her friend Clarissa in a flowery crepe dress and it rained. The crepe shrank and when she came home Tyna and I had to peel her dress off her plump arms and it left coloured patterns on her skin. She and I have been eating custard creams. I have a lovely secret inside me—Jesus loves me. And there she is, ankles together, her knees wide apart because she's fat, and I hate the way she's sitting. It's not well bred. Then she smiles at me and I know I love her so much. I do want to be like her. I heard Tyna once tell someone that Bigga saw Aunt Amy's son come out of the moneylenders and so she gave her nephew all the money she had because moneylenders are terrible people. Everyone knows how kind she is. She wouldn't ever, ever leave me, I know that. The man sitting beside her stands up to get off the bus. I go and snuggle next to her and stroke her knee. At the next stop we too get off.

At last I'm in my own bedroom. I close the door quietly, kneel down by my bed and open wide my arms.

> *O Lord with shame and sorrow/I open now the door/Dear Saviour enter, enter/and leave me nevermore.*

For days, weeks, my feet do not touch the ground. I have a Saviour who promises to be eternally true (unlike my father), who loves me (unlike my father), who created me to know him and love him in my unique way (unlike my father who made me and then threw me away). I'm happier than I've ever been.

And now I've seen the Light honesty compels me to tell the nuns and my school friends—in the nicest possible way—that they have an imperfect understanding of salvation and are somewhat at risk. For the Pope, Purgatory and Penance have taken a tumble in my eyes. If only Catholics read the Bible they'd have found this out for themselves. But do I find them diligently reading it every day? No I do not. And fancy having church services in Latin! If only they'd had them in English, the Skinners say, the scales would have fallen from their eyes years ago. I must do something about this.

Every morning we stand in line at Assembly.

'Close your eyes, girls . . . all together . . . . Hail Mary, full of grace, the Lord is with thee. Blessed art thou amongst women . . . pray for us sinners . . . .'

'Pray for us sinners'. Indeed! Just who do they think the Virgin Mary is? Prayers are for God only. I'm sure Mary knows this and she wouldn't like it one little bit—she's sounds like a lovely person I'd like to meet and is probably embarrassed at all the fuss. But any mention of praying to Mary, mother of Jesus, or any of the saints, calls for tightly closed lips and a sour face. So closed and so sour I've been hoping that someone asks why and opens up a big juicy chance for me to preach the true gospel.

How do the nuns take all this? They are less than pleased. My history homework comes back looped with red ink pointing out my errors. In Religious Education lessons when I question whether Purgatory exists, Sister Vincent is provoked to say 'I can tell you this, even the Archbishop of Canterbury will only get to Heaven by dint of the Pope's prayers as he crawls through Purgatory on his hands and knees'.

'What a terrible thing to say'. Mr Skinner's distrust in the Roman Catholic church goes up in leaps and bounds. I find this exciting and feel myself to be a bit of a heroine, bravely sticking to my faith amid all this heresy. You could say I'm a champion fighting the dragon of evil. I get invited to Sunday lunch more often. I'd rather eat anything in the vicarage with the people of God than be with my family who do not go to church regularly but play solo whist on Sunday afternoons or listen to the wireless or fall asleep . . . and are not beyond having a glass of port and lemon. Whisky even for Eddie and his sons.

'Come here, Yvonne'.

When Reverend Mother says 'Come here', you come. 'Here' is not her study but a store room, nothing more than a long thin cupboard lined on both sides with wooden shelves from floor to ceiling. There's a wall at the far end in front of you and a door closing behind. It was probably a chambermaid's pantry in the original mansion bought by the nuns and once upon a time had shelves heaped with crisp white sheets and bolsters and pillows, perhaps even a chamber pot or two. Now it's a very special place. It's like being invited into the Tower of London, for here are the Crown Jewels. Here are new exercise books stacked in precise piles, colour coded, russet for history, blue for Religious Instruction, turquoise for squared maths pages. Paper is still scarce after the war. To get a new exercise book you have to show your old one to your form mistress who examines it page by page to make sure every inch has been covered. When, oh bliss, you are given a new exercise book, you first have to draw a pencil line down the middle of each page, back and front, and write everything in two columns to make it go further.

But Reverend Mother has not called me in to chat about the paper shortage. She is Irish, wears rimless spectacles and has a round face which registers every fleeting feeling. To-day her cheeks are flushed and her lips curl in disgust.

'I have heard you've been questioning whether Limbo really exists', she says, 'I have heard that you have been saying the Pope is not infallible. I have heard that you think Purgatory is a made-up place'.

She pauses. What can I say?

'You know best, do you? Better than the Holy Fathers, better than all the Cardinals and Councils. Do you know what that is, Yvonne? It's Spiritual Pride, the Sin against the Holy Spirit, the one sin which God can never ever forgive'. At this moment she catches sight of a rogue exercise book, a russet among the blue. She leans forward to put it in its place and straightens up a few more piles. In the silence her words pile up in my mind. Put like that it sounds terrible and I am very wicked. My heart pounds and I can't seem to get enough air. I put my hand on the shelf to steady myself.

'I hear you come into school with tracts from the Protestant Truth Society. And girls are reading them'. It's true. The Skinners think I'm very brave, smuggling in anti-papist booklets, then handing them out in brown paper envelopes from the saddle bag strapped to my new drop-handlebar bike in the bicycle shed. Being banned material, they go down well.

She pauses and here comes the punch line 'You are fluent for your age, Yvonne'. She's broken the rules because no one ever tells you if you have a talent or a skill, as a safeguard against the terrible sin of pride. I thought 'fluency' should be a good thing but the curl of her lip makes it sound like leprosy.'By circulating your lies, you are putting at risk the most precious thing your friends have: their faith. You have become a fanatic. We shall have to strip you of your vaunting pride'. Not only am I a liar but I'm also something along the lines of a canker in the midst of young tree full of promising apples. I must be cut down.

'This is a warning. Either you stop this activity this very day or I shall take your scholarship away'.

It means she's expelling me. Bigga can't afford the fees.

The interview is ended. For a moment a new dilemma wipes out what's just been said. We are facing one another in the narrow passageway and the only door is behind me. Even if I flatten myself against the shelves and try to make myself as thin as paper to allow her to walk out first, Reverend Mother would have to brush pass me, touch me cloth on cloth. It is unthinkable. I have no choice but to turn round and walk out ahead as a rude person with no manners would do. I run downstairs to the cloakroom to go home. I fumble for my bike in the shed, eyes blurred with tears.

As I cycle home I ask myself what Bigga will say. She was afraid I'd be nun, now I'm something worse—a fanatic. And I'll have to leave the convent. I keep telling myself that it's alright: God has a plan for my life. Do I believe that? I find Bigga at the kitchen table dunking a digestive biscuit into her cup of tea. It's Thursday, half day closing. I tell her my tale and she listens. Her face shows that she's on my side but she's pale and tired.

'That's all I want', she moans, 'we turned down your 11+ scholarship so we've lost that for good. Where's the money coming from to pay your fees?' There's a pause. 'And what's more, I want you to help me to night, homework or no homework. I need you to slice some rashers on the bacon machine, weigh them and wrap them neatly in greaseproof paper. Then I need the sugar weighing'.

You have to concentrate with sugar. It drives everything else out of your mind. With a tin scoop I slowly empty an open-mouthed sack as I tip pound after pound into blue paper bags which stand up like fat erect soldiers, bellies full of sparkling crystals. I'm nifty at pressing the paper at the top of the bags down with my thumbs and in one movement folding it over into a secure package, essential if it is not to be spilt on the floor and make damp crumbs of glue. Gradually I become aware of Bigga on the phone to Tyna in the living room. Her voice gets faster and louder.

'The Pope isn't going to hang up his hat and cope and go down to the dole queue if he discovers that one naughty convent school girl in Bedford is going around telling everyone who'll listen that Limbo's a bad idea. And that Purgatory's a load of rubbish. How dare they! Cheeky buggers!'

This wicked word swings round the living room and the Swiss cuckoo clock hears it and so does Scheherazade and I hear it too. For the second time that day I cannot believe what I'm hearing. Things must be very bad if she has to use a word which must never, never be said out loud. The first time I heard it was when I was on a bus.

'What does 'bugger' mean?' I asked.

'It doesn't mean anything. But it's very, very wicked. Don't ever let me hear you say it again'. I don't argue but think it's a waste. The sound is cosy, makes me think of snug-as-a-bug-in-a-rug. The only word I can think of which rhymes with it is another nice word 'rugger' which I sometimes watch on Saturday afternoons with Aunt Amy's son Kenneth. And if it doesn't mean anything why the fuss? I can understand why it's wicked to say 'bloody' because that means Christ's blood which he shed for me for my sins on the cross. That's much worse.

I lie in bed that night and can hardly wait for Sunday. The Lord is on my side! I don't mind being talked about now. The Skinners will be mightily impressed. Now I'm really something special. Not everyone gets threats like these. The Skinners will probably dig out a book or two about the suppression of non-Catholics through the ages. Could it be that I'm a real live 20th century martyr suffering for my faith? Wow! Can you get any better than that?

It soon fades. The next day I go back to school and watch my language. My saddle bag only contains homework. It's not the threat of having to go to a secondary modern school which worries me, as I'm not sure what it is. Nor am I driven by wanting to care for Bigga by setting her free of an extra worry about fees. I'm just a coward. I'd have to explain when I went to another school I'd been kicked out of one already. I already carry within me a father that couldn't be bothered and a mother who won't say I'm her daughter, but no one can see that. They are secrets inside me and I look just like other people. But public disgrace I cannot face. And Tyna would never understand. She'd blame me for upsetting Bigga and get very cross. What's clear long before Sunday is that I'm not the stuff martyrs are made of. My faith is real enough but I'm fed up with being special. It's a mug's game. I'm afraid that the Skinners (and God) are going to be very disappointed in me and they'll just have to put up with it.

10

A CROOKED FACE

I've only once tried to slide myself under the glass and into the picture and that was at Tate Modern when I saw for the first time Edward Hopper's *Summertime, (1942)*.

I couldn't help it. A girl is standing on the steps of a porch looking straight out onto the world. Her frock is white with puffed sleeves, a nipped-in waist, and her full skirt stops just above her knees. She has my teenage figure—the frock's tight because overnight her body changes directions. It's a puzzling time to be alive. Her straw hat is like my school panama, though set at a jauntier angle than Bedford in the 50s would allow. Her feet are not shod with Sensible Lace Up Shoes; there's even a glimpse of black heels. She's alone and the street is empty. The grey walls of the building are bleached white by the sunlight. She can feel the heat on her cheeks and legs, and the breeze which stirs the curtains through a window flung half open. One hand rests on a pillar for support; the other is tucked behind her, not giving anything away. She looks as though she's unprepared for what is to come. A porch is a liminal place of transition between the interior she knows and the big wide world outside.

What will she do next, the girl with the steady gaze? Her feet are poised as if about to move. The pavement spread out before her looks as if it's been made in heaven—or a fairy tale. White and unblemished, it gives nothing away. No sign of use or misuse, no scuffs, chewing gum or tyre marks on the road. A tabula rasa. Peace and silence. But what if something is coming down the road, too horrible to imagine?

In my hand is a tiny black and white snap of Bigga and me standing in Tyna's porch at Lowestoft one sun-filled Easter. I'm wearing a similar dress. There's a matching photo with Tyna beside me. We didn't know what was coming. We're framed in an arch set in a pebble dash wall. Tyna's wearing a short-sleeved striped summer dress and her arm is wrapped round my waist. Bigga looks tired. By now I'm almost as tall as her. Why, oh why, didn't I think of taking a snap of the two of them together? It was the last time I had the chance.

One airy spring day a couple of months before my 'O' levels, I drag the ironing board into the living room, directly behind the shop where Bigga is serving. The iron, which should have sped like a sledge over my crisp white Aertex blouse ready for tomorrow's netball, wobbles and wavers. I'm reciting Latin verbs in my head ready for a test next day. Bigga walks out of the back of the shop and sinks into an arm chair.

'I don't feel very well'.

I don't look up. 'I expect it's the flu'. The Latin verbs continue to canter. It's not that I don't care—I tell myself that I help in the shop when she asks, stacking shelves, filling glass vitrines with Borax and Rennies, weighing biscuits into paper bags—although my heart isn't in it.

'I feel sick and a bit dizzy. I don't know what's the matter with me. I feel very queer'.

'It's probably flu coming on. Aunt Mary said how poorly she felt last week. It's nothing. Everyone's got it'. As I speak fear prickles my skin and throat. I speak louder, with more authority. 'You'll be OK in the morning. It's nothing'. I lift my head from the ironing board. Then I know it's not nothing. Bigga's face is crooked and very still, her eyes are fixed but not looking at me and a tiny trickle of saliva dribbles down one side of her mouth. Her body looks as heavy as lead, her hands grip the arms of the chair tightly as if she were on a fairground ride, her feet are together but her red crepe dress is spread tightly over her knees which have fallen apart. She's not looking at me and I don't know where she's gone.

I switch off the iron and move slowly across the room towards her. I've never seen someone so ill or so absent. What's going to happen next? To her? And to me? I hope I went to kneel beside her and cup her cold hand in mine and gently kiss her cheek and stroke her face. But my memory has picked up scissors and snipped away sights and sounds. I must have said something, 'I'll ring for the doctor, just in case . . . I'm sure there's no need . . . there's nothing seriously wrong, better just to make sure . . .' There's no response.

Perhaps she can't hear me. I'm trying to comfort her, but it's me that's frightened. She doesn't even know I exist. I want someone to say in a very loud voice, 'It's nothing. She'll be fine in the morning'.

Years later it's as if someone is flicking through a photo album made of black card. Now you see a page, now you don't. Here is a picture of Bigga lying stretched out on her side on the grey uncut moquette couch which matches the arm chairs. She has a cushion under her head. She's too heavy for me to lift so how did she get there? Did one of our customers come into the shop and then I called them to come through to the living room to help? Turn over the page of album and there she is being strapped onto a stretcher, bound and tied as if she were a mad woman about to break loose. Seeing my stricken face the ambulance man says, 'Don't worry, we have to do this to take care of her'. No one explains that they're afraid she may roll off because now she has lost control of her body. I want to throw my arms round her to hug her but she's moving away from me. She doesn't even know I exist.

On to the next page I can see a stretcher being manoeuvred like a large parcel over the counter and out to the ambulance someone must have called. The last picture is of Dr Leahy on his way out, half turning to me, 'It's hardening of the arteries', he says quietly, 'It cuts off the blood supply for a time and causes difficulties'.

When he's gone friends and neighbours call it a stroke. So far I've only met illnesses which have turned out well, either curing themselves like colds or flu, or being cured by doctors. I haven't yet met an ailment which wriggles out of control, beyond the reach of anything, even a miracle. Could this be one? I feel very cold and start to shiver.

Did I sleep alone that night and the weeks ahead? Or with a neighbour? I don't remember. I must have opened the shop the following morning and the mornings after that. When customers step on the shop door mat a bell rings and they need serving. Shops, like shows, must go on. I stop going to school regularly. Aunt Amy comes to help from time to time and together with other friends we manage. Commercial travellers and wholesalers who call round with their order books each week or fortnight are patient with me and prompt me into drawing up sensible orders and handling the accounts. Customers nudge me and forgive me when I get it wrong. At least the misery of food rationing is over.

Tyna makes a flying visit from Lowestoft to see Bigga in hospital.

'How ill do I look?'

Tyna says, 'I've seen you look worse'. Bigga smiles and is comforted.

I say nothing. It's not often the three of us are together with no one else around and here the two of them are talking in code. They must have done that for years. The difference is that now I can understand it because I know I'm Bigga's child and they're remembering when I was born and Bigga's life was hanging in the balance. I want them to stop.

'Do you like the roses we brought you, Bigga?' I say quickly and the danger is past.

When we kiss goodbye, Tyna and I go to the surgery to see Dr Leahy.

'What will happen next? How soon will she be better and come home?' Tyna's words sound awkward, 'I mean, how is she?'

'I'm afraid it's not something we can do a great deal about. We'll do some tests and she will get better after a spell in hospital and then some convalescence but I'm afraid it will get gradually worse,' he turns towards me, 'I'll see that she's in good hands'.

Tyna goes back to Lowestoft next day because Uncle Jack doesn't like being left alone. His doctor thinks he may have emphysema.

At night I picture Bigga's arteries hardening. It's what her face did too that morning, fixed like concrete when it's setting. Is that what's happening inside? The Old Testament is full of stories about what happens to people who harden their hearts and none of it is good news. They didn't obey and they get struck down right, left and centre. When I can bear it no longer I share my fear with the Skinners. We don't see much of each other now what with running the shop and having to be careful at school what I say about Purgatory and the Pope. And my O levels looming.

'Can it be a punishment from God?'

'Never! Yvonne, you know God better than that'.

And I do. Then perhaps it's my fault, not hers? There was that business over my scholarship. The nuns nearly took it away and after that her face looked old. She hasn't got much money because she has to buy my uniform and I need a bike to get to school. I shouldn't have been born. I want to shout at her 'Why did you drag me into the world by the scruff of my neck and kept me like a performing animal to be clever and good?' Often at night I think what my last school report said 'Yvonne is too absorbed in personal interests'. It's true. All I do is think about myself. Bigga is far, far nicer. People cheer up when they see her. They don't cheer up when they see me. I keep remembering last summer's Sports Day. I was sitting with Sister Brigid watching the tennis.

'What are you going to do when you leave school, Yvonne?'

'I'd like to help people, perhaps be a social worker'.

She soon put me right.

'Ah, Yvonne, look at Susan over there.' Susan is pretty and charming and laughing at the centre of a group of girls, 'Now Susan has the right personality. I think there are a lot of girls who admire you', says Sister Brigid slowly, 'But I don't think you have many friends'.

During the day there's no time for thinking about the friends I haven't got or anything else, except the shop. People rally round—including Aunt Amy—to help out so that I can go to school on eight days in July to take my O Levels. I pass the eight I'm allowed to take (no one can take more at our school as it would be pure showing off). It's the day I was planning to dazzle everyone with my brains, but I only get the top grade in two. Anyhow it doesn't matter. The important thing that day is the delivery van which breaks down and some angry customers who are pretty fed up when I tell them we haven't got what they want.

Bigga recovers enough to come home, hoping to pick up her former life. I move into the Sixth Form and sort out A levels. If I'm no good at social work perhaps I could do science and be a missionary doctor and heal people in a jungle or a desert. But they say it takes seven years to qualify so that's no good. I settle for History (because I'm good at it) and French (because Sister Odile teaches it). There's a school trip to France but we have no money. I can read French but refuse to speak it because I cannot bear the dissonance between what I hear in my head which is how the French nuns speak and the rubbish which comes out of my mouth.

Bigga is soon showing signs that she cannot cope with a shop and house, so decides to sell up. She gives her furniture away to her nephew Kenneth. The last thing we do when we move is roll up the stair carpet and put it in the back of the van. Some small belongings—my books in particular and the picture from my bedroom—are packed in cardboard boxes and taken to be stored in Aunt Clarissa's substantial mansion on the Clapham road. She's a friend Bigga met while both were doing voluntary war work. They shared a love of the theatre and on one occasion went up to Town to see 'Blithe Spirit' in the West End. Bigga loved to tell afterwards how she (poor) was wearing her only luxury, her musquash coat, and Clarissa (rich) was in a jacket made out of a blanket, fastened with safety pins. During the interval they sucked humbugs produced by Clarissa from a Colman's mustard tin. Clarissa has been to a Swiss finishing school and her house is full of beautiful furniture. It's also full of cats which seem to take kindly to the many possibilities opened up by cardboard boxes, even before we leave the house.

Meanwhile Bigga answers an ad in the local paper for a residential housekeeper's job. We move across Bedford to the home of a respectable bachelor, a civil servant with grey hair and a grey suit, living in a terraced house in a quiet street. It is probably the only career move open to her, but it's an unhappy choice. Bigga is not cut out to cook and mend and clean, but things are amicable enough for a short while until the man is suddenly diagnosed as having a brain tumour and dies a few weeks later. Aunt Amy takes us in while Bigga looks for another job.

11

WHITE HOT SHEET OF THRILL

Bigga is slumped in one of Amy's green leatherette arm chairs beside the fireplace. Her maroon cardigan hangs loosely from her shoulders, her brown skirt is stretched across her outspread knees and her ankles are crossed, feet in the fluffy blue slippers I bought her for Christmas with the money I earned delivering letters at the Post Office. On the other side of the fireplace sits Amy in an identical chair, immaculate in a pale grey woollen crepe dress she made for herself. On the tiled mantelpiece stand three carved ivory elephants which forever face the window lest they bring bad luck. Amy leans forward, picks up a burning coal with the fire tongs and delicately manoeuvres it back into the grate. Everything this large lady does is delicate: tiny flowers made of icing on a wedding cake, a miniature posy in an egg cup. Finely stitched quilted satin cushions in egg shell green decorate the three piece suite in the front room. Of course we hardly ever see them because the room is kept for special occasions like Christmas and funerals. If you feel like dying I imagine it's the best place to be.

What is Bigga thinking? Is she remembering that once she had a career, then branched out in London to run her own business with her closest friend? The war smashed all that up. Then Tyna leaves. She hardly ever sees her because it looks as though Jack's lungs are faltering. He wants his wife by his side at all time. Now Bigga's future is in a job for which she's temperamentally and practically unsuited. She's lost her home and most of her possessions. Does she think about whether there's anything left in her bank book? Is she wondering if she'll ever feel well again?

What is Amy thinking? The perfect wife, mother and sister, cook and seamstress, pillar of Clapham church, founder-member of the village Women's Institute and the Mother's Union. Is she mourning? Eddie's gone for ever. He never knew what it would be like to settle down with her and her village. He died the very week in which he'd planned to retire from his work at Peterborough. Instead her sister Gertie is here, now crumbling before her eyes. Plus her sister's ill-begotten daughter.

'Isn't it about time that child left school and did an honest day's work and started to look after you? My two boys left school after School Certificate and have never had a day out of work since'.

Perhaps Aunt Amy never said that to Bigga. Perhaps I just imagined it hanging in the air. It's real enough at night when the question creeps into my bed and bites me awake. But she might well have said it because Inskips don't stay on at school. Our pride and joy is getting every girl and boy in the family into an apprenticeship: Cliff a printer, Lance a painter and decorator, Clarence a draughtsman, Erna a dressmaker—that's what we do best. We're all proud of Uncle Eddie's framed certificate on the wall saying he was a Member of The Institute of Welding, but he didn't go to university. Why am I the only one who imagines she's special enough to stay on in the Sixth Form and take exams?

There's no one I can ask what to do. I've rarely seen the Skinners since we sold our house and Bigga became a housekeeper, and when I do I can't talk about leaving school because they're sure God wants me to go to university and who am I to question God? And although the nuns—Sister Odile in particular—are very good to me, I feel that after my little talk with Sister Bridget information about my family difficulties should be on a need to know basis.

Miss Lois Dalgleish, a tall, willowy Australian with fair hair which is nothing but curls, steps into the convent to teach history to the Sixth Form for a couple of years. She and I fight like cats and dogs all through the A level syllabus, especially over the Reformation, slinging statistics at each other about the body count engendered on both sides by heresy and martyrdom, and ridiculing in genteel language each other's most precious beliefs. Red ink is her weapon and mine are mumbled, sullen, barbed remarks. I still have a 23-page hand-written letter she wrote to me one holiday putting me right on this and that. She has endless patience. And she has plans.

In the summer holiday at the end of my first year in the Sixth Form she caught the bus to Cambridge and met an acquaintance at Kings College. She came back with the idea that I might take the Entrance Exam for Newnham College, one of only two Cambridge colleges open to women. It looks lovely on the postcard but no one at the convent has been to Cambridge and I'd have to take the exam in my fourth term in the Sixth Form, which is a bit early.

'In Cambridge there are eleven places on offer to men for every one open to a woman', Miss Dalgleish does not want me to raise my hopes, 'So the Entrance Exam is nothing for you to get excited about'

When I tell Bigga she says, 'You can only do your best. That's all anyone can do'. I leave her to tell Aunt Amy, in case she's cross. When I get called for two days of interviews she says, 'If that's what you want . . . I only want you to be happy' I write one of my long affectionate letters to Tyna with the news that I've been chosen for interview and get a long affectionate letter back full of the price of coal and how she and her friends played cards until 3am last night and the fire had nearly gone out, but she forgets to mention the interview. That's better than her making a fuss about it.

The cat springs up and stalks off, head and tail held high, pretending nothing untoward has happened.

'I'm so sorry—I didn't see your cat there'.

I am one of a string of interviewees who will sit on Miss Behrens' beautiful sofa that November morning in 1954, hoping for a place at Newnham, but I'm probably the only candidate to sit on her cat. And the only one with a sordid secret inside her: my father could be mad or bad and he's certainly missing. He could be walking past Kings College at this moment, or crossing a desert. He could be dead. Or not.

So far this slim, elegant, cat-loving woman, who will quiz me about my enthusiasm for History, knows nothing of it. Nor is she likely to, if I can help it. Her room—now a little hazy with cigarette smoke—is full of exquisite furniture and pictures. Last night over dinner I was surprised to find that some of the girls selected for interview came from schools which prepare pupils every year, their teachers being friends or even fellow students of the dons. I love the gossip. Miss Behrens is said to be formidable. She never went to school but grew up in a rich and complicated household surrounded by servants and governesses. She can't remember when she couldn't speak French and German. Students and colleagues are said to be fond of her, if a little in awe. Her capacity to generate awe did not diminish: she wrote what some say is her most remarkable book when she was eighty one.

Before upsetting the cat I'd felt calm. If I fail to get a place—and I expect to fail—it doesn't matter. I know the odds. But nothing can alter the fact that I'm one of the Nearly-Chosen who got an interview and when I'm old and grumpy I'll be able to take this memory out as if from a picnic hamper and feel better for it.

'I notice you were born in London. What part?'

'Hammersmith. We moved away soon after war broke out'. What's this got to do with anything? I daren't ask but I don't like this sort of question. It's too personal. What will she say next? 'What is your father's profession?'

Instead she says 'And have you applied for a place to read History at Oxford too?'

'Well, no. I like Cambridge better'. It's the truth, but not the whole truth and nothing but the truth. Perhaps Bigga's training in putting the best face on things is coming in handy. How can I say 'Cambridge is cheaper to get to for an interview—I came by bus—whereas Oxford would have meant a train fare? And what's more, most people think it's a waste of money for the nuns to pay the fees for one Entrance exam, let alone two.

'Has anyone from your school ever been to Cambridge? Would I know any of them?'

'No, I'm afraid not'. I sense from this question that she's on my side. Perhaps as an outsider I'm a mystery, worth taking a chance on? For a moment I'm swept with a longing for Newnham and what I'll miss by not getting a place.

'And now I hear you are thinking of switching to Economics? Her voice is cool, 'I believe the Principal spoke to you?'

'Yes, Miss Cohen did suggest it when I met her earlier this morning'. The Principal, an agricultural economist, sounds fun. I'd liked the stories told last night by some on the girls in the know: her zest for life, her eccentricity, how she sits cross-legged on the floor and throws a packet of ciggies across the room to the needy.

'You must think carefully about this. History and Economics are so very different. One is analytical, the other inductive'. I can't work out which is which, so say nothing to be on the safe side. 'Why are you attracted to Economics?' I shift around on the luxurious cushions.

'I like making new patterns with ideas'. I must be careful. To get in to Newnham I spent yesterday swearing that History was my great passion, and life would hardly be worth living without it. Today it looks as though the Principal has too many wanting History places but too few candidates for her subject. Girls and economics? Not a pairing which many schools think about. Well, if there's a place going in economics, I'm all for it. I want to be wanted and I don't care what I study as long as I get a place, somewhere where I can belong. If anyone had said 'Would you consider spending the next three years studying the language, culture and literature of Ugaritic, that ancient Semitic culture?' I'd have said 'It's just up my street. I think of nothing else', which surprises me considering I'm no good at languages.

In my last interview I make a fool of myself. I'd ended an essay on my History exam paper with a throwaway remark suggesting that my head was full of startlingly original ideas if only I'd had the chance to share them but now there was no time, never thinking I'd meet the examiner in the flesh.

'You left your last essay unfinished, Yvonne. What would you have said if you had the time?'

I'm appalled, and gabble some nonsense.

'How interesting. Were you using 'agrarian' in a special sense?'

She doesn't contradict or humiliate me. It's as if she has an eternal spring of hope that her students might come up with something original if she listens hard enough. By not exposing me as a fool she enables me to see my own foolishness. It's bracing and I love it.

I needn't have worried for a moment about being poor or about having half my parents missing. No one shows the slightest interest in where I've sprung from, not then, nor for the next three years. The only sticky moment came when one tutor said as she was walking out of the room, 'I wonder if the Chairman of Westfields' Trustees is a relative of yours? If so, do give him my best wishes', but she closed the door as she spoke. I've never heard of Westfields. Is it a college or a department store? And what are Trustees?

Back home I can't wait to tell the story of my interviews to the Skinners. They praise God and so do I.

'We have some news too. Our niece Grace is coming to stay with us. She's going to try for a place at Newnham to read medicine. She's lived in China all her life where my sister and her husband were missionaries', adds Mr Skinner, 'Had to eat egg shells to keep up her supply of calcium—she spent three years in a Japanese internment camp'.

In December the telegram boy brings the golden envelope: ECONOMICS VACANCY OFFERED NEWNHAM WRITING. I tell Bigga, then grab my bike and dash to school. I run up the stairs, scattering the news to the boarders who are in the Homework Room, before knocking at Reverend Mother's study door, her study this time—not the cubby hole where we'd had our last interview. In a couple of minutes the boarders gather round on the landing outside and start to sing 'For she's a jolly good fellow' and Reverend Mother leads me out to them.

'Look at her, she looks as though she's heard that she's going to be executed in the morning', says Reverend Mother and it's true. Remember Tyna's brother in the photo trying not to smile. Smile is smug. Smile is self-satisfied. Don't do it. Anyhow maybe the telegram went to the wrong address. Fancy me thinking I was good enough! But I must be polite, so I smile to order. The smile spreads throughout my body. I've never felt anything like it. When she was accepted by Newnham, Miriam Margolyes, the actor, put it like this: 'I've had joy, but that kind of white-hot sheet of thrill that ran through me . . . I've never had that since . . . . the pleasure of it warms me still'. Joan Bakewell looking back on when it happened to her said it was like the promise of 'a starlet going to Hollywood'.

I'm also thinking that now I have somewhere to live during term time for the next three years. And it will be a war-free zone. No talk of Switzerland or a man called Ro who might or might not exist, no letter lying in ambush in a drawer.

Shortly afterwards Bigga and I move from Clapham to Wrestlingworth, a village lying equidistant from Bedford and Cambridge, to live in an 18thC farmhouse where Bigga is housekeeper, this time for a farmer whose wife and daughter have recently left him. Sometimes when I wake up in the morning in my low-ceilinged, luxurious bedroom with its window overlooking a pretty country lane, I think I'd swap it all for my kidney-shaped dressing table and its mirror which I'll never see again. I even miss Aunt Amy's orange and brown rag rug. After all, now I'm the housekeeper's daughter who's sleeping in the real daughter's room. On 'our' dressing table is a silver-framed photograph of her—she'd slightly younger than me and used to go to the convent—with her father and mother. Why was she allowed to have one of each? She's on an exotic cruise, wearing an evening dress and leaning over a table covered with fine china and cutlery, while white-jacketed waiters hover over her like guardian angels. I wouldn't mind tearing it up into tiny pieces.

The farmer is pleasant and easy going. From time to time he takes us sailing at St Neots and Offord D'Arcy. When Bigga has time off I occasionally run the house. Sometimes his wife comes back and then she takes over.

One of the pluses of this move is that the farmer can get me piece work during the summer holidays, picking peas, strawberries and blackcurrants at nearby Cockayne Hatley. No matter a small circle of hot pain in my back means I can hardly stand at the end of the day. I offer it up to God—old habits die hard. I urgently need some money for Cambridge: my priorities are an evening dress, a coffee set and a small portable radio. As for the evening dress, I shouldn't care about clothes since I'm a Christian, a citizen of heaven and am required to consider the lilies of the field and how they grow and how even Solomon in all his glory was not arrayed like one of those. That said, I need one for the annual College Commemorative dinner and who knows when an evening dress might come in handy? And the radio? Never mind that the only one I can afford has reception so poor it sounds as if the orchestra is playing on cardboard boxes, it will keep me company.

So each morning I cycle to the fruit fields to join a group of women from neighbouring villages who've never met a student before, although we're only a few miles outside Cambridge.

'Do you have to make your own bed?' they ask, 'Does someone wash your cups up for you?' When I tell them that I've heard men have bedders who do this for them every day but girls do their own, no one is a bit surprised.

They can strip a row of strawberry plants or blackcurrant bushes stretching across the length of the field when I'm only a third of the way through. They enjoy talking about sex and I love listening. Here under this huge wide sky we women can say the unsayable. I haven't a single thing to add as yet but I don't miss a word. One grandmother tells me, 'When I got married I didn't know where a baby come from even. My Mum told me nothing. I were that innocent, I were. When I were having my first baby I say to my Mum 'Where do the baby come out, then? Do it come from the belly button? Or have I got to be cut down there?'

'No', she say, 'It come out from where it went in'.

'I were that surprised I didn't believe a word she say so I say, 'You're pulling my leg'.'.

'No I aren't', she say, 'Grow up, girl'.

Bigga and Tyna never mentioned sex. I didn't want a word from them anyway. Mrs Skinner had told me everything I needed to know about having babies, and made it sound pretty straightforward. And here in the Suffolk fruit fields under the open skies us women can talk and laugh easily.

'What about you, Dora?' asks one woman, 'What happened the night old Tom come to your cottage?'

They've heard the story many times before but Dora, who has a more fragile grasp on understanding the world than most, answers each time with a simple account ending with 'It were all over his shoe, it were'. The other women laugh. Sex is fun. Their jokes are straightforward, different from the ones I used to overhear Tyna and Bigga telling at home and sometimes catch on the Home Service on the wireless. Those jokes seem to depend not on what you say but on the way you say it. Here the women's laughter is never cruel. They are tender towards Dora and throw handfuls of fruit into her panniers to help make up the weight.

'We make sure she get her fair dues', they tell me.

I get my 2 A levels, and my grades don't matter as Newnham chooses you if you pass its own Entrance exam. Two are enough to get me a County Major Scholarship, which will pay my tuition and residence fees for the next three years. On Sunday afternoons I walk across Clapham fields with my cousin Lance, who's ten years older, and with Aunt Amy's frisky cocker spaniel, Howard. Lance enjoys being the Labour rebel in a Tory Inskip family and never fails to turn up wearing a bright red tie. He tells me it's the rate-payers of Bedford and the tax payers all over England who are footing my bill.

12

A MAP OF WHERE MY HANDS CAN REACH

I travel to Cambridge from Bedford on the Oxford/ Cambridge railway line which Mr Beecham will soon axe. I pay sixpence to leave my bike at the station, and join the queue for a taxi. A tall young man ahead of me folds himself into the cab at the head of the queue and mutters 'Selwyn'.

The driver jumps out and grabs my suitcase.

'Where to, young lady? Newnham? Good. It's next door to Selwyn College'

I join the young man on the back seat and he retracts into a cringe as far from me as possible. All I can see are slim fingers and elegant nails.

'Thank you for letting me share your taxi', I say in my most polite Convent school voice. Such froward behaviour as speaking seems to confirm his perception that I'm after his virtue. Silence. The young man now leans forward, buttocks clenched on the edge of the seat, elbows glued to his side, fixing his eyes on the dinginess of Station Road and the carvings on the Catholic Church. When the driver asks if I want the Porters' Lodge I say 'Yes' and hope for the best. As I climb out of the taxi and pay my fare the Selwyn man uncurls, and sighing, settles back into his seat for the remaining few hundred yards. There are no farewell hugs.

At the Lodge the Head Porter runs a pencil down the admissions list and I try to keep up. Is my name there? Am I in the right place? What if I had to go back to school and say there'd been a mistake and they didn't want me?

'Please show this young lady to her room'. I follow the Housekeeper along the corridor and want to dance.

'It's up three flights of stairs, I'm afraid'.

I don't care if it's up Everest. I want to run to the top, turn round, fling my arms open and hug her. I have a right to be here. Cambridge is expecting me. Someone has prepared a room for me. My own room. This is as good as it gets.

A college porter is standing in my room, puzzled. My green rectangular trunk sent in advance fills the space, lying on its back, helpless as a tortoise. It's on loan from Aunt Clarissa and has travelled the world. It's locked and the brass corners on one end reflect flames from the gas fire, at the other end they nearly reach a shabby Victorian desk. A thin bed is to the left, with a blue Utility arm chair standing stiffly by its side as if visiting a patient in hospital. I put my suitcase and three string bags on the floor: out spill a kettle, some cutlery, books and a huge pack of what Bigga and I always keep handy, Dr White's extra-large sanitary towels, the only type to staunch our monthly flow. I catch sight of myself in a small mirror. I'd thought long and hard about what to wear so as not to look ridiculous: a tight black polo-necked jumper made of fine wool and a mid-calf-length scarlet circular skirt with a belt which I'm hoping will show off my one good point, a tidy, nipped in waist. Perhaps I'd seen a *Picture Post* photograph of Jane Russell in *The Outlaw* in my dentist's waiting room? I made the skirt out of a circle of felt. No boring seams—just cut a hole in the middle. I'm longing for the time when I can afford a sewing machine. A scarlet scarf at my neck made out of the leftovers is clipped in place by a black ring Bigga bought me in Lowestoft when we went for a week's convalescence with Tyna and Jack. I know I ought to miss Bigga but I don't want to think about her or anything outside Cambridge.

'It's the wrong way up. It doesn't open from the top like other trunks. You need to stand it on end and open it like a wardrobe'. The porter hesitates. I'm not used to talking to grownups like this, telling them what to do. It feels like talking in a foreign language but if I don't say it now, I'll have to call him back later and that would be even more embarrassing.

When he's gone I open it out fully from top to bottom by splitting it in half, like splitting a peach down the middle to get the kernel. It has drawers and straps and buckles and chrome bars which unfold like arms to greet you. Dangling from them are fixed wooden coat hangers.

I pull out two sheets, some pillow cases, towels and white damask napkins—all on the required list—to take downstairs to the housekeeper. Today I still have one of the napkins with 'YVONNE INSKIP' in spindly capitals

I picked out in black Indian ink. Then out tumble nighties and knickers, vests and bras—Tyna has always said I'm not what you would call a careful packer. I lift a turquoise pique housecoat out of one of the drawers. It has fine black lines swirling around like a watermark on best quality notepaper. Making clothes for Cambridge had been a bit like preparing a trousseau. The nuns' sewing lessons had not been wasted, for this, unlike the skirt, needed yards of hand-sewn seams. I can imagine myself, pale and interesting, perched on the window ledge surrounded by piles of dark, impenetrable books, sash pulled tight to show off my waist, wide flared skirt touching the floor.

Out of the other drawers come a radio, a pale gold brocade evening dress with a (homemade) peacock green velvet stole and a coffee pot with six tiny cups, all together costing £20, money I've saved from fruit-picking. I start to hang my dress in an alcove covered by a cretonne curtain which stands in for a wardrobe, but instead sink down on the bed. I look around at my very own room. I ought to write and tell Bigga I've arrived safely. What I cannot know is that another new student, Sylvia Plath, is in a nearby room writing to her mother. She might have been describing my room: '*I don't know how I can begin to tell you what it is like here in Cambridge! It is the most beautiful spot in the world . . . My room is . . . on the third floor, and . . . I love it dearly. The roof slants in an atticish way, and I have a gas fireplace which demands a shilling each time I want to warm up the room (wonderful for drying my washed hair by, which I did last night) and a gas ring on the hearth where I can warm up water for tea or coffee . . . I love the window sofa—just big enough for two to sit on, or for one (me) to curl up in and read with a fine view of treetops . . . . I can't describe how lovely it is'.*

There's a knock at the door.

'I'm Jennifer and I've got the room next door'.

'Come on in . . . I'm in a mess . . .'

Jennifer is awesomely beautiful: almond-shape dark eyes, long lashes, heart-shaped face. In fact, she looks exactly like Bridget Bardot. Later people whisper that she goes to some provincial film premieres as her double. She picks her way across the floor, avoiding the kettle and a milk pan and settles in the Utility chair where the light from the window falls across silky dark hair swept up into a pony tail. Two wisps escape the rubber band to brush against those lovely cheekbones. I think of my photograph of Bigga at the fancy dress party. She was a beauty too. It's safer if, like me, you're not.

'Coffee—a cup of coffee?'

Jennifer looks like a girl who goes to racy places like espresso coffee bars which are out of bounds for convent girls. Well, I've never before owned anything so beautiful as my coffee set, pale apricot with a black design like Japanese script. From this moment henceforth and forever I'm never going to use normal-sized cups like we had at home, especially those full of milky tea with spoonsful of sugar. I light the gas ring under the kettle and pour water on a spoonful of Nescafe into a cup only slightly larger than those in the dolls' china tea set I used to have. I have not yet heard of ground coffee and percolators, but this tastes brilliant—not like stuff from the Camp coffee bottle we had at home.

Later Jennifer and I walk to the railway station to pick up our bikes. People walking towards us slow down as they pass and can't take their eyes off her. It is as if I'm walking beside a naked woman. I get used to climbing the three flights of stairs to our corridor and finding men-in-waiting who turn towards me when they hear footsteps and then turn away disappointed. No one ever stands outside my door. At this rate how am I ever going to marry a vicar—or anyone else for that matter? God's plan for my life is a man without secrets who'll give me a new name and a home and children and the old Yvonne Inskip will be dead and buried, and I've got three years in which to find him.

In my first term I'm asked to sign up with a Cambridge GP and for reasons I don't question this means a medical examination. Perhaps it's someone's research project? I undress to the waist. The doctor is delighted.

'May I get a photograph taken? It will be anonymous, of course. It will only be used in a medical journal to teach doctors'.

My back is what excites him. The most perfect specimen he has ever seen.

'Your scabs and scars of old wounds are only in the places where you've scratched or squeezed the spots'.

'You mean they mark out a sort of chart, a map of where my hands can reach?'

'Exactly so'.

I'm glad to be useful to the doctor but I'm ashamed of my greasy skin. For years acne has been one of life's little crosses and various remedies have been suggested mostly wrapped in some degree of humiliation: advice about more frequent washing, more green vegetables, various evil ochre ointments and green lotions that smell of sulphur. Nothing has helped and I have known that the remedy is literally in my own hands. I can't leave my skin alone. I pick off scabs in the hope that there will be new shiny pink skin underneath and the blemish will have gone. But mostly I'm too early and the tiny wound bleeds again until it forms another scab. It's a race between my fingers and new skin to see which one gets there first. When the damage is repaired, it's usually at night, before I wake up to wreck it again.

Maybe it's all Rose of Lima's fault? I wanted to be like her years ago. She spoiled her complexion by using pepper and lye, an alkaline solution households used for washing and cleansing. She chose to do it. She was determined to put men off so that she could guard her chastity. I don't want to put men off. I have no idea how to put them on, but have a feeling that spots are not a move in the right direction.

'Do you have any problems you'd like to tell me about?' I'm grateful for the doctor's good intentions. 'Boyfriend problems or something like that?'

'No thank you, my life is in the hands of the Lord'.

'Anything wrong at home?' the doctor persists 'Would you like to talk to a colleague of mine? Not a skin specialist, but a psychiatric colleague'.

Why didn't I blurt out 'Anything wrong at home? You must be joking. As far as I know my father cleared off when I was a baby. One of my mothers left when I was eleven . . . my birth mother has never admitted she had me . . . she's had a stroke and is not getting better . . . we have no home of our own . . . do I have to go on?'

Instead I say 'I'm a Christian and God will look after me. But thank you for asking'.

If the doctor had then said 'If you ever have a problem and change your mind, come back', I'd probably have said 'Thank you but the Lord will help me solve any problems I might have'. And that would have been the end of that. But instead he said 'Well, if you ever feel you'd like to talk to someone about anything at all let me know'. Those careful words left a door open which I went through the following term, but for the moment I say nothing and walk away from the clinic with my piety intact.

At Newnham's Annual Commemorative Dinner I wear a brocade evening dress the colour of a field of corn and feel superior to all the pastel pink and blue net frocks which were last seen trailing down the aisle behind a bride. I sit next to Grace, the Skinners' niece, and the latest daughter in a vast tribe of intrepid missionaries. She's hoping that God will call her to work in South America but so far he's been keeping his plans up his sleeve.

When the Queen visits the college a week or two later together with the Principal she sweeps through the Hall amid a wave of curtsies. A camera catches the Duke of Edinburgh pausing to talk to the girl in front of me.

'Where do you come from?'

'Mauritius'

'And what are you studying?

'Mathematics, your Highness'.

'Excellent', with a grin, 'You'll be able to manage the family budget perfectly'.

Yes, I think, yes. My economics degree will come in handy managing our house and family on a vicar's stipend. I'm in the right place.

It's during this term that I see Uncle Jack on what was probably his last trip out of Lowestoft. He and Tyna break their journey to Bedford when they roll up at Newnham on a BMW motor bike. It's his pride and joy which he had saved for all his life and, apart from his clothes, a few sticks of furniture and tens of thousands of Woodbines, the only thing he ever possessed. He used to spend days and weeks stripping bits of it down, laying each piece meticulously in order on the concrete garden path, cleaning it and putting it back together again.

'Would you like to see round the college?' Tyna and I have just had coffee in my tiny cups, but Jack has had a mug of tea with three sugars. We tour the buildings and then step out into the grounds glimmering in soft autumn sunshine. The three of us stand by the sunken garden with its discreet ornate fountain. I cannot believe my good fortune at being there.

When they leave, Jack slips a ten shilling note into my hand.

'Why?' Tyna asked him as they walked away, for they were hard up. Jack had to turn up morning and midday in the hope of work and never knew whether a ship had docked or if he'd be laid off for the rest of the day.

She told me later what he said, 'I felt sorry for the poor kid. She must get lonely with all those long corridors and big rooms'.

13

PRAYER AND PASSION

I'm in the ballroom at Dorothy's Café and it's breakfast time, but I have not danced the night away. I'm here for a meeting. Tables and chairs for a hundred are scrunched up together between fat ornate pillars. The room is filling up.

At Newnham in 1955 you could open doors at random along its long corridors and find a sherry party, a poetry reading, a study group on Trade Unions, a Gestetner rolling out Labour Club pamphlets, an arts magazine being pasted together, a prayer meeting, a play rehearsal, a novel being written, a gramophone beating out Elvis Presley records or a rowdy tea party . . . And which door do I go through? A prayer meeting of course. I've signed up with the Cambridge Christian Union or CICCU, (pronounced 'Kick You' by those of us who are in the know) and this morning I'm bright and early at one of their uplifting breakfasts.

I'm looking for a place for Grace and me. We see a lot of each other. Her passion for spiritual things puts me to shame. In the light of eternity the world around her—King's College Chapel, the Backs, crusty bread and home-made raspberry jam for tea in Hall—is but a backdrop for the real dramas of life which lie in the soul. Once she was given some lilies and when they didn't open quickly enough she peeled the petals back. I walk over to the only empty table, set for five, and drape my Newnham scarf—gold, blue and grey—to reserve a chair for Grace. We've both had deadlines: I cycled to the town centre at midnight last night to catch the London post for an essay to Eric Hobsbawm, my Tutor. He wants to know if a teenager like me can spot a mid 19C watershed in Britain's economic development. First I had to look 'watershed' up in a dictionary. Is Grace going to get here in time? The room is filling up fast but no one joins me. About a dozen women are here but they came in groups and sit at their own tables.

About two minutes before the start my shoulders relax when I catch sight of Grace standing in the doorway. I wave. She is tall and stooping, light boned and pale. She has a demure walk as if her legs are lightly joined at the knee so her ankles swing back and forth like a pendulum. She puts her hand on my shoulder and whispers that she had a puncture. Breakfast is being served swiftly by waitresses in black dresses and frilly white caps and aprons. We order coffee and toast. The room is now full of handsome athletic men, some born from generations of fathers who could choose to take as their wives the most beautiful women they met. To me, my fellow students in their uncrumpled suits, pearly skin, and hair which knows its place, radiate prayerfulness and spiritual passion. I feel weak with excitement. The seats at our table are the only empty spaces left in the room.

I cannot remember who the speaker was that morning. What he said must be recorded in my Archives folders among the sheaves of notes I took of the talks and sermons I heard in my first year: every precious drop which might shampoo my soul is bottled and corked. The trouble is that I'm a collector, not an archivist, so couldn't be bothered to note what was said by whom, when and where. Since it all came from the Holy Spirit it was OK to miss out the middleman. But I do remember resting a book on the table that morning, Catherine Marshall's *A Man Called Peter,* a book about her husband, a penniless immigrant from Scotland who became Chaplain to the USA Senate in 1947 and died suddenly of a heart attack. I'd heard they were even going to make a film of it starring Richard Todd.

The speaker, just introduced, catches sight of three men who appear at the far door. He points at Grace and me.

'Over here. There are some spaces at that table'.

The men obey. Everyone sits and waits in silence. The one in front, the tallest of the three, is wearing a Harris tweed jacket and an impassive face. Next comes a man, small but perfectly formed, who smiles at everyone but looks at no one, wearing a navy blazer. Bringing up the rear is a man whose blonde hair has not recently seen a hairdresser, startling in a room full of short-back-and-sides. He walks face downward, narrowly missing several gilt chairs. His eyes watch his feet as though a moment's inattention might result in one of them flying off and landing on someone's plate.

'Excuse me, are these seats free?' the tall man looks straight at Grace.

'Yes'.

'Thank you'. In unison they turn their chairs so that they have their backs to the table and to us, so as to give the message their full attention.

The speaker begins. Instead of listening I'm thinking the speaker can't be a Cambridge man or he would know that men and women don't sit at the same table. There's nothing in the Bible about it, of course. It's just that it would be froward and indelicate for men and women who hadn't been introduced to sit together. I can't just blame religion. It's probably upper class manners. Someone said that only ten years ago at Trinity College a physics lecturer wouldn't begin until men and women were sitting at separate tables. That's how it is.

A waitress glides silently over to take orders from the three latecomers.

'No, nothing at all' they say quickly and she disappears.

They must be rich. They've already missed one breakfast they're entitled to in their own college and now they're dismissing another they've paid for because the entrance ticket includes the cost of breakfast. Will they go on afterwards and eat bacon and egg somewhere else? Why are they saying 'No?' Because to eat would mean turning their chairs round and acknowledging the existence of one table and two women? It might even involve asking for the silver-plated milk jug or for the Golden Shred marmalade with its curvy spoon slotted into a chrome handle, dangling, nearly touching, sweet and innocent. Better go hungry than fall into temptation. Suddenly I'm angry—all this stuff about Christians being one in Christ and they can't face sharing a spoon.

I look up. The neck of the tall man in front is hard to miss since it blocks my view of the speaker. It's a handsome head with smooth dark hair kept in place with mathematical precision. I'd like to stroke it. It's glossy. Would it be sticky? Brylcream, I guess. We used to sell a lot of that in our shop and I'd recognise it anywhere. I wonder how I'll know whom God wants me to marry? I move my head to the side and capture slices of reflections of the audience in the diamond panes of the mirrored walls. Perhaps my future husband's here. How will he find me?

At that moment the tall man places on the table beside him a spiral notebook. The maroon cover bears his name 'Edmund Gorse'. Still eyeing the speaker, his slim fingers with perfectly shaped nails slowly turn the narrow-ruled pages of up-to-date lists of people to pray for, headed Daily List, Weekly List, Monthly List and Emergency List. I look down on my own dirty fingernails and vow to do better. I can't read the names as the writing is so tiny and lots of it is initials anyhow. On a blank page Edmund begins to take notes. He must be one of the Sound, sound in doctrine and sound in practice. The Skinners have told me what I should look for: a Sound man who never oversleeps and so never misses his Quiet Time with God every morning, who prays and reads the Bible for at least half an hour; a man who doesn't drink alcohol, doesn't have doubts, swear, smoke, look longingly at women, go to the cinema, buy Sunday newspapers or even use public transport on the Sabbath, unless in an emergency when God understands. Edmund Gorse probably gives a tithe, one tenth, of his grant (or more likely of the allowance from his parents) to God through God's earthly agencies like church or missionary societies. This still leaves quite a lot left over if the cut of his tweed jacket is anything to go by. He has shifted his chair slightly so as to write things down and my knees are nearly touching his back. We are very close.

'Watch and pray', the speaker is winding down. The room fills with polite clapping. The tall man, Edmund that is, turns round and looks at me for the first time. He's surprised—and so am I.

'Aren't you the young lady who hijacked my taxi when I'd just arrived?'

'Well, I . . .' His friends are watching with admiration. Edmund has been alone in a taxi with an unknown girl. Sensing their shocked approval his face is transformed.

'You must admit, Edmund', interrupts the short man with the smiley face, 'there are worse fates than being carried off to an all-ladies' college. I'm Piers, but the way'. We all shake hands, 'this is Edmund and that's Luke. We three were at school together'.

'At Monckton Combe, I assume?' It's a gamble. I'm only guessing. The only man I've met who's been there is Grace's brother but I've heard her family talk of it as being the school where good Evangelicals send their sons. I take the chance to show off because if I'm right it proves I'm not an outsider.

'Well, yes. Do you know anyone there?'

Grace takes over. It seems to me as if she knows everyone worth knowing in the Church of England. Her uncle is a bishop and in church circles her family credentials are impeccable. Being with her is like being with minor royalty.

Edmund turns to me, 'What do you think of the address?'

'I wasn't listening very hard. I'm preoccupied with a book'.

'What is it?'

'I'm just re-reading *A Man Called Peter*'.

'Oh, an excellent book', says Piers 'Should be compulsory reading for every clergyman and his wife'.

'I haven't read it. Why should they read it?' Luke asks.

'Full of sound advice. A clergy wife should treat the great and the lowly the same. And have a sense of humour'. I hope I have one. I need it now because I can't help noticing he's doing all the talking and it's my book anyway. 'She's got to be a good cook: impromptu supper with the family and someone homeless as a guest one day, lunch for 200 at a stewardship campaign the next'. Edmund and Luke are listening hard. Can they expect this from their own chosen ones one day?

'That isn't all', Piers is warming to the subject, 'Catherine Marshall says a church feels that its minister and his wife belong to them and they want to be proud of their possession. There's a bit about how ministers' wives need to dress becomingly and to be as attractive as possible'.

Edmund looks alarmed at the prospect of imagining an attractive woman, let alone turning her into a clergy wife and climbing into bed with her as his lawful wedded spouse. Piers looks flustered as if he's realized where his tongue has led him. Grace doesn't seem to be listening and I wish the floor would open up and swallow me. Am I in the presence of a parade of beautiful imaginary women walking across the minds of these men and am I coming off much the worse for it?

Luke, who's been mostly silent, turns to Piers and says quickly, 'I've just remembered you paid for these tickets, Piers. I must settle up with you.

He opens a tan pigskin wallet to pull out a ten shilling note. Tucked in one of the compartments I can see a bright pink ticket which can only mean he goes to the theatre. So Luke is likely to be Unsound. He's a frivolous Backslider who's lapsed into worldly ways and might, for example, be found on a dark night going down a narrow passage on his way to Jesus Lane and the ADC to see a play or even a musical. You can't be too careful.

On the way home I ask Grace, 'How do you think it went?'

'Well at least they talked to us'.

I can't believe she's saying this, although it's exactly what I'm thinking. What the two of us should be doing is running through the sermon we've heard, picking out all the juicy bits we could profit by, not discussing young men.

'Edmund is a member of the Plymouth Brethren'. Grace knows everything. That rules him out. They have to marry within their membership and I'm Church of England. To join the Brethren is a step too far. What's more Luke is Unsound and Piers is shorter than me.

Grace has a room in college which doesn't yet have a gas fire. It's freezing until the coal fire has been lit for hours so she often joins me in my room at tea time. I'm on my knees balancing bread on the toasting fork. She has put the butter in a dish in the grate to make it easier to spread.

'What do you think 'dress becomingly' means?' I ask.

'Well' she said 'You mustn't be extravagant or draw attention to yourself'. Grace's clothes are made by her mother from remnants of material bought at the street market, 'Why do you ask?'

'I think I need to buy some clothes', I hear myself saying, while rescuing the butter which is now so hot it's nearly liquid.

The next morning a little shopping is called for. I walk out of college through Newnham's beautiful Pfeiffer Gates. Just imagine, they got smashed by male students in 1921 in protest against women being admitted to titular degrees. It must have cost the earth to mend them. I'm so, so glad I'm alive today and not then.

This is the morning when I feel it is my Christian duty to 'dress becomingly' and even 'be attractive', if that is what a clergy wife should do, so I go to the boutique opposite Emmanuel College. I buy a silvery grey dress in fine lawn, with tiny tucks and pearl buttons, a white collar and everywhere the suggestion of a Puritan maiden, except that round my waist goes a fine leather belt plaited in a riot of colours, with a silver clasp. And clearly I must have a summer frock in jade green glazed cotton, edged with sherbet pink, so cunningly cut and stitched as to show off to the very best advantage the places where I go in and out. I'd be mortified if anyone commented, but very glad if someone would show by just a glance that they noticed.

Perhaps the new clothes tipped the scales. One morning I look in the mirror and see staring back at me above the jade green and the sherbet pink a pale, greasy, spotty face. I hate my spots, but nothing—not even earnest prayer—can stop my fingers picking away at them until they bleed. I remember that the dermatologist offered me the chance of a chat with one of his psychiatric colleagues. I make an appointment.

14

FLYING AND FALLING

When the day comes I stride down Lensfield Road towards the clinic determined to look confident and not glance over my shoulder to see if anyone's noticed me. I half expect to find a sign saying 'MAD PEOPLE THIS WAY PLEASE' with a pointy black arrow at the bottom. What if someone does see me here on the doorstep? An appointment with a psychiatrist is nothing to be proud of. But I'm past caring. I want the chance of 'a chat', and if my blotchy, distressed face and spotty back will open up an introduction, that's fine by me.

Dr Sheldon is about my height, stocky with wavy brown hair. A bit like Rupert Davies who played the definitive Maigret on TV a few years later. His handshake is firm and friendly.

'Would you like to sit here? Let me tell you what I know about you—you're a First Year student at Newnham reading economics and I've read your medical notes about the acne'. He pauses. 'What would you like to tell me about yourself?'

'What do you need to know? What would be helpful to you?'

'Well, let's start by you telling me about your room at Newnham'.

I'm startled. Why hasn't he begun by asking me about my family? I've been rehearsing a narrative about what's happened so far, crafting an emerging and dramatic plot which shows me in rather a good light. What a waste! But clearly this is not the moment.

'I love it. It looks out on to tree tops—it's a bit like an attic. It feels special'.

'Have you done anything to make it yours?'

'No . . . oh well, I've covered the tatty old wicker wastepaper basket with wine coloured paper and glued my favourite quotations on'.

'Can you remember any?'

'Oh I can remember them all. I've been collecting them for years'.

'What's the shortest one?'

This day we sailed on. W.S.W.

'What's so special about that?'

'Christopher Columbus wrote it when things were desperate. They nearly had a mutiny on their hands. In the log book they'd hidden from the crew the fact that they were finding more sea than they'd bargained for—there seemed no end to it. But a few hours after that entry was written, they discovered America!'.

'Does life sometimes feel like that to you? A bit of a burden, just keeping on keeping on?'

'Yes, it does, though I know it shouldn't'. I say loud and clear as if he's deaf, 'Coming to Cambridge means I've got everything I've ever hoped for'. He waits. I search for something to say. Nothing too personal. 'I heard two old ladies in front of me in the Market Square the other day talking about their shopping and one said 'Well, that's the morning done'. I know just what she meant. I feel that when I go to bed. I'm glad to have got through another day'.

Silence. What's the matter with me? 'You're never satisfied' is what my mothers used to say to me'. I dig my fingernails into my hands to stop feeling sad.

'Would you like to tell me about your parents?'

I tell the tale of having two mothers, then one. And no father. What's more, I say, I was actually living with my real mother all the time, though our relationship was a secret shared by only three people and that did not include me. Every word feels like a heavy stone I have to pick up and hand over to him. I can hear my voice. It sounds like someone else, flat, bored, as if I'm reading from a telephone directory. I pause, hoping he'll say something normal like, 'Oh, I am sorry. What a shame'. or show some interest like, 'and what about your father? Where's he?'

I wait but he leaves the silences hanging in the air. So I have to go on, 'I once found an old letter which said I was adopted and I got very excited about that. But when I got older I only had to look in a mirror and see whose child I was. My mother never admitted she'd had me'.

He asks one question: 'Do you feel angry with anyone in your story?'

'Of course not. Anger is stupid and wasteful. We should love one another. It says so in the Bible. And we didn't get angry at home. My mothers said it was a waste of time.'

He lets that pass. 'We know your skin is a bit of a problem. Is there anything else you'd like to mention?'

'Well, when I was younger I used to be worried about going mad . . . yes, there is one other thing. It's very silly and it doesn't trouble me much', I pause, 'I'm afraid of falling'.

'Do you mean stumbling against something or losing your balance?'

'Neither. I can't explain. When I'm on an escalator I have to grip on to the rail, peg myself to something solid, because—oh this sounds so stupid—I'm as much afraid of floating up through the air as of crashing down. I can't explain'.

'Let's go back to your waste paper basket. Who is the person you quote most often?'

'Oh it has to be the aviator Antoine St Exupéry. It's in French but I can't speak French. In English it's *I can't wake up to my own fulfilment unless I'm called there by someone else . . . who in turn only exists through me.* It sounds much better in French. *(Je ne puis m'éveiller à moi-même sans y* être *appelé par un autre . . . mais cet autre* à *son tour, il n'existe que par moi')*

'I don't think I've read anything by him'.

'I did his book *Terre des Hommes* for A level. He describes the magic of flying over an empty planet, the silence, the beauty. It was in the days when planes were held together with string and rubber bands'.

I suddenly see myself as he must see me, a silly romantic girl. I've been here before. When I told Reverend Mother I'd learned chunks of Rupert Brooke's poems by heart, she laughed at me, 'You've fallen in love with his profile at the front of your book'.

But I can't stop myself, 'Saint Exupéry kept taking risks. Once he crashed on a narrow cliff above an abyss and spent three days in the Egyptian desert hallucinating. He describes tasting coffee and biting into a warm croissant in a café after he was rescued by a passing Arab on a camel'. I dare not go on to point out that he died young, his plane tumbling into the Mediterranean—no doubt under a cloudless blue sky—and was never seen again. It would be too much.

'What other quotations from him did you put on your waste paper basket?'

'How mysterious everyone is. How our own garden wall may enclose more secrets than the Great Wall of China. He imagines the skull of a dying slave as a treasure chest, stuffed with images of coloured silks, festivals, plantations, and white Moroccan towns, lost forever'.

'Anything else?'

'Yes, how a group of aviators clubbed together to free a slave from the Moors. They flew him to Agadir, then gave him a bus ticket to Marrakesh and a thousand francs so he could look for work. But no one could stop him squandering the money on golden slippers and bangles for dozens of street children. St Exupéry said as a slave the man had felt weightless and now he took the first chance he could to bind himself to others with the ropes of human relationships.

Otherwise we fly away . . .' my voice dies away, 'How did you know that this links to what I said about floating and falling?'

'I didn't'. Dr Sheldon says, 'Perhaps being parentless is to be untethered, but it's you who made the connection, not me'.

Dr Sheldon and I meet fortnightly for two terms.

'It would really help me to help you if you could write your story down and let me have it next time we meet', he says at the end of the first session 'and keep a journal for your eyes only. It would also help if you'd keep a record of dreams which you can tell me about'.

So each fortnight I bring him a dish of dreams. It's as if he sits there behind the desk, white damask napkin tucked under his chin, knife and fork poised in his hands. In my journal I note that he says my dreams are 'analytically very good because the more strongly things are repressed unconsciously, the clearer they become consciously'. In other words I'm so repressed there's no need for my dreams to plunder the dressing up box and hide behind a twirly moustache and ginger wig. I walk in week by week and unfurl colourful banners of improbable events. I'm like a back-to-front medium with a message from another world which is meant for me but I can only access it through someone else.

I don't like the secret, uncensored journal he told me to keep. When I open it I have to cover up the previous page with my hand so as not to read the last entry. Its despair and self-disgust is like a tide of sewage.

At times he and I turn to sex and violence.

'Has anyone ever assaulted you? Been intrusive?'

'Well, yes, and the police were called . . . I was about 14, walking along a Clapham lane lined with a thick hedgerow. I was reading and eating an apple when there was a rustle in the hedge. I looked up and saw a boy about my age spring out and run in front of me, blocking the path. He began to touch me and say nice things about my body'.

'What did you decide to do?'

'I didn't decide, there was no time. The next thing I saw was his head jerked backwards and he threw himself back into the bushes. I'd hit him between the eyes with the apple core. It gave me time to run. I ran until I got to a Lodge leading up to the Manor House and hung around holding on to the hedge with both hands. I was too embarrassed to ring the doorbell. When I'd got my breath back I ran on to the end of the lane until I got to Bedford, then walked back along the road'.

'What happened then?'

'My mothers called the police. A nice woman PC interviewed me. She was worried in case it had been worse and I was too embarrassed to tell. They caught him—he'd been behaving strangely in children's playgrounds—and said they were pleased to have my testimony because they thought I was a reliable witness'.

'And were you?'

'No, I never got a chance. I sat for hours on the stairs outside the courtroom, then the boy changed his plea to 'Guilty''.

'How do you feel about it now?

'If I'm honest, rather pleased. I sort of won'.

'And having a stranger touch you and praise your figure? How was that?'

'I didn't notice'.

I'm beginning to feel that Dr Sheldon may have the answer to everything if I hang around long enough.

'I still don't know why I can't speak French'.

'Have you any thoughts about it?'

'I've no idea'.

'Let's look at the facts. The nuns wanted you to speak French but you wouldn't?'

'Couldn't'. I put him right.

'Or 'couldn't' But on the other hand the nuns wouldn't let you speak about things you wanted to say, talking about your faith, for example, which is very important to you. They forbade it'.

'Yes, I had to keep silent or they'd have taken my scholarship away'.

'I wonder if your unconscious has been getting its own back? Our bodies and minds are like stubborn donkeys. We can force them to go a certain way, we can ill treat them—up to a point. But they have ways and means of protesting, of making themselves heard'.

'But why did it pick on French? Why not chemistry or algebra?'

'What does France make you think of? Say anything that comes into your head'.

'Glamour, the can-can, frills, people talking a lot, waving hands, drinking wine, people talk about 'a dirty weekend in Paris . . .'

'What would you call a woman who went on one of those?

'A sinner'.

'Anything else?'

'A fallen woman'.

'Let's look at what 'fall' means. When do we use the word?'

'Well, ... countries fall when the enemy wins . . . when you're unhappy you feel 'low' or 'down' . . . when you can't do something you say you're 'floored' . . . we say someone falls pregnant, you fall ill . . . you could be 'a fallen woman'.

'Do you think you know anyone who might have been what people describe as 'a fallen woman?'

Silence.

'I think your fear of French—and of falling—may be to do with your fear of being 'a fallen woman', which is what some people, including I think your Aunt Amy, might call your mother'.

'Is that why I encourage my spots, to make myself ugly and therefore safe because no one will want me?'

'What do you think, Yvonne?'

'Perhaps I'm afraid of being like her'.

'You don't have to go on being afraid, Yvonne'.

I believe him.

At my last session we tidy up a few loose ends.

'But what do you make of my fear of going mad? I won't, will I?'

'I think it was the way you rationalised the anger in you. But let's look at it . . . tell me what a mad woman would look like'.

'The only mad woman I've actually seen is little old lady in Bedford when I was a child. She roamed around the streets asking questions out loud about the missing men in her life which no one answered'.

He lets that pass so I try again.

'A mad woman would have thick scarlet lipstick—put on crookedly—and black pencilled eyebrows with false eye lashes like a cow and toes peeping from her shoes. She'd be stroking her long matted hair or winding it round her finger'. I pause.

'I think things are changing for you, Yvonne. You had to be very good all the time and 'madness' would give you an excuse for thrashing out, making a noise, being colourful, breaking something, even hitting someone. Doing all the things you'd never do. Now you're finding it easier to say what you feel. You don't have to apologise for everything. And the world won't end if you upset someone. You won't always get it right—none of us do—but you won't go mad'.

At the end of the last session I walk to the door and turn to say good bye. I have just bought something else: a stunning edge-to-edge coat in apricot, and wear it over the jade green dress. I'd handed my 'memoir' over to him at the beginning and never saw it again. But I do have the journal which records that this is how it ended.

'I like your coat', he said, 'It's beautiful'.

So this is what it feels like to be complimented by a man. I walk out into the street, and the people and the birds singing in the trees seem to be in a halo of light.

I never see him again.

15

A STUDY OF MAN EMBRACING WOMAN

The Principal of Newnham doesn't understand why I want to drop economics. 'Be under no delusion,' she writes at the end of my first year, 'Under the new Professor you're not likely to get a higher class of degree in Anthropology than in other subject'. She thinks I'm ambitious. But I'm not. What possible advantage would even a First Class degree be to me when my vocation is to become a vicar's wife; leader of the Mothers' Union, ready with 200 home-made mince pies to hand out after the Midnight Christmas Communion service; and a dab hand at rounding up the Sunday School on a day trip to Wicksteed Park, Kettering? No, my trouble is that economics has let me down. I have some important questions lined up which it won't listen to. Why are women so poor? Can we find fairer ways of sharing things out? What good are families? Now I've found a new subject which people jokingly call 'the study of men embracing women'. It's Social Anthropology. Sounds promising. I've talked to anyone who will listen—including Dr Sheldon—about changing subjects. What better way to get answers than to find out what's going on in the rest of the world and learn from them?

If I'm going to switch to Part II of the Tripos in Social Anthropology, I've got some catching up to do. So for six weeks in the summer vacation I'm given a glorious room with a large balcony overlooking Newham gardens, and the sun never stops shining. Books cover the floor. Listen carefully, they say, and you'll find that every human being from the Andaman Islanders to Zulus has the same set of problems: how to cope with birth, death, hunger, danger and disorder. You'll learn how at times it's possible to heal without hospitals; manage without money, policeman and plumbers; trust the spoken word because there's no written language. You'll be amazed to find rational cognitive patterns without science; political order without a state; spirituality without a church.

I can't wait.

So I turn up to the first lecture and anthropology lives up to its promise. The library copy of Malinowski's '*Sexual Life of Savages*' (1929) used to be locked away, only handed out to postgraduates with written permission from their professor. Now there's a less pessimistic view of its corrupting influence on the young, but it has to be specially asked for. I ask, but am disappointed to find that only the title is risqué, the rest is about kinship, marriage and mortuary rites. But in one anthropology book I catch my first sight of a photo of a naked man. Later experience teaches me that the man in the picture has an unusually long penis, but at the time I assume it's standard issue.

I'm curious about penises for two reasons. First, I'd like to know as many facts as possible about what difference it makes to its owner. Step into any room and the men there are likely to better educated, richer, more travelled and more used to being in charge than women. Men certainly seem to get all the best jobs. Why are we so different? Is it in our bodies? We have to take the ebb and flow of our lives for granted, cope with the menarche and the menopause. Are we less inclined to master the world because we have to live co-operatively with ourselves? I want an answer.

Secondly, I'm not going to be an outsider. I want to join all the women since time began who know what it feels like to have a lover. By the end of my second year my theoretical knowledge of sexual practices worldwide is probably unequalled among most 20 year olds. Because so many legal, ritual and economic institutions depend on marriage and family patterns I sometimes feel anthropologists write about little else. As for practical experience—nil.

But to be honest I'm more interested in family patterns than sex. I've read descriptions of some weird sexual practices but in the end they seem a bit limited and repetitive compared with deep relationships which have infinite potential, if poets and novelists and spiritual writers and the Bible are anything to go by. You usually find them in a family or close friends. But what is a family? As a student I feel I'm standing in a market place of ideas from across the world, all jostling for attention. Every one of them is sure they've got it right and God is on their side. Weddings can take place in minutes or over years. In one place multiple wives is every man's dream but elsewhere it's a nightmare. You might be able to select your marriage partner freely, or your extended family may have the right one lined up for you. It's as if each culture is making similar garments but following a different knitting pattern.

What matters is that every child must be born into a bunch of specific adults of both sexes who accept life-long responsibilities. Usually there are backup contingency plans: one or more specific adults or groups linked by blood or marriage who expect to retain their glue and stick to the child through thick and thin. Meanwhile the children learn that they have reciprocal responsibilities as they grow up. Nothing is left to chance. I really like that.

Of course anthropologists point out that it doesn't always work, but then what does? Supposing a man dies childless. The argument runs like this: he'll be a lonely ancestor journeying through the after-life, and not in the mood to do you any favours from beyond the grave. No problem. His wife can conceive a child in his name through his brother. But what if she's sterile? Or dead? A mere detail. A surrogate will have a child on her behalf. So you can have ghost marriages between two dead people. I couldn't foresee when I was 19 that within my lifetime science would catch up with this degree of sophistication. Now we provide living ghost fathers and mothers who supply sperm and eggs and wombs for those in need. Societies can thrive on consensual legal fictions like these, because the child is what matters.

I screw up courage to ask my tutor, Dr Edmund Leach, if we could have an extra-curriculum group discussion about family patterns.

'Certainly, get some chaps together here in the Arch and Anth Museum and I'd be pleased to come'.

I can't do it. I haven't the courage to ask my fellow students and risk them saying 'No'. But I don't have to wait long to find out what Dr Leach really thinks. In the early 1960s he will scandalise the nation with his Reith Lectures. He bitterly attacked what he called 'the cereal packet family', a daddy, a mummy, a small boy with an even smaller girl ecstatically marching hand in hand across the cardboard cereal box. He attacked the contemporary family because two parents is far too small a unit for safety. He didn't foresee that anyone in their right mind would choose to be a lone parent.

Back in my room I read accounts of initiation rites, taboos, incest, funeral ceremonies, divine kingship and witchcraft. I learn to interrogate everything, asking 'What's its function in that society?' The answer comes back that in order to find out you have to go among real people, learn the language, feel the pain. I listen to lecturers who in their fieldwork have been exhausted by heat and fever and starvation; have listened attentively to men with upstretched arms singing praises to their ox; who've talked to leopard-skin chiefs and watched how a Kachin from East Burma was slotted in to the kinship system of a village hundreds of miles away within a couple of hours of arriving in Eastern Assam. It's a tough and heroic life. 'Field research in anthropology is what the blood of martyrs is to the church', said C.G. Seligman. This is the sort of talk I understand.

But I continue to worry about women. Everywhere I look they get a raw deal. Gods take sides and it's shocking. You can tell a 'righteous' man by his many wives and cattle, but if a wife dies in childbirth, she was 'unfaithful'. Some say 'Women's heads are tougher than men's so they can carry heavier loads' and others that 'Only men's fingers are nimble enough to embroider prestigious ceremonial robes'. Even here in Cambridge it's less than ten years since women were allowed to graduate. Still no woman can be ordained priest.

What of my Christian belief? Anthropology inoculates me against ever again believing in an arbitrary God out there who intervenes at will. St Iraneus in the third century remarked that the glory of God is a human being fully alive, and he gets my vote. Rocks of new knowledge tumble into my brain and wear away some of my beliefs. From time to time I visit the demolition site and in particular check out what's happening to women. Nothing much yet to report but clearly there's now a space to keep an eye on.

For example, the Gospel writers tell the Christmas story of the Virgin birth. Now I'm discovering that dozens of not dissimilar stories are told about how gods come into the world in irregular ways as a means of showing how special they are. Am I worried? Certainly not. The story of the Virgin Birth is saying what cannot be wrapped up in words. It's reaching down to deeper eternal truths. I'm not going to lose any sleep wondering about gynaecological details. After all, I've avoided enquiring about them all my life.

16

TEMPTATION

The fact is that after a year of waiting I'm getting anxious. Too many members of the Christian Union—men who will no doubt be future bishops, canons, deans and archdeacons—come back at the beginning of each term transformed, beaming and jolly. They shyly admit they're engaged to be married. These are people who watch each other but have not lifted their eyes in prayer meetings all term to look at a woman, no doubt bearing in mind that the New Testament is pretty strong on a man's impure thoughts. Each probably thinks it's his Christian duty to check that no one breaks the rules All the more surprising that the Lord seems to be more relaxed about such things during the vacations.

And just look at whom they choose. As a would-be anthropologist I can't help seeing them as an endogamous tribe, who only marry within their own group. Their fiancées for the most part are the daughters, sisters, cousins and nieces of current bishops, canons, deans and archdeacons. The girls, however bright, leave private schools not bothering much with exams, and hang around for a time doing clerical work in, say, a bishop's office. Some families do a swop with friends on mainland Europe, each ending up with an au pair. Then the girls get snapped up. I, on the other hand, am not getting snapped up. Why can't I have men standing waiting for me in the corridor like Jennifer? Just one would do. I'm not greedy.

Then I find in my pigeon hole an invitation from the Cambridge Pastorate, a Christian group without membership rules, open to anyone. I ask Grace to go with me to a vicarage garden tea party on the lawn of Holy Trinity Church next Sunday'. I don't tell her my motives are not strictly theological.

Next Sunday she and I join the Cambridge Pastorate. I sit alone, half-hidden in a large wicker chair at the edge of the grass and watch a tall slim man stride across to Grace and make her smile. He's older than most of the men here, his hair is fair, already receding, his nose and lips thin. He wears a navy blue blazer and a summer Emmanuel College tie—white with discreet cerise and blue stripes. His trousers are immaculately pressed. I watch him walk away, moving smoothly and graciously across the lawn, like a dancer. Now he's sitting down on a swinging striped sofa between two women, carelessly, at ease. He doesn't seem to know or care that such brazen behaviour breaks the rules. He goes up to Grace and says something which makes her laugh. Is he flirting with her? Could be tantamount to serious intent. What are the rules here? I don't know any more. I ask around and, yes, he is preparing to be an Anglican vicar. I wonder what his name is. I start to go to Pastorate events regularly.

I make friends with Bill Skelton, the Chaplain of the Pastorate. He's in his thirties, unmarried and stunningly good looking. He's a bit of a hero—lots of medals—having been a distinguished night-fighter pilot during the Second World War. He's also the nephew of the Duke of Somerset, whose coronet he carried at George VI's coronation, but I didn't know that, and only a few people could have foreseen the turmoil and tragedy which later shaped his life.

'Would you be interested in joining us on the Pastorate Mission to Hornchurch in September?' Bill asks, 'About 50 or us are going, we'll do door-to-door leafleting, hold special services and meetings in people's houses etc. It would be good to have you with us'.

At our first team-building meeting to prepare for the mission, we cram into Bill's room in Clare College, sitting or standing on any space we can find. We've been asked to bring one book and, in turn, say why we chose it. The blonde older man, whom I now know to be Richard, says he's writing an essay on 17th century English mystics. He reads from John Donne's poem *Extasie.*

> *. . . all severall soules containe/Mixture of things, they know not what,/Love, these mixt soules doth mixe againe/And makes both one, each this and that.*

And my heart does a handstand.

The book I've chosen is a fat volume, *A History of Western Philosophy*, written by Bertrand Russell. I'm trying to show off, but it's not going to work. No one has told me that the book is regarded by people in the know as a pot boiler, written when Russell began to trade on his genius by writing for ordinary people. I've chosen it because, though I wouldn't tell anyone, I feel linked to Russell. I once read that he was afraid of going mad. His father, mother and sister, all real people with real names, had died by the time he was three, which is sad, but he was luckier than me. He grew up with people who'd known them. He'd have heard stories which might have made him hate and love them. At least he'd got someone to get his teeth into.

A fortnight later I'm sitting on the same bit of floor and it's just as crowded. Bill's talking about Tolstoy's *Resurrection* which I've not read. It's the story of the fallout from one night when an aristocratic nephew seduces his aunts' maidservant, Katusha. She conceives, is dismissed and descends into poverty and prostitution. He thinks no more about his one-night stand until years later by chance he sees her in court facing serious charges. His life is propelled into new and dangerous channels. Suddenly I feel panicky. The walls crowd in on me as though they might topple down. I look round to see how I can escape, but I can't leave without scrambling over a lot of people and making a fool of myself. My heart is pounding so loud I'm afraid people will hear. It passes but after that I always sit near the door.

When Bill has finished I go straight to Heffer's bookshop and buy a tiny navy—blue hardback copy of *Resurrection* in The World's Classics Edition, which I still have. I gulp down page after page. When I get to the seduction scene on page 68 I stop. I can hardly bear the pleading, the scolding, the arms which lifted her up just as she was, in her 'coarse, stiff chemise' and the click of the latch. Her words ring in my ears 'Oh don't, you mustn't! Let me go!' while she clings closer to him. In my edition there are seven tiny dots across the page to signal what happened in the prince's bedroom. They are the most eloquent dots I have ever seen. A huge wave of feelings I've never experienced before bathes every cell in my body. For a few seconds I am a stranger to myself.

In September a local paper is impressed—probably amused—by the sight of a Cambridge crowd of students coming to sort out Hornchurch's spiritual life. A press photographer persuades the men to line up like beauty queens with placards round their necks. Richard is third from the front. When the photographer wants something less formal he wanders into the church hall to snap a couple facing each other on hard wooden chairs: Richard and I are planning an evening meeting in someone's house which Richard will chair and I'll give a ten minute talk. I'm stiff and upright and alert, my hand-made scarlet felt skirt wrapped round my legs, notes clutched in tight fingers. He's sitting back, relaxed. He's called a mature student, older than the rest of us, some of whom are, like me, straight from school, others having done two years' National Service. He has an other-worldly look, composed and meditative, a little austere until he smiles. His smile, for me, lights up the whole church hall.

When the mission's over Richard suggests that as we both live in Bedford we travel back together. I can't believe my good fortune. In the train he startles me by saying, 'Have you thought that if we took a razor blade and cut out every reference to poverty and injustice in the Bible, there'd be very little left?'

'No I haven't . . .' What with that and my free scholarship at Cambridge and what Lance told me, I vow to vote Labour for the rest of my life, but I say nothing.

When we reach St Pancras he says, 'Shall we have something to eat here? It's nearly 1 o'clock'.

I want the conversation to continue. He leads me across Euston Road to an ABC café. We sit at a table with an

HP sauce bottle on it and my powdery tomato soup comes with a grubby spoon. He's certainly not trying to impress anyone.

'How long have you wanted to be a priest?'

'When I was working in Southern Rhodesia I had a spiritual awakening. I was clear I had a vocation to the priesthood', he pauses.

'What do your parents think about it?'

'Nothing much. They say it's up to me—after all I'm 25. I must be six years older than you'. I love to hear him talk—his voice is low and silky and sexy. 'Nothing is straightforward, he continues, 'Prayer just doesn't seem to work for me . . . there's so much suffering. Then I think perhaps I could help by living a different sort of life'.

On the train back to Bedford Midland station, as we slow down at Luton station, he says, 'I spend too much time thinking about myself and wondering what other people are thinking about me. If you really want to know, I want to be totally dedicated to God. I think being a celibate monk may be the only way to do it'.

When term begins Richard invites me back to his college, Emmanuel, to a magnificent suite overlooking Front Court, with two bedrooms and a tiny kitchen at the back, which he shares with Chris, another ordinand. When I arrive I'm surprised to find girls everywhere, either nurses from Addenbrooke's Hospital or Cambridge Maternity Hospital, or trainee teachers from Homerton College. While Chris, wearing an apron, is busy in the kitchen, Richard is draped elegantly against the tall mantelpiece, chatting to a circle of admirers. When he suggests he and I go to Evensong at King's College Chapel and we walk along King's Parade—a zone free of iPods, admission charges and baseball caps worn backwards—I tingle with delight. He chose me, not any of the others. And when he touches me, slipping a warm hand in mine, I know that I want that hand, once given, never to let mine go. I feel for the first time that I have somewhere to go and someone to go with.

In the next few weeks I discover there've been lots of others before me, even a fiancée while he was working in what was then Southern Rhodesia. When he shows me the books on his bookshelf, I can't resist slyly looking to see if there's yet another affectionate message on the flyleaf. Well, there's nothing I can do about the past. He got it wrong, it's OK, I forgive him. It's his future choices I'm interested in.

We see each other several times a week and often go to Evensong at Kings College Chapel as a mid-afternoon break from studying. Day after day I sit at a desk in the University Library—anthropological facts and theories dancing on the page in front of me—while I'm hoping against hope that this is the afternoon when he will appear. I don't allow myself to pray that he will come. I tell myself that's not what prayer is for. But often he comes all the same and when I see his familiar outline my heart leaps with joy. I get to know King's Chapel well. There's a dark oak screen. Henry VIII has his initials carved on it, as does Anne Boleyn. They say it can only have been put there between 1533 when he married her and 1536 when he had her executed. Not very long. Sex and religion do not mix well.

This poster says that too. I took the picture in Interlaken in the 90s: one clergyman, gazing at another, name unknown, an elderly man in a dark suit, lips pursed, eyes troubled, his head encircled by the black halo of his hat. 'We wish everybody a beautiful Sunday'. The caption is bland and kindly, but the picture is not: a minx with a wide smile leans against the man in the poster. She's young, impatient to get his attention; carefully placed so that we can see her while he cannot. But he can feel the weight and warmth of her bare arm on his shoulder, her breath on his neck, perhaps to whisper in his ear. It's a gesture which only those very close to him would use. He looks troubled, as if he's being touched by something not altogether wholesome. What should he do next?

A few months after Richard and I met, we are in my room at Newnham and I'm lying face down on my bed, Bible open in front of me, chin cupped in my hands, bare feet waving restlessly in the air. We're studying Psalm 137 together, a psalm later made famous by Boney M in *By the Rivers of Babylon,* though understandably they underplay the bit about dashing little ones against the stones. There's not an obvious link from the psalm to an argument about celibacy, but I've managed to make it because I can think of little else.

'Look, Rich, I know what you mean about being a monk. Of course people give things up when they've got a goal . . . mountaineers or athletes . . . the nuns at school, Newnham dons . . .' I'm getting carried away, 'but I don't see why anyone should have to give up having a wife . . .'

Out of the blue it's: 'I love you, Yvonne'.

I get up quickly, swinging my legs down on the floor. He's sitting staring at the fire. He could be talking to the kettle. I'm alarmed. I can't let him love me yet. I meant to tell him I'm not what I seem, but not now, not here. I was going to break it gently. He doesn't know what he's letting himself in for.

I hear someone say in a pompous, self-important voice, 'I think you should know that I have no idea who my father is and I didn't even know who my mother was . . .'.

'Yes, I know'.

'How do you know?' my voice shakes.

'Your vicar told me at Christmas. He felt I ought to know before I got too involved with you'. I try to take this in. They've been talking about me in secret. So I'm faulty goods which need a pre-sale warning?

'It's not a problem, Yvonne. I love you', he turns towards me and stretches out his hands to take mine. 'Look at me. I'm not asking you to marry me because I don't know whether God would have me marry. I've told you from the beginning that I may be called to be celibate. Marriage is too easy, too cosy'.

'Oh'. Is this the best moment in my life so far? Or the worst? What's the good of love on those terms? I certainly don't want to give up sex before I've tried it. I privately consider priestly celibacy a Roman Catholic nonsense but do not think this is the moment to say so. I've just copied out in one of my journals Charles Kingsley's words warning young men against 'books and sermons deprecating as carnal and degrading those family ties to which they owe their existence . . .' Three cheers for Kingsley.

'If I married I'd be distracted by worrying about money. And how could I do a good day's work in a parish if we had broken nights with children crying?' he wants some reassurance but I don't know where to start, 'But in the last few days I wonder if God has been saying to me 'Think of sacrificial marriage. Although you will be distracted by a family, I want you to marry Yvonne'

'I understand perfectly', I reassure him, though I do not understand a word, 'Nothing could be worse than cosy marriage. I agree. Let's forget you said what you did'.

I'm frightened he'll say something I'll regret. Things are happening too fast, he could say he doesn't want to see me again.

'Let's go out and have a Chelsea bun at Fitzbillies'.

Later that night in bed I twist and turn in anger. How dare he see me as a liability? What the hell was he talking about when he said 'sacrificial marriage?' No sex please, we're Christians? Sorry, love, not tonight, it's Lent, come back in 40 days'? And what was I talking about when I said what I did about 'cosy marriage' being terrible. What's wrong with being cosy? Sounds lovely to me. Think of John Bunyan. A fine upstanding Christian if ever there was one. He said parting from his wife and children was as bad as 'pulling the flesh from my bones'. Perhaps he said it as they were dragging him away to put him in Bedford Jail. Well, it all worked out fine. When he got to prison he wrote *Pilgrim's Progress*—the first international best seller written by a member of the working class. Think of what we'd have missed if he hadn't written it. Marriage hadn't held him back.

I pull the bedclothes up over my head. Richard wasn't joking when he talked about being a celibate priest. This is deadly serious. Would I get in the way, be somewhere I had no right to be? No, not that again. But I keep coming back to the fact that I've prayed that God will lead me to the right man and here he is. If he asks me to marry him I'll have to say 'Yes' and take the consequences. I fall asleep thrilled that whatever happens now nothing can quench the fact that I've been loved by a man. And above all a safe man, unlikely to go the way of my father, but returning to my bed night after night.

When I wake up next morning I'm pretty sure that God's celibacy plans for Richard, even if they ever existed, do not stand a chance.

A month later on a February evening, I'm sitting on the floor by the gas fire in my room, leaning back against Richard's legs. He's in the blue chair struggling to learn New Testament Greek and I've covered the floor with bits of an essay on cargo cults in Papua New Guinea. We're drinking Nescafe and sharing another Chelsea bun from Fitzbillies.

'Yvonne, it's no good. All this uncertainty . . . I can't go on like this . . . it's getting to my work'. He closes his Greek grammar. 'I've just had an essay back and my tutor didn't like it'.

I'm alarmed. It's all my fault? Am I already a millstone round his neck? Is this his way of saying good-bye? I dare not speak.

'If I asked you to marry me, how long could you wait?'

'A long time'. I stare into the flames flickering in an orderly line across the gas fire.

'Lord knows what the Bishop might think. A priest with a family costs the church much more. I don't want to go to theological college with a black mark against me'. I can't see his face but his voice is heavy with misery. He seems to wait for me to say something comforting but I can't think of anything, 'We'd have to keep it a secret'.

'That's no problem'. He's picked the right person here. I'm used to keeping secrets. Where would I be without them?

'Would you wait six years?' he pulls me gently to my feet and holds me by my shoulders. I'm very still.

'Look at me', he cups my chin in his hand, 'It'll take that long. Finish my degree here, then two years at theological college, and after I've been ordained I'll have to wait at least a year because bishops don't like you to marry when you're trying to settle into a parish'.

'That's not fair'. I don't argue with the maths but am stung into saying, 'It's a hypothetical question. You say 'If I asked you . . . ?' What am I supposed to do with that?'

'OK. That means you've vetoed it. It means I can't discuss it with you anymore. We'll talk about something else'. He snatches up his jacket.

'I'm sorry. I didn't mean to upset you'. This is going all wrong. Why am I being difficult? He loves me—and I can put up with anything. I face him and slip my arms round his waist, 'I expect you've forgotten what it's like to be in love for the first time', I plead, 'That's what makes me a bit jumpy'. I might lose him. I might lose him. I glance at my watch. He'll have to go in a few minutes. At 10pm all visitors must leave Newnham and I can hear footsteps already along the parquet wooden corridor outside my door. Jennifer's man, no doubt. It's rumoured she's engaged and is going to leave Newnham at the end of term to get married. I should have talked to her about boyfriends but now it's too late and she's so beautiful I'm just not in her class.

'I'll come with you as far as the Porter's Lodge. Wait a moment while I put on a coat and shoes'. We walk downstairs in silence. What if this is the last time I see him?

But instead of saying good bye at the door Richard turns and says, 'Come for a walk with me'.

We go to Fen Causeway, a bumpy, tufted meadowland with raised tow paths lining narrow water channels. There's a mill with its lighted windows making restless angular patterns in the water. We barely speak until we get to a small wooden bridge only a few yards long and covered in flaking white paint, which crosses a dry ditch filled with prickly thistles and rusty weeds.

'I've seen you open up like a flower these past few months. I loved you even before then, before I knew I did'.

I lean over the handrail of the bridge and look down onto the muddy weeds. I'm finding it hard to breathe. 'You look beautiful'. I don't believe him for a moment as no one has ever said anything like that before, but it sounds comforting.

'It's all because of you'.

We walk hand in hand round the Fen, seeing nothing, saying nothing until I break the silence, 'Shall I tell you something?'

'If you like'.

'Oh, my words are worth more than a mere 'if you like''.

'Please will you tell me?'.

'I'm thinking of my love for you, Richard, and I'm frightened. There's something heroic and self-satisfying in giving up everything you hold dear for God'.

'I don't understand'.

'It's what attracted me to becoming a nun when I was young. Later I prayed that God would call me to be a missionary, like Grace. I can feel it again now. I wonder if I should sacrifice my love for you, so that you could be a better priest? Perhaps I must look for my true vocation somewhere else?' I turn and look into his eyes.

'Do you mean you're thinking of giving me up?' he asks.

'I don't think we'll have any peace until we've decided'.

'I can't help thinking that's when our troubles will begin—if we go ahead'.

He grabs my hand and we walk quickly back to the bridge, 'It'll have to be a step of faith. If we knew for certain we would not be trusting God'. It's as if he's talking to himself. He takes my hand roughly in his and kisses me lightly, almost shyly.

'Will you marry me?'

I look up at the bare twigs on the trees which are chopping the moon into pieces.

'Of course'.

At the weekend we go shopping for fish cakes and a jar of tartare sauce. We walk past a narrow window displaying engagement rings in a shop opposite Kings College and suddenly we're no longer hungry. I choose a second hand ring with a band of five small opals costing £8. There's a beautiful big black opal from Australia which costs £12 so it's not in the running. The jeweller explains that opals are tricky. I must be careful as they expand in heat and might push open the tiny golden claws and fall out. I like the idea of a ring which needs to be cared for.

Four days after he'd slipped the ring on my finger (only to be worn when we're alone, of course, for our engagement must be a secret), Richard is in my room waiting for me and I'm running back from the college library along the polished wooden parquet corridor in my stockinged feet when I slip and fall. We both agree it's nothing, just a sprain, and he leaves for dinner at Emmanuel College. When I can't put my foot to the ground I realise I need help. I don't want to bother Richard by ringing from the Porter's Lodge to ask him to take me to hospital. That would be a terrible start to our engagement, suddenly turning into a burden, someone who needs looking after. He's got an important essay to write.

When everyone has gone to dinner and Newnham corridors are deserted I make my way on one foot down three flights of stairs—hopping or shuffling on my bottom—and ask the Porter to ring for a taxi. I share an ambulance back from Addenbrooke's Hospital, my broken leg in plaster, with a man from Corpus Christi who gives a riotous account of how he broke his ankle skiing. I wish I too had a glamorous story to tell about my leg, broken a week after I got engaged.

That night, as I lie awake telling myself to get used to the pain, I try to remember what was it that Dr Sheldon said about flying and falling?

17

BLIND LIGHT

Blind Light (2007) is a brightly-lit glass room filled with dense mist, an art work by Anthony Gormley. You watch people vanish as they go in, then seconds later reappear as shadows when they move close to the walls. Inside visibility is down to as little as two feet, so you feel as if you are drifting at the bottom of a sea. White light is worse than black. Black is familiar. At any time we only have to screw up our eyes and black is there waiting for us. Each night we rehearse it when we go to sleep. Outside, my daughters saw my hand and didn't know if it was a friendly greeting or a cry for help. I could only stay a minute or two, needing them to lead me outside where I'm tethered to the real world.

While I was inside *Blind Light*, I thought of our engagement. It was as if wanting to be a priest generated a white light which flooded our lives with scruples and scrutiny and drama. It blinded us both.

Richard walks into my room at the Wrestlingworth farm, the bedroom which really belongs to the farmer's daughter, not the housekeeper's daughter. He's only allowed in because everyone now knows we're engaged. I'm sitting on a stool upholstered in powder blue satin in front of the dressing table. I want to show him something: a summer nightdress I've just made out of a flimsy pink and white striped seersucker fabric. It's sleeveless and strapless, really just a floor-length tube, trimmed with white broderie anglaise and a wide pink sash.

Richard's the man who will stand up and say publicly that I am his and that he will never leave me. In return I'll give him a '*colossal reservoir of faith and love . . . to swim in daily*—Sylvia Plath's words which I read years later. She even said that her new husband, the poet Ted Hughes, would '*somehow (fill) that huge, sad hole I felt in having no father*'.

I move towards him. Richard's everything I'm not. He's rooted. Apart from a short time in Africa, he's lived all his life in one house with one set of real parents. And he has a distinguished spiritual provenance. His ancestors belonged to a Christian denomination founded in the 14th century in Bohemia, who sailed the world to teach, heal and preach love and justice. It's all beautifully recorded: they were a scattered community who had to keep writing journals, reports, sermons and letters to bind each other together. I love him so much. He kisses me and holds me tight. He can feel my back, my hips, my breasts through the fabric. I've always longed to be held like this by a man.

And what do I say as I sink down on the real daughter's powder blue candlewick counterpane, sun streaming in through the low window, and pat the space beside me?

'Tell me about your grandmother'.

'She was born in Antigua, the daughter of Moravian missionaries. They were advanced in their ideas—built settlements with schools for girls as well as boys'.

'Separate, of course?'

'Of course. She married an Irish missionary in Jamaica and had seven sons. She brought them across to England in twos and threes to Fulneck, a Moravian boarding school in Yorkshire. She was already several months pregnant with her eighth child when she made another crossing. They travelled on a banana boat because it was cheap. She hated bananas for the rest of her life.'

'Was your father on the boat?

'Yes, he was 10 years old, the second oldest, coming across to Fulneck to join a couple of older brothers. I've got a sweet, affectionate letter my grandmother sent to her husband when she arrived in England. She misses him dearly, she says, the younger children too, and assures him she's in the best of health. I'll show it to you one day'.

Every time he talks of the future with me in it my heart misses a beat.

'By the time the letter arrived in Jamaica my grandfather was dead. She went back to collect the rest of the boys and then came back to Bedford with the eighth child, another boy. She brought them up singlehandedly in a small terraced house'.

So that's what Christian marriage can lead to . . .

'How do you remember her?'

'I knew her when she was old, sitting with one ear close to the wireless, spectacles on the end of her nose, atlas a few inches away from her eyes, listening to the news and following every twist and turn'.

Richard has a smile which lights up the universe, and a voice to die for when he reads love poetry to me, but there are days when smiles and love poetry are the last things on his mind. I'm standing by the alphabetical rack in Old Hall Newnham where we pick up our post. There's a note in the 'I' for 'Inskip' pigeon hole and I recognise the hand writing. Another cancellation. It'll be 'an essay to write . . . a book to read . . . Evensong . . . it might rain . . . it's too hot . . . I'm tired as I got woken in the night by a noise'. Richard still cannot decide between marriage and celibacy and picks at his doubts like scabs. He loves me, he loves me not. He says it's nothing personal. I cling on for dear life and sit on my bed reading spiritual books and underlining all the sad bits about life being a vale of tears. I know what I'd really like: a couple of minutes alone with God when I've backed him into a corner. With his undivided attention, I'd ask him what on earth is going on. I might even him a piece of my mind. Failing that I need someone with skin on. I decide to make do with Bill, the Pastorate chaplain, the one who inspired me to read Tolstoy's *Resurrection.*

On the day he comes round I dress with care, a suit—pencil skirt and cropped jacket in a pebbly tweed of black, white and turquoise with a tight black sweater. I wind a long thread of tiny aqua shells round and round my neck and it makes me feel better. There's a knock at the door. I pour coffee into two small apricot cups.

'How's your mother getting on, Yvonne?' I offer him a tiny bowl of coloured sugar granules which are hard to melt but look handsome. 'The last I heard I think she was having to give up her work as a housekeeper'.

Bigga is the last thing I want to talk about. She made her choices and has to live with them.

'She's back with her sister now and a social worker is trying to fix up lodgings . . .' I hesitate, 'Bill, that's not what I want to see you about . . . I don't know how to put this . . . I might break off my engagement with Richard. I know I made a promise and you shouldn't break a promise . . . . but sometimes he tells me he's very much in love with me, another day he says he doesn't feel anything and can hardly bear to see me . . . I don't think I can go on like this much longer'.

Bill's advice is robust.

'Stop praying! Stop digging and delving inside your head! Throw away all those spiritual books! Go out and feel the warm sunshine on your skin . . . . find a tree with blossom and stand underneath it . . . . look at light and shade on buildings . . . . Walk along the Cam and listen to the river . . . . enjoy each present moment'.

All this is well and good. But in the meantime 'What shall I tell Richard?'

'Don't break off your engagement. Of course you're afraid. You can live with that. How can a sensitive and alive person ever feel secure?'

It wasn't until I read his obituary in *The Times* 40 years later that I discovered where that last question came from. He knew all about blind light and how sex and religion were uneasy bedfellows. He was a homosexual priest at a time when to have sex with another man was a criminal offence. The church suffered a huge loss when he turned down a bishopric offered to him by the then Prime Minister Harold Wilson.

After Bill has gone I look down out of my window. Someone's mother is taking photographs of the leafy green collar of leaves edging the building, then she turns to capture the washed-out mustards and golds of the trembling birch trees. The woman is large. Does she remind me of Bigga? I can feel her mountainous stillness and concentration. I want to be a mother like her. Richard will give me that. When she finishes, she tucks her small black unremarkable camera with its cargo of bright beauty inside her handbag, and walks away, her flowing pink skirt swaying from side to side, nearly touching the ground.

But a slippery engagement is not my only problem. Sex, bloody sex, makes itself felt in another way. Apparently Richard wants too little of it, my mother had too much. Or at least Aunt Amy could be forgiven for thinking so when Bigga goes back to hospital with another stroke and then returns to live with her. I catch the bus home to see them both.

Bigga is pale and unsteady. She turns to me and says', I did the washing up last night'.

'You did no such thing. You said you were cold. You sat by the fire while I washed up. I did the lot.' Amy is indignant. She looks straight at me, 'She wouldn't be in this state if she'd looked after herself. She can't stay here with me forever, you know'.

Of course she can't. I'm inclined to believe Amy's version. Bigga's memory is miserly. It doesn't give her the words she needs and at times she's a stranger to us both. Where will it end? Where will she go? And where do I get a bed when term ends? I can sign up for a mission at Charmouth with board and lodgings for a fortnight; Cadbury's offer a month's unpaid work experience and will pay a student's keep; and I can cook at a children's Christian summer camp and eat and sleep with them. Richard's parents have a spare bedroom but his mother is wary. If Richard and I stay up after she goes to bed she comes down from time to time for an Asprin or a drink of water. I can understand—a fiancée with bad blood in her veins could get herself pregnant like her mother and ruin everything. She wants her only son to be a priest before he's a Daddy. She gives me a manicure set for my 21st birthday. I vow to learn to cut and shape and tame my nails but old habits have returned. My back's bleeding in half a dozen places, my heart beats in strange patterns and sometimes—but only when I'm in bed at night—I can't stop shivering.

I need advice. Our family doctor has known my mothers and me since I was four. Should I do the decent thing, I write to ask him, leave Cambridge, get a job, find somewhere to live, and look after Bigga? Neither of us has a penny apart from my grant and her Old Age Pension but perhaps we could manage.

> *. . . I am quite certain that your mother needs to have someone with her most of the day . . . at present the arrangements at Clapham are quite satisfactory . . . If events there do change, then I shall do my utmost to see that she is cared for in some way. It is to my mind important that you take full advantage of your training . . . you can best help your mother by succeeding in this task. I do not wish you to feel in any way that you are failing to carry out your duties as a daughter . . .*

Dr Whitmore even insists that he, not I, is the one to break this news to Bigga and Amy.

Meanwhile my work has been going downhill and in my final term my Tutor Dr Lesley Cooke asks me if she has my permission to contact our doctor for a prognosis. Would it set our minds at rest to know that Newnham College has found a pocket of money? If things break down at home, the college would pay for residential nursing care for my mother until I finish my Finals. When I tell Aunt Amy she says she doesn't intend to accept charity from anyone, never has and never will, and Bigga is alright where she is. But she must say they do look after you at that college. There remains the rest of the term and Finals to get through. Richard and I are still engaged—just—and his parents and aunt will be coming up to celebrate his graduation. Bigga is coming too. Amy says, 'Your mother's got a right to be there. She's worked for you all her life'.

On Degree Day Richard looks handsome as he takes his mother, aunt and me out to lunch, then goes off to have a studio photo taken. Bigga arrives by taxi, excited, bewildered and clumsy but thrilled to be there. I'm ashamed of her shapeless figure, her cheap hat and vacant smile, and hate myself more and more. Inside me is a truculent child blaming her for getting us into this mess. I look terrible with long tangled hair, an ill-fitting short black skirt belonging to my future mother-in-law and a crumpled white blouse. I stand uneasily in a crowd of expansive parents, their happiness and pride spilling over and threatening me. After the ceremony I steer Bigga through the crowds, collect her belongings and get a taxi to the station, where I meet up with Richard to say good-bye. Bigga and I are off for a week's holiday with Tyna because they both believe the bracing air of Lowestoft will do her good, which fills my eyes with tears when they say that, because I know that nothing can prevent the damage building up inside her.

Reader, I marry him. I was the one who made it happen. I lived for a year in an attic in a Walworth vicarage, without theatre tickets, make up, sweets and outings but with meagre food and darned stockings, in order to save £10 a month from my ICI salary. (I couldn't help noticing that a male student from Cambridge with a third class degree who joined at the same time was already being paid 50% more, but what else should I expect?. I also organised the wedding for £14 11s 11d, excluding the dress which Bigga bought me in a sale, the most elegant wedding dress I've ever seen, and sometimes I slip into it even now just because I can. And excluding also the cost of flowers from the florists Moyses Stevens. They're demure, understated and ravishing, a blessed relief at a time when brides are expected to drag half a greenhouse full of stuff with them down the aisle. It's a bridesmaid's posy, the collection among colleagues where I work doesn't run to a bridal bouquet.

I get up one October morning to prepare toast and boiled eggs in my attic for everyone and then go downstairs to make Whitstable sandwiches (shrimps, lettuce, cucumber and Heinz salad cream) for a DIY wedding reception in the vicarage lounge. I prepare two bowls of punch: one for our families with plenty of rum and red wine in it, the other for our Christian friends, innocent of any alcohol. After the ceremony I organise the signing of the register in the vestry. The wedding photos show Grace, who is my bridesmaid, in a wrap-around paisley dress made by her mother, nursing a bunch of chrysanthemums bought by her mother. She is standing next to Bigga and both look happy. Tyna is absent as Jack needs her. Aunt Amy looks disapproving and has told everyone I could have done better for myself. The future she disapproves of is my life as a curate's wife in Scunthorpe.

For the first few months of our marriage we live apart because Richard has to finish his residential training for the priesthood at Lincoln Theological College and I'm working at Millbank and living in my attic. I catch the train from London to Lincoln from time to time after invitations like 'Would you like to come up for Holy Week? I'm not sure that we would be able to sleep together'. When Richard is ordained we move into the curate's house which is small, pretty, detached, like a child's drawing with a straight path up to a front door flanked by two neat windows. On a trip to Bedford to see Bigga Richard and I call in at Clarissa's house to collect those cardboard boxes I stored with her. The cats have commandeered them for years. Everything is stinking and rotten, including the carved Swiss box I used to fill with Tommy's sleepy kittens when I was a child.

18

THE PAPERS TO PROVE IT

At last my time has come. It's early evening and I'm lying wrapped in a gaudy patchwork blanket crocheted by Tyna. The sage green bedroom curtains shut out the dark, our newly-painted pale primrose walls glow in the electric light. This is where my first baby will be born.

I didn't know I was pregnant for the first four months. I'd had a pregnancy test—you hand some urine over and Ian, our doctor and friend, sends it to an unsuspecting frog, who's injected with it. If she produces eggs within the next 24 hours, the test is positive. But not in my case. When I eventually went to see Ian again because I wanted my periods back, he felt my belly and said 'Never trust a frog. You're 15/16 weeks gone. Sorry about that . . . no doubt in the future they'll think of better ways.'

I've never felt so well, so alive as I do during pregnancy. I'm flooded with warmth towards my own mother, Bigga. How could I have been so callous? She's generous and impetuous but she makes life interesting and who am I to judge her? We need to talk and I promise myself that after the baby's born we'll do just that.

When my contractions begin to grasp and claw at my belly I take my mind off them by cutting up some cornflower blue material on the kitchen table to make a summer dress. I'm wonderfully prepared. I've read every book about babies I can lay my hands on. Trudie King insists they can only be fed by the clock even if they're crying their hearts out. Clinical Theology says the first 9 months are a 'womb of the spirit' and if you leave babies to cry you propel them into depression and despair when they grow up. I'm confident I'll know what to do when the time comes.

When the waters break Richard phones the midwife. Thirty minutes later a stranger walks in, a tiny woman, compact, grey haired, looking smart in her blue uniform. But she's the wrong woman. 'My' midwife, Mrs Denny, the one who's been looking after me for months, has flu.

'How are you? How are the pains?' asks the midwife.

'Fine' I say, irritated because I haven't got 'pains'. 'Pains' is loose talk and not what I want to hear. What I've got are contractions—but this is not the moment to argue.

'Oh, that's no good, you can't be 'fine' if you're going to have a baby'.

'But I've been to classes and done my exercises . . . deep breathing and panting . . .'. My voice fades away. I'm not quite as sure as I sound. My body seems to have risen up and taken me over. She's right. I'm in deep, deep pain. This isn't how it's supposed to be.

She unpacks her things. Richard stands by my bedside and she waits for him to go. He doesn't. She hesitates, then turns to him, 'Are you thinking of staying here in the bedroom?'

'Yes. We talked about it with Mrs Denny. I know it's unusual for fathers to stay but she was quite happy about it'.

I can see her struggle. Every part of her wants to order him out of the room—a man, someone who would get in the way, someone with no business there, a member of the sex which causes all this trouble for women anyway. He's not wearing his dog collar but she knows he's the curate, 'a man of the cloth'. So she can't bring herself to say the words. She turns her back on him and gives me her full attention.

'How old are you?'

'Twenty four'.

'Never mind, sometimes you old ones surprise us'.

My heart sinks. I know Scunthorpe brides marry young because their boyfriends make good money in the steelworks as soon as they leave school, but I do not want to hear that I might be too old to have a straightforward birth.

She then promises to take me as far away as she can from the horrible things which are about to happen to me. Her kindness to her mothers, as she sees it, is to knock them out. She prides herself that they don't feel a thing when they're in her hands.

I don't know what I inhale or what drugs I'm given. Suddenly the bedroom and Richard have gone. Time collapses. I'm running down black corridors silently screaming, I'm outside my body, I'm searching for myself, I glimpse me from time to time. Now I'm in pieces, now I'm a black inky blot spattered over a page. Now I'm underwater drowning. Air, I want air. I want to gulp it down like water because I have a thirst which never will be slaked.

I come round suddenly, open my eyes and have no recollection of having given birth. I wasn't even in the room at the time. But I must have been, because Richard, in the familiar grey pullover Tyna knitted for him, is standing at the foot of the bed, facing away from me, and I can see a beautiful baby with rich black hair peeping over his shoulder. Then Claire is in my arms. I'm a mother and she's my daughter.

'Congratulations, my dear. 8lb 8 oz. Not a single stitch needed. You were a very good girl', says the midwife, 'I only wish all my ladies were as little trouble as you'.

Three days later, John Yates, our vicar, comes to celebrate Holy Communion by my bedside. It's a way of thanksgiving. Richard, his curate, holds my hand. Half way through the service Panic leaps on my bed like a rabid dog, savaging my mind, violent and pitiless. I'm going to die because my heart will burst with its thick sharp rhythms. My blood feels vinegary and prickly as it races through my veins. I must get away from Richard and John. I fantasize springing out of bed, knocking over the chalice of wine, scattering the round white hosts on the bedside rug and sprinting across the corridor to the bathroom where I could pretend to be sick—not mad, which is what I feel. Instead I lie stiff as a log and let everything happen around me. When the service is over and John has gone I try to explain to Richard what happened. Am I going mad? He is kind, reassuring but doesn't understand any more than I do. Perhaps, he wonders, everyone feels like that and they just don't talk about it?

John's wife Jean brings snowdrops for Claire when she is a couple of hours old, a gift she repeats on Claire's birthday every year of her life. I've never held a baby before and count time lost when she is not in my arms. She's the most beautiful, precious creature in the world. I'm brimming over with milk—clearly my body is designed for this. I am deliriously happy. And have never been so terrified.

People in the parish bring grapes and flowers and a home-made Scunthorpe plum loaf.

'Eat each slice with a crisp apple and a slice of Cheddar. You'll soon be up on your feet again', they tell me.

Pretty cards, mostly pink, congratulate me from the dressing table, showing rows of sweet, rosy-cheeked babies who mock me from their radiant mothers' arms. I wonder what planet these mothers and babies have come from, because the picture I've got in my mind is on no one's pretty card.

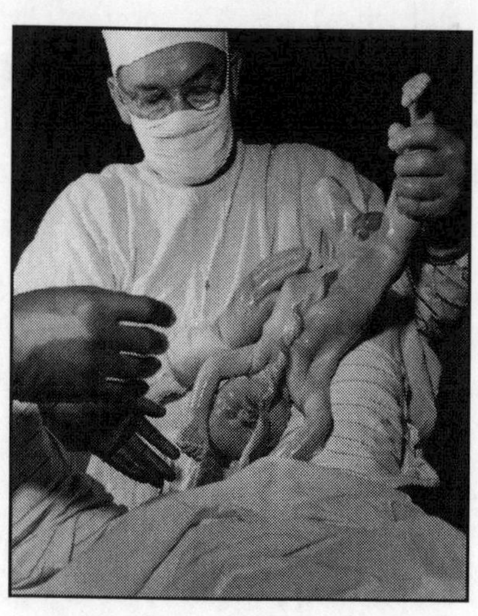

It's this one by Wayne Miller, picturing his father delivering his son. Miller helped curate *The Family of Man*, a famous exhibition at the Museum of Modern Art in New York in 1955. I bought the book when I was a student. This baby dangles like a trophy, like a fish caught by an angler. The uncut cord is like a coiled spring and the baby is full of a dark strength and energy. Helpless infant? No, someone who's going to turn everyone's lives upside down.

What I'm not prepared for is Claire's lack of composure. It's as if she has arrived, looked round at the world and found it wanting. I try everything: my breasts, a warm nightie, a snowy terry-towelling nappy, caresses, lullabies, routine feeds, random feeds—nothing works. It's not that she's a whiney, sickly baby. She's full of life and energy but she cries, cries, cries and I have never heard such a terrible sound. Is she bored? Tyna says in her letter it's a sign of character and I hope she's right.

Meanwhile Richard has his vocation. Meals are on time, beds are made, the washing pegged out on the line and ironed when dry. When the frost freezes the clothes into weird shapes I bounce them along the floor to make Claire laugh. I walk everywhere because the pram is too big to go on the bus and I do not ask for lifts in our car. That's for parish business. I do everything to make sure Richard sleeps through the night, even if it means curling up on the cold lino by Claire's cot ready to pick her up if she makes a noise. This is part of my vocation. Richard is not a monster. Our friends see us as an avant garde couple: *Guardian* readers, radical in theology, politics, contemporary art and poetry, and up to speed with the latest theories on psycho prophylaxis and natural childbirth. Richard was with me when the baby was born, for goodness sake, at a time when most fathers didn't turn up for what many people, including some doctors, saw as a pretty disgusting process. It's simply that New Man has not yet arrived.

But Panic is a terrorist who's never more than a few seconds away. He walks beside me up and down Scunthorpe High Street as I go shopping; he sits in the empty chair as I'm chatting to friends over a cup of coffee; he cuddles up on the sofa while Claire is at my breast. When I have a panic attack I say, 'At least I'm feeling something. I'm not numb like I am when I'm depressed'. When I'm depressed I say to myself 'This isn't as bad as a panic attack, when I feel I'm going mad'. Eleanor's stories flood back. Panic puts his paws on my shoulder and licks my ear. I feel his hot breath on my cheek when he says 'You're going mad. You'll soon be locked up'. What do mad people do? Perhaps they smash windows, slash cushions with a knife, talk nonsense like Bigga does sometimes. I hear steps on the pavement outside and imagine two men in white coats walking up the path to bind me to a stretcher like they did Bigga, I wrestle the image to the ground and stamp on it. I live life like a cartoon character where each step of the staircase appears as you put your foot on it. The cornflower blue material is never stitched into a dress. What keeps me sane is daily life: clean your teeth, answer the phone, puree the carrots in the Mouli grater, make cool pastry for an apple pie; steep nappies in a bucket of Napisan. And Claire's laughter is an energy burst which tugs me back to what going on outside me.

At my post natal check-up, Ian says 'Time cures most things. There are a few drugs but I don't like giving them to nursing mothers. You never can be quite sure of the effect on the baby. I think you can manage without them'. Wise words despite the fact that no one yet knows that the widely-prescribed drug thalidomide is causing terrible birth defects. 'You're not the sort of person to give in, are you?'

'No, of course not'.

But I am. I get an appointment with a psychiatrist at Scunthorpe War Memorial Hospital who's sympathetic and thoughtful and listens well. Someone tells me he's Turkish and as I wind my story round Catholic nuns and Protestant theology, he hints that this territory is not entirely familiar. But he starts by clearing one problem out of the way.

'When you were a child you found a letter saying you'd been adopted. What did you feel when you read that? Were you sad that you'd never known your parents? Or did you want your real parents to be dead?'

'Yes, of course. Then I could imagine that my parents had wanted me. They'd have gone on loving me but they couldn't take care of me'.

'So then death, their deaths in this case, would have solved your problem'. He pauses, 'Do you ever think death, your death, would help now?'

I'm astonished. Things are bad but not that bad. 'I never for a moment think of suicide. My life is a gift from God'. For a moment I feel better.

'Are you afraid of hell?' It's not a question I'm prepared for.

'No, I don't believe it exists'. I know that if I did it would be more to do with a terror of turning up somewhere unexpected, unannounced where God had turned his back on me, than of fiery flames.

He's to the point: 'I think it's clear why you're depressed. Just think of your own mother. Just imagine how she felt. Perhaps she wanted you—she was getting on for forty and you were probably her last chance to have a child. She wanted to show you off and be congratulated, but she had to hide you because you were living proof of her shame. Or perhaps she was horrified to find herself pregnant. For a start she was an intelligent woman and would have known that childbirth, probably by a caesarean section, was a risky operation then for a 40 year old. She might die. Did she blame the man who'd made her pregnant? Did she blackmail him? Where was he when she was going through this?'

He leans forward 'What you probably don't know is that babies—even very young babies—pick up these feelings. As a new mother you're reliving the conflict your own mother experienced all those years ago. Your mother did not own her embodied emotions and they've passed on to your unconscious. You are paying the price for her actions.'

I believe he can see the stitching between events which is invisible to my eyes. I'm not to blame! It's Bigga who's the villain. She was rash and deceitful. My father too of course. The Bible says 'The fathers have eaten sour grapes and the children's teeth are set on edge'. But what's the point of blaming a man who to all intents and purposes doesn't exist? I walk out of the hospital light-headed with relief. No drugs are offered nor any further appointments. But this well-meaning psychiatric intervention has one sad and unintended effect. I'm free to see myself as a victim. It's my comfort blanket. I wrap it round me for the remaining months Bigga and I have together.

Reluctantly I visit her from time to time, now she's in a geriatric hospital at Clapham. I tell myself I don't go often because we have little money for train fares. As I walk down the ward towards her I'm ashamed when I see her face light up and vow I'll come more often, but I don't. When she falls asleep I think obsessively about the plant Myrtle, named after Myrrha whom the gods turned into a myrtle bush. When she had her first stroke the doctor talked about the hardening of her arteries. I've watched Bigga over the last eight years turning from a moving living person into someone whose veins grew into woody twigs and one day she'll end up a corpse, stiff and unbending as a tree trunk. Why did this happen to Myrrha? Something about punishment for a forbidden love, I half-remember. I know I don't dare to look the story up in my book of classical tales when I get back to Scunthorpe. She wakes and I stroke her hand but it's too late. I feed her mashed potatoes and mince and then rice pudding and she opens her mouth for each spoonful as trusting as a child. Each time I come she has slipped further away from my love or reproach. I'm more and more sorry that I judged her harshly and only when it's too late do I want to hold her in my arms and tell her I love her as I used to as a child.

The phone rings at 6am and Richard goes downstairs to answer it. We're staying with his parents at Bedford which means Claire in the carri cot at the end of the bed. We've had a bad night and I'm sitting up, Claire in my arms. Her eyelids flutter and I pray that they'll close. Richard puts his head round the door and says softly 'It was the hospital. Bigga developed pneumonia late last night and died at 3am. There was no time to let us know'. I hand Claire over to him, swing my legs slowly over the side of the bed and walk to the window. I gaze at the empty street. Nothing to see. Nothing to feel. Silence.

'They said it was a peaceful end. She won't have felt anything'. Richard is the professional, he has seen death many times. I trust what he says. I know I should feel pain but I can't pick it up. It's out of my reach today. Getting through the next hour, the next minute, getting through life is as much as I can cope with. I've nothing left over for death. I'm silent. Richard, carrying a now sleeping Claire in the crook of his arm, walks round the room and puts his other arm round my shoulder.

'Say something, Yvonne, or cry—it'll do you good'.

'I can't'. Knowing that a hand grenade of panic could explode at any moment doesn't leave much space for anything else, although in the last few months I've begun to feel better. I bend down and kiss Claire's cheek, then turn to Richard. He pulls me towards him with his free hand and kisses me warmly. His hand travels down the small of my back and he holds me firmly against him.

I pull away, take Claire, now sound asleep, from him and stroke her hands. 'Bigga adored you', I tell her, 'She bought you a tiny doll's pram just like the one I used to have. You made her very happy'. Still no tears.

'Yvonne, you don't have to worry about a thing. I'll ring the Co op as soon as they're open and fix up the funeral details and let people know, especially Tyna'.

People turn up at Clapham church for Bigga's funeral because she's a village girl and an Inskip. Richard and I sit in a front pew. I think I can smell the white lilies on the altar and remember that Aunt Amy used to ban them from her house. Had she heard the legend that the lily sprang from Eve's tears when she discovered she was pregnant? Pregnant and being thrown out of the Garden of Eden. Did they make her think of Bigga? I feel very tired and want to close my eyes. My Holy Picture from Sister Regina had lilies. Bigga didn't like me using a Holy Picture anyway. I should have torn it up into little pieces and thrown it into the fire. She and I used to sit in this very pew and say together a prayer from Evensong about how 'we've left undone those things we ought to have done and done those things we ought not to have done . . .'. I want to squeeze her hand and say 'I'm very sorry'. It's too late. I'll never hear her voice again and she'll never hear me saying that or anything else. She has slammed the door in my face.

The organ plays Aunt Amy's hymn 'There is a green hill far away' which she chose because their mother sang it to all her children to get them to sleep. The congregation knows it well and the sound fills the roof tops. Richard and I lead a little procession out through the porch to stand awkwardly by the grave where Bigga will rest with her parents. No companionable man to lie beside. Then we walk down the beech avenue to Aunt Amy's house for the wake.

When everyone is going, Aunt Amy asks me to stay behind. She settles down to put things straight. We sit in armchairs facing one another each side of the fireplace.

'Your mother never told us she'd had a baby', she begins, 'The two of them told us a pack of lies about adoption. And we believed every word. I've never forgiven them for making such fools of us'.

'I expect it was easier to believe than not to believe?'

'Yes of course it was. No one in our family has ever been in a scandal. Gertie and I were decent honest girls, well brought up. You didn't go chasing after other people's husbands. So when she brought you along we couldn't see what was staring us in the face. Until you started to look like her. Then we knew alright', she pauses, 'I used to say to Eddie often enough 'If only she'd come to me and told me what she'd done. I'd have forgiven her everything'. She fixes her eyes on me, 'What I couldn't stand was all those lies'.

Now I understand. For years I've heard the roar of a sea of anger in her voice but it was not her sister's sexual laxity, nor my birth, which called up the storm. It was the cover-up. The two sisters had once been very close. Amy had taken her sister's part when young and cared for her at home when old. But she had never been trusted, she'd been lied to, treated like an idiot. They've been tangled together for decades in a mesh of pretence which each year became harder to tear down.

This was the moment Amy gave me a large brown envelope stuffed with Bigga's 1935 diary together with a bundle of papers and postcards. I recall Amy saying 'Your mother gave these to me. She had nowhere to put them. She said I was to give them to you. I don't know what's in them'. And Amy, unlike her sister, would never, ever tell a lie.

This is the moment I snap the lid shut on my past. I don't need to look at the papers. Yvonne Inskip is dead. I'm Yvonne Craig now. I'm no longer an illegal immigrant on this planet. At last I'm tethered to this beautiful earth. I've even got the papers to prove it: my marriage certificate and my daughter's birth certificate.

But what lingers with me is one of the last full days I spent with Bigga. I go with her to a hospital clinic because she needs to be assessed before being admitted to long-term geriatric care in Clapham Hospital. It must have been a particularly miserable day for her because the Hospital used to be the Poor House for the indigent. The villagers saw it not as a sanctuary but as a place of disgrace and a prison, to be avoided at any cost. They wouldn't walk past it if they could take another route. What they couldn't know is that one day an immigrants' detention centre called Yarl's Wood would be built there, another place of detention for those with no choices. And that one day it would be burned to the ground.

The consultant asks her to strip.

'Where did this scar come from?,' he points to her belly.

My virgin mother doesn't say a word. Instead she lifts her hand slowly and gestures towards me. I look away quickly, embarrassed. The scar lies like a chain locking in her secret from Amy and from me. It is the first and only time she acknowledges that I am her child.

I help her to put her clothes back on. Neither of us speaks of what has happened.

19

SCUNTHORPE

Tyna will be here in an hour. I hardly know her now. My most vivid memory is the day she and Jack called in at Newnham College and Jack tucked that ten shilling note into my hand. She couldn't come to our wedding: for years she's been watching Jack's lungs silting up, wrecked by the coal dust, grain, asbestos and chemicals he lugged around as a docker. He's been comforted—but not helped—by tens of thousands of Woodbines. Her letters tell me how he tries to keep warm in winter and sits by the empty black grate in summer, his back to the French windows, with less and less energy to go out and tend his chrysanths or to poke about in his greenhouse, which is falling to bits. As money's tight Tyna finds a part time job at Pye's TV factory at the end of the road but on the first morning Jack has a relapse and sends for her to come home. After that she hardly leaves the house. When Jack dies, four days after Bigga's death, Tyna loses two of the people she has loved most. This morning she caught a train to come and see us.

Home is now the curate's house, a Scunthorpe prefab on a friendly estate built in a hurry after the war. In the middle of a square of dog-stained grass is a church-cum-community centre which looks like a giant shoe box. Its flat roof, folded over the walls, fits like a lid. I'm in the kitchen staring at our garden; nothing but weeds, a clump of lusty rhubarb and a slim, arthritic and cankerous apple tree just high enough to savage the washing line. This is my last chance, before Tyna comes, to get rid of the envelope Aunt Amy gave me. When I first looked through it, it seemed to be mainly pretty postcards saying '*Sorry I haven't been in touch*' and '*I've been ill/overworked/abroad*'. They all end bleakly with: '*All the best, R*'. No love or lust anywhere. There's a tiny 1935 diary of Bigga's, plus some birthday telegrams from R, some to Tyna, some to Bigga. My birth certificate shows up with names of people who never existed. And there are three hand-written notes to Bigga from the Bank of Scotland, plus a type-written business letter addressed to a Mr R. Strub, an ugly name and I've no idea how to pronounce it unless you make it rhyme with 'pub' and 'grub'. Since no one's going to say it out loud, it doesn't matter.

I walk into the living room and stand over a wicker waste paper basket like the one I had in Cambridge. The quotations are still wrapped round, but look weary. I know I could tear Bigga's paper remnants into tiny pieces and toss them in. Or I could take a match out of the box in the cutlery drawer and let them burn to ashes in the sink. I could bury them in the rhubarb patch and leave them to rot. It wouldn't take long.

But not with Bigga's body so recently in the grave. I've never seen a dead body, not even while it's still up and running as it were, in a funeral parlour, fleshily occupying a whole coffin. By now it will be decomposing in the churchyard. What's left of her? Gifts from her friends—smooth, starched, snow-white hand-crocheted table linen, stored like an unused trousseau—together with a handful of tiny black and white photos, most of whose faces are unknown. They must stay, and are already tucked away in a dressing table drawer. The undertaker gave me her gold signet ring. It should have been a wedding ring. I'll get rid of that as soon as possible. Sell it. It might make ten shillings

I slide the envelope between the tablecloths and make sure they travel with us whenever Richard changes his job. After the prefab, the church provides us with a six-bedroomed terraced house which had been a 'hotel'. When we move to Bristol it's a 23-roomed Victorian vicarage, then on to a newly-built disaster 'in the Italian style' on the edge of the city, where water ran down the electrical fittings and individual stairs were of a different height. Naturally the architect won a prize. With each move I find a space in the new house where you put things to die, not yet ready to throw them away. Richard thinks I had the papers and postcards for at least 20 years before I showed them to him.

Through the kitchen window I see Richard drive up in our grey mini. Now I'm a grown woman Tyna's a mystery to me. Bigga was my easy-going mother, casual, fun—and unreliable. If she got cross she flared up, got scary, shoved the furniture around. But she flared down again quickly. You knew where you stood with her, even if you'd rather be standing somewhere else. But Tyna went on smouldering. She was the strict one and she made the rules. When a hot bath was a weekly treat, daily washing had to be regulated.

Make sure you wash down as far as possible, my girl', said Tyna, 'Then up as far as possible. Then wash possible.'

I needn't have worried. Tyna and I meld together perfectly. I love cooking, she loves washing up. She loves billiards on TV, I like early nights. Money is tight so we shop together for over-ripe cooking tomatoes and jars of out-of-date yoghurt. She eggs me on at auction sales and we come home with bargain lampshades and cutlery balanced on the push chair. Best of all I have given her another readymade, another little girl, a 'grandchild'. It's love at first sight. Claire gets a companion whose default position is 'yes' to the world: games, jigsaws, walks, stories without end. And Richard is Tyna's special favourite—he can do no wrong. Although I complain how unfair this is, I secretly like it. It's as if she's saying 'Hey, you made a good choice there!'

Everyone loves her.

'I wonder why she's so different from the scold who brought me up? Is it because she no longer has to keep Bigga's secret?'

'Perhaps it's nothing to do with that', Richard is sceptical, 'Perhaps she's decided that caring for people is what she likes best and what she does best'.

'Maybe she remembers what it felt like when her own mother died and how cruel her stepmother was,'

'She probably thinks there's enough pain in the world already without anyone adding to it'

Our next door neighbour comments, 'That woman hasn't got an unkind bone in her body'. Bus conductors haul her shopping on board, nurses can't do enough for her after her cataract operation; social security officers press help on her and a teenager on a bus shares a bag of crisps. Each year I count the days to her visits: six weeks every spring and six weeks every autumn. I make the most of the freedom she gives me, especially by joining a national campaign *Every Child a Wanted Child*. And I'm getting better. I know I am.

I'm dripping Golden Syrup in a whirly pattern onto Claire's bowl of breakfast porridge. I turn the wireless on. I catch Sylvia Plath's name. Since Cambridge days I've been keeping an eye out for her whenever she's in the news. She and I live on different planets but we're both married, I have a child, she has two. I feel proud I've been at the same college as her. I put the spoon down on the sky-blue Formica top and it sits in a golden pool of syrup. I listen. She prepared bread and milk for her two children while they were asleep, sealed up their bedroom door, went downstairs and put her head in the gas oven.

I sit down beside Claire and stroke her hair and tears roll down my cheeks. But an altogether cruder me squats on my shoulder and whispers in my ear, 'She's dead. You're alive. The colour is coming back into your life'.

I wonder, if Sylvia had had a Tyna, would she still be alive and writing poetry today?

I don't mention my panics and depression to Tyna, nor a heart which begins to flutter as if it's in a Georgette Heyer novel and needs a strong dose of sal volatile to keep it going. The doctor says it's nothing, but I wonder. I don't want to be the curate's poor wife who's never been the same since she had a baby, and then turn into the poor curate's wife. Saying things out loud, even to Tyna, gives them a physical presence in the world. Anyone can grab words and twist and shape them. As long as everything is going on inside my skin, I'm safe.

Instead I write in secret. *Inferiorwoman* walks into my life and I rather like her. *Superwoman* is strutting her stuff in Shirley Conran's book of that name and the sluts of the world need to fight back. Fifteen years later *Inferiorwoman* will make an appearance in the *Observer*.

Inferiorwoman lives in a household where dirty nappies soak in the Napisan bucket under the sink. Her kitchen floor needs washing but she tells herself it's a comfort to any woman who calls to see the curate about a christening or a wedding or to hire the church hall for a party. When she offers her a cup of tea the visitor only has to look around and it'll put a spring in her step when she thinks of her own spotless tiles. There's a kitchen cabinet in one corner with a big white enamel flap which is never closed. Guess what's there? a grubby Baby-Gro, some fat wax crayons, half a bottle of milk, a pile of brown envelopes . . .

Inferiorwoman sits on pretty chairs rescued from a church hall. She paints them a different colour each time she moves house. When there's nothing left to sit on, she stuffs floor cushions with old tights. She's never tasted prawn, lychees or tabasco in her life, but her Lincolnshire plum loaf (eaten with Cheddar cheese and a crisp apple) is worth waiting for, and she's learned to call bacon-and-egg tart Quiche Lorraine. Her children's teeth do not rot and fall out because there's no money for sugary drinks. Electric knife sharpeners, ironing sleeve boards and hostess trolleys do not get a look in, along with perfume, hair dye, false eyelashes, hats, hairdressers and depilatory cream. She counts on the fingers of one hand items to be ironed; a friend gives her a hand crocheted bedspread to console her for all the continental quilts she'll never buy. She never mislays passports since there are none—abroad exists only in colour supplements or in black and white news. Holidays are spent camping in beautiful wind-swept Cornwall. To go to the Mayor's Ball she makes an evening dress from remnants of cloth and a Mary Quant pattern: a scoop neck, black satin high yoke and a long slim wool skirt in a small chequer board pattern of black and white.

She lives in a prefab and in the summer sits with her neighbours on the low garden walls putting the world to rights. One neighbour sees her trying to chop down a small, pesky apple tree which savages the washing line. He gives her a hand. She'll paint the loo purple and silver, lay tiles, and even do some plastering—jobs which on the whole priests don't get round to. She starts a drop-in Stork Club in the church hall, with speakers on breast-feeding, child benefits, but most of all family planning. No more unwanted children in the world. Inferiorwoman gets invited to speak at the Rotary Club and the Lions Club and to write in the local paper. When her second daughter is two she's diagnosed with congenital dislocation of the hip and treatment involves being stretched for eleven days on a rack in a way that a medieval torturer would have been proud of. It would have

> *been easy to treat if diagnosed at birth, but is easily missed if there's no family history. Inferiorwoman only has 50% of her family history . . .*

When Susannah's discharged from hospital she spends a year in a frog-shaped plaster. Some of Richard's friends at the steelworks, where he's just been appointed Industrial Chaplain, put together a contraption made of scrap metal so that I can wheel her outside the house. We move into a long slim six-bedroomed terraced house in the centre of Scunthorpe. Trade Unions meet here and social workers drop in to have a sandwich with their colleagues at lunch time. Labour party ward meetings are in the front room, and a WEA lecturer comes weekly on the ferry from Hull University.

A current slogan *Every Child a Wanted Child* seeps into every part of my life. Wanted, loved and cared for. With parents. Is that asking too much? Everywhere I go I find children who didn't ask to be born and have no one to protect them. In Susannah's ward a little boy in a glass cubicle slowly dies of burns. He'd been put in a bath of scalding water. He lived with his father and a 16 year old housekeeper, who's caught the train back to Scotland and can't be traced. Later, when I'm 31 and pregnant with my third child, I'm sworn in as a magistrate in Lincoln Castle. One day I meet a man in the dock who'd spent his childhood in care. He looks us straight in the eyes and says, 'No one has ever looked after me who hasn't been paid to do it'. Now he faces prison again because everything else has been tried. We think three months would do, though we know we're sending him back to paid minders. A message is passed up to the bench from the dock. Would we consider four months on compassionate grounds? He'd rather be inside for Christmas.

The social enquiry report says he was conceived by a casual encounter on a Cornish beach.

It's the moment when TV discovers that ordinary members of the public have opinions. I have three advantages: clergy are paid little so I'm not only articulate but poor, and from a town (Scunthorpe) that's a bit of a joke. I become Rent-a—Pauper on any subject to do with mothers and sex and children, including women in prison, women as priests, women and violence. I'm very optimistic. The future looks rosy now that a women can take a pill and not rely on a man 'taking precautions'. No more abortions, no child cruelty, no child poverty. It'll mean every child knowing who its parents are.

Aidan is born in the best room in the house, on the ground floor with tall French windows and long, long curtains with bold Impressionist irises. It leads on to a tiny garden, at the end of which runs a 'ten foot' or snicket, a path between the backs of two rows of houses. There my daughters play with the Italian children next door, who give us bundles of sugared almonds wrapped tightly in pink net every time someone takes their First Communion. Now it's snowing and I spend a blissful day with Aidan in my arms, watching them play with their buckets and spades, making a snowman with a carrot nose and shiny black eyes of coal. They wrap my Newnham scarf round the snowman's neck.

'Now he's warm as toast,' says Claire.

20

BRISTOL

On the day Neil Armstrong steps onto the moon, we drive down to Bristol where Richard is taking up what used to be Terry Waite's job: Diocesan Laity Training Officer. In Scunthorpe we'd both swerved left into politics and new perspectives. Social issues became as necessary to us as our daily bread. But in Bristol Richard has different priorities: experiential learning. Terry was one of several pioneers—including radical priests who'd been expelled from South Africa for multi-racial work—with a new approach to group work and training. He took it first to Uganda and ultimately Lebanon. In English churches in the 70s if we wanted to learn about leadership, handling conflict and problem-solving we turned to facilitators who ran experiential workshops. Lectures from experts didn't count.

Richard often works away from home. He's on the right in this press photo, dressed in white vestments, at Worthy Farm and the Glastonbury Festival, celebrating Communion outside the Jesus Tent. I hadn't realised until I was married that for some people there's something uniquely erotic about a priest. My secret knowledge of him is very beguiling and has a sharp edge of power. I trust him.

To keep in touch with his experiential work I join him in a mini-lab at *The Inn On The Park* in Park Lane, Mayfair, run by a team from the Esalen Foundation in North California. The children have a blissful day with Tyna.

'Trousers!' Alan Watts pauses, then looks down at his crotch. 'I hate trousers!' Four hundred people stand patiently in front of him. We feel beneath our bare feet the luxurious gold carpet of the hotel conference room and over our heads hang five glittering chandeliers. There are a few cushions by the walls but no chairs.

'Castrative!' he exclaims, 'but today I wear them. I'm in England . . . in Mayfair,' another well-timed pause, 'where they don't even know the meaning of the word. Wouldn't notice if their balls dropped off and bounced along the pavement.'

A few embarrassed sniggers. I am silent. So is Richard. Alan throws out his arms in a huge embrace as if to enfold us all.

'There are two ways of experiencing this workshop. You may hear the truth, feel the love, see far ahead. Or something more important than all those things will block you. You get to choose. You think effort will solve your difficulties, trying harder.' He's right about that. 'You're wrong. Totally wrong. I want you to feel what happens when you let go. Start by concentrating on your breathing. Don't change it, just be aware of it. Close your eyes . . . slowly let your breath out . . . let it come back by itself, when it feels like coming back.'

I panic, gulp down a mouthful of air, swallowing it like water in a drought. I open my eyes a crack and peek at Richard. He's miles away, beatific smile, arms limp by his side. Curses, I'm never going to get the hang of this. I relax my shoulder blades so hard they practically bang into each other.

'Now you'll notice your breath gets slower and deeper and comes from your belly.'

.My breath takes fright at these words, plunges down as far as my collar bone, then jumps out.

'Now I want you to make as much noise as you can while you're moving round the room. Leap and jump as high as you can, and take as much space as you need. Draw deep down into those marvellous wells of energy inside you and you'll find treasure there. I'll tell you when to stop.'

We do as we are told. The ones who frighten me most are those men who look as though once they were given names like David or Tony but now call themselves something so exotic it needs to be spelt out very slowly. Some wear caftans and all have a low, gentle speaking voice as if every word is a gift they are kind enough to hand over. These are the ones who grab an opportunity to leap into the air and scream as if there were no tomorrow.

'Stop,' says the circus master and we stop. 'Not a single word is to be spoken,'

No chance—no breath.

'But I want you to turn to the person nearest you and greet them non-verbally in any way that seems appropriate.'

Panic. Dotted all over the room will be the usual No Mates and I'm one of them. It started with gym at the convent when you had to choose partners. But no, lo and behold, the woman almost facing me smiles and lays her hands gently on my shoulders. She's slightly shorter than I am, wavy hair, sturdily built, looks calm and capable. I lift my arms to cradle her elbows. She slides her hands down my arms until she's holding my wrists. We gaze into each other's eyes. A minute or two of silence. Then she leans forward and whispers in my ear 'You've got the pulse of an airline pilot. Congratulations. Trust me, I'm a nurse.' Suddenly she lets go of my wrists, slips off her floaty cream cheesecloth top and gives it to me, her hands asking for mine. What can I do? In a trice she's got the precious top I made out of a cream green-sprigged Mary Quant fabric. Good job it's crepe and a bit stretchy, I think, as she just manages to wriggle into it.

Then we're told to get into groups of six and sit cross legged on the floor in a ring.

'Go round the group speaking one at a time without interruption and select the one person in the group you could manage without. No comment, no answering back until everyone has had their say. Then the group decides who's out. When I'm the chosen one I don't argue. I could see it coming—I'm the Older Woman at 35, all the others look Twenty Something. I wriggle backwards out of the group and they close ranks. What does surprise me is how angry I feel. I tear into the group until I crack their wall of linked arms. When I tumble inside their guilt melts into laughter and relief that it's over.

At lunch Richard joins the queue at the counter. I go downstairs as I feel more at home on the floor below where regular hotel visitors stand around in shoes. But I do go back upstairs and manage to get through the rest of the programme of chanting, dancing, music, breathing and paying attention to 'the here and now'. The promised 'enhanced sensory perception' and 'drug-free altered states of consciousness' work, at least for a while. When it's all over we cross Park Lane and stand at the bus stop among men and women who glow and shimmer, haloed with grandeur and beauty. Even the trees of Hyde Park looked freshly painted.

But back at home in Bristol my real passion in life is condoms. Why condoms? Because they're safe and cheap and the quickest way to prevent a nation of unwanted pregnancies. While the Delfen Foam Complete Unit with Applicator in Purse costs 68p, condoms are 30p a dozen. The snag is that they're not easy to buy. *Which?* magazine, started ten years ago by Michael Young in a converted garage in Bethnal Green, has inspired local groups to do their own surveys to highlight problems. They've been looking for good value among electric kettles, sunglasses, aspirin, cake-mixes, scouring powders, non-iron shirts and British cars. In Bristol, notebook in one hand, sometimes push chair in the other, we're on a hunt for condoms. Chemists are coy—while 95% sell them, only 5% put them on the counter on display. And rarely do they have shop assistants of both sexes to make life easier for the bashful lover. We dream of having ads as centre spreads in all the tabloids, but in the meantime we write up our results in a pamphlet with a striking op art cover Bridget Riley would have been proud of.

A few weeks later I get a phone call. 'I'm being hounded by the press,' it's the Bishop of Bristol, 'they want me to blast Ann Summers to hell and damnation because she's opening a sex supermarket here. I've invited a few people to meet her for tea on Friday. Will you come?'

I meet a young woman who speaks movingly about how useless she feels because, since opening her shops, she gets 200+ letters a week from people with sex problems. Ann Summers is pretty and blonde and waves her hands helplessly.

'It's the last thing I expected,' she says.

'Perhaps you could put posters on the wall so that you can alert shoppers to Marriage Guidance or the Samaritans?' asks the Bishop.

Two of Ms Summers' managers, nattily dressed and poised powerfully behind her armchair like china dogs on a mantel piece, move in swiftly. I understand why a week later when I visit the shop.

What do I find? Lush carpets, low lights and improbable black underwear pinned like insects to the walls. Racks of shining armour too, trays of electrical apparatus and knobbly plastic, everything red, black, purple, silver or gold. It's a fantasy world, a fairy tale capsule. No, it has a religious feel—candles, perfumes, paraphernalia, special costumes to perform the rites, testimonies from devotees and disciples, training manuals for the neophytes—all offering heaven-on-earth through sexual play. You could argue that when sex works well you wonder for a moment why you waste time doing anything else, but this shop is ridiculous. And the Bishop's suggestion is a non-starter. You couldn't have a poster showing real people with untidy hair or crooked toe nails in a place like that. It's make-believe.

At the 1970 National Conference of the Labour Party I get the chance to propose a motion advocating free contraceptive advice as and when and where it's needed. One of my heroes, Jenny Lee, is the seconder and her speech makes sure we win. I give Tyna some press cuttings, although all my campaigns pass her by. I could've been out playing tennis or the piano or poker—anything which makes me happy is good enough for her. She picks up a cutting running a story about the vicar's wife from Bristol who wants sex on the rates.

'Oh, I like that bit about your flowing raven black hair,' she says.

It's on the tip of my tongue to say, 'Is it as dark as Bigga's was when she was young?' but how can I say that if officially I don't know Bigga is my mother? I want her to tell me what it feels like for her to adore everyone's children, but never have her own. Or how she coped with being both mother and non-mother, the person on whom Bigga relied not only to share child care but also to manage disinformation. But what might she say if I rocked the boat?

When Clover, a friend from Newnham days, posts us the keys to her flat near Marble Arch we take a holiday. By chance Susannah and I are walking past the Swiss Embassy. On an impulse I grab her hand and say, 'Let's go inside.' At the counter I ask if they have any information about an R. Strub who had lived in this country in the 1930s. Having Susannah standing beside me gives me courage. I can feel her warm hand in mine. The official simply turns round, digs into a drawer of record cards behind him, pulls one out and holds it up in front of me. The first thing I see is a tiny passport photograph of someone with a haircut not unlike

Adolf Hitler's. This is my father, moustache and all, and it's not quite what I expected. Then there's his name and date of birth, together with his wife's name and those of their four children, two boys, then two girls. He'd died in 1944 in Westminster. I'd have been seven then, which fits in to my memory of Bigga saying, 'Uncle Ro is dead.'

The official waits patiently while I tear a scrap of paper from an old letter and write the details down. When I look again I notice the card also says he and his wife divorced in 1941, when I was four. He'd married again two weeks later—but not to Bigga.

Back in Clover's flat I realise what I've done. That card is talking about real people, probably alive and well. I hadn't banked on discovering a family, only one person, a father, a dead father. When I think about them I can only imagine Lowry's thin anonymous figures, striding across somewhere exotic like an Italian piazza or the Champs Elysees. I've never been abroad so the image is somewhat lacking in detail. Stick to the facts, I tell myself. What's real? When I was four—instead of walking along the streets of Bedford wondering when I was going to start school and which school would be best—I'd have been the last thing on his mind. He'd clearly lost all interest in his third daughter and her mother. Instead he was negotiating a divorce and setting up home with his new love.

When I get back to Bristol I'm tempted to tell Tyna I've seen my father's picture. I'd love to ask her if he really did look like Hitler. Instead I write to the Swiss Embassy to ask where any of the Strub family might be living now.

A member of the consular staff replies, 'I do not have the present addresses, but it seems to me that your relatives are probably living in Great Britain.'

I leave it at that, but my success with the Embassy has unsettled me.

'You're just like your mother,' Tyna says one day out of the blue, scrubbing a sheet stained by a leaky period before putting it in the washing machine, 'This mark means you've got lots of iron in your blood. That's good. But you're both very hard to wash for'. So it's true. It's the first time she's said 'your mother'. A little child inside me says, 'But you're my Mummy, you said so.'

I've got to settle this once and for all. I've still got the envelope Aunt Amy gave me. I get out my birth certificate and spread it on the table. It's a horrible raw pink, the colour of false teeth. The only real people on this form are the Registrar Mr P Nicholls, and me, a mewling and puking baby two months, one week and five days old. The rest of the characters are make—believe. My 'mother' is a hybrid, her birth name Gertrude Annie true enough, but she has stolen Tyna's surname, Maund. My 'father' is Herbert Inskip, who never existed, though 'Bertie' was the name of Bigga's fiancé who died of TB.

OK. If Bigga and Tyna needed a certificate packed with lies; I need one showing where I really sprang from. How can you be real if your parents don't exist? The General Register Office at Somerset House needs to do a little tidying up.

'I am applying to have my birth certificate changed because I know it to be false.' I point out that my parents as shown never existed. I say I now know the identity of my mother and can back up the claim with documents, photographs and one witness. I'm bluffing, of course. The letters and documents in themselves prove nothing and my witness is Tyna whom I describe as being 'frail but of a sound and lively mind', which she is, but whom I would never ask to testify. And I want my certificate to show a blank space because that's what my father is. A blank space.

Mrs Cross, the Registrar, is equally firm in her reply: Mrs Gertrude Annie Maund was the informant. She would have been asked to check it before she signed 'in acknowledgement that the particulars recorded were correct' and she swore that it was so. Only she can undo it. Since she died more than twenty years ago, 'your birth entry will remain as it stands.'

I try again but I'm no match for Mrs Cross. It's the first of several dead ends but my sympathy's with her. Hang biology, you still need to have to have social order. A baby must be born into a cradle of responsibilities and rights woven by consenting adults if it's to survive. I agree with her: if individuals could shuffle their ancestors around at will—or delete them altogether—then children and young people might fall through the net, and there'd be chaos. Blood should not always be thicker than ink.

Richard is relieved. He's always warned me against a family search. Many years ago he married an only child who soon became an orphan. He's an only child too and likes it that way—finding a cluster of in-laws isn't a priority. 'And think how you might get hurt,' he says.

When Richard's contract ends we move out of our lovely storm-proof Victorian house and into a nearly-new vicarage at Whitchurch on the outskirts of Bristol, designed so badly that once when Richard looked out of the French windows in his study, he saw two strange men in the garden eyeing the house. What are they doing? They'd been sent by the Diocese to size the place up for demolition. It was the first we'd heard of it. It will come to that eventually but not yet. Instead the building leaked and crumbled throughout the decade we were forced to live in it.

Life feels like that too. By now I've been a Bristol City and Avon County Labour councillor for some years. When a journalist from Bath turns up at an Avon County Council Planning committee, is she telling the truth? She writes about each councillor in turn including 'the intellectual woman—very intense she is, must be Oxbridge. She cares desperately about absolutely everything and I suspect she never accomplishes a thing . . . There (the councillors) sit—most of them never opening their mouths—and getting ten quid a day of my money.'

`Perishing cheek,' says Tyna, when I read it to her, 'I know for a fact that you only get 50p an hour for baby-sitting expenses. Nowhere near ten quid.'

I'm not doing much better in the parish either. It's tiring being married to a wonderful person who's always out being wonderful somewhere else. He counsels some of the women who live on the estate with their well-meaning husbands and turbulent children. They tell me they find him gentle, thoughtful and patient. Some count the days until their next appointment, the next time they can browse among their innermost thoughts and find some surprises. A few find him sexy, a slim, tall figure, greying hair now, presiding over the Family Eucharist. He's wearing a pale honey-coloured cassock and has a ceremonial stole glittering with sheaves of corn in gold thread and bunches of podgy velvet grapes draped over his shoulders. His hands dip into the silver chalice and rub the wafer between his fingers in the moment of Fraction. Down and down they dip, dipping out of sight and only I know where they go and I'm not telling. One parishioner hands me a letter saying she's in love and would like to share him with me, and as propositions go, I can think of more appealing ones.

The husbands like him too, perhaps because he never takes sides.

What's troubling me far more than a predatory woman or two is my chilling need to be visible. It's as if I can't stop showing people that I exist. It doesn't matter if I get good or bad publicity. Dr Johnson put it well, 'I would rather be attacked than unnoticed'. The first time I stood for election, I knew I'd be annihilated. *Don't Be Vague, Vote for Craig* was the legend on Labour party leaflets Claire and I pushed through hundreds of letter boxes. On election night my Tory opponent almost needed a wheelbarrow to carry her ballot papers around while I got one measly pile. But I continue to put my face on controversial TV whenever I'm asked, get photographed on peace marches, preside at public committees and in court. I crouch inside a small grey van touring the streets of 'my' ward on election night with a loudspeaker on the roof and try to find words to blare out to innocent passers-by, and wish I were dead. All that happens in the day time, but how much longer can I put up with nightly flashbacks of embarrassment and self-loathing and occasional panic attacks? My heart wobbles all over the place. 'Neurotics are often very tough,' says John Lancaster in his *Family Memoirs,* 'they have to be to withstand the blast furnaces of their own neuroses'. Can't I get it into my head that I'm not special, that I don't have to make myself special? Special things have happened to me, that's all.

By the time this floor-length Dollyrocker frock is no longer fashionable, and Richard's turquoise shirt with flamboyant tie is an embarrassment, I realise that my 20 free-wheeling unpaid years at home have got to end. Claire, on the left, in aqua and orange, moves into the room I had at Newnham to study physics. Susannah, in a stylish scarlet and blue trouser suit matching Claire's, is now at secondary school and Aidan long ago grew out of multi coloured boleros Tyna crocheted for him. I join the staff of Wesley College as Tutor in Human Sciences. It's a theological college which trains women and men for the Methodist ministry and I love the job, working with distinguished colleagues and feisty dedicated students.

I'm now earning some money. There's only one way to spend it. A house. I've been homeless once, and once is enough. Clergy live in the house that goes with the job. They don't own it. One day they retire. What then? What if Richard died? What if he left me? A single parent family is a frail coracle.

When the local Co Op Funeral Director rings to arrange a funeral service for an elderly lady in the parish, I contact an estate agent. Her cottage is 300 years old; walls are a foot thick; two rooms up, two down; there's no hot water and the bath in the kitchen is full of slugs. I write to Tyna explaining how awful it all is.

'Tyna, I love the flagstones and the tiny windows and low ceilings. And that big Belfast sink in the kitchen is wonderful. But you like modern things. But we could do it up for you. Suppose we did, would you like to live down the road from us?' I don't mention that the stairs are so steep the curate had to help the undertaker carry the stiff corpse out of the bedroom—we can put in new stairs. But I send her a sketch map pointing out the snags: 'If you gave up your place on *The Windsor Castle* pub darts team at Lowestoft, you probably wouldn't find it easy to find another team in Whitchurch'. Then I list all the organizations she could join instead. Tyna, now in her mid-70s writes back:

> *The Sunshine Club is bound to be full of elderly people and I'm never much of a one for mixing with them. If I joined Wives and Friends I'd have to turn out in all weathers. Beetle Drives are a waste of time. I'm not sure about the Mothers Union because I've never been a mother. But the weekly whist drive sounds just up my street!*

'I've never been a mother.' That's very straight talking from her. But Tyna and I never seem to find the right time for a conversation, even after she's moved in to live with us in the vicarage for a year while Bon Cottage is stripped and rebuilt. When it's ready, despite being a newcomer and quite deaf, she plunges into a dizzy round of card parties, church socials, harvest suppers and whist drives. We buy her a dart board which she hangs on her living room wall so as to keep her hand in.

Aidan is her special friend. He used to run away to Bon Cottage whenever we fell out at the vicarage. His class mate David often visits with him. David is Welsh, he is sturdily built with dark wavy hair and blue eyes and wears a black leather jacket with lots of chains. I'm a bit in awe of him. But each time they say good-bye Tyna gives David a kiss and a hug and slips a Mars bar or a large Kit Kat into his pocket.

Supper is over and I'm alone. I scrape the remains of the smoked mackerel salad into the bin and stack the dishes in the sink. Richard is out on a visit to arrange a christening. The phone rings in his study: someone wants to know the time of the Remembrance Day service next Sunday. While I'm sitting at the desk talking I notice that the hem of a sage green curtain has unravelled and is trailing on the floor. I stoop down to find out how big a job it will be to mend it. A strip of Sellotape? Will a safety pin do? Or do I have to get out needle and thread? As I straighten up I knock a small notebook off Richard's desk. I notice a timetable of group exercises used by the facilitator when he went to a residential Gestalt workshop a month ago. I'm curious to know if any are new to me. I pick up the notebook. I do not expect to find extra-curricular activities.

Silence. The caller at the other end of the phone keeps talking, wanting to know when the service will be over. I put the phone down as slowly and carefully as if it were made of egg shell. The room is very solid and still. The curtain hem gapes and gawps at me and I kick it. An electric typewriter in front of me has a half-written letter about a baby's funeral arrangements. It's about the cot death. Dry-eyed, on the same sheet I type a stream of words I didn't even know I knew. They are from my days and weeks and years in court, words which pour into the eyes and ears of magistrates from witnesses' written statements and evidence spoken, words stacked neatly on some memory shelf until they're needed. This is their night, the moment they've been waiting for. No spaces, no punctuation, just the foulest words I can think of.

I pull the paper out of the machine, screw it up and throw it in the waste paper basket. I feel nothing. Aidan comes back from David's house, we have a cup of coffee together and he goes to bed. I walk back into the study and close the door. I look down and find my hands tearing at the thin lilac cardigan I'm wearing. I slip my arms out and wrench it apart until the seams break and the stitches scatter. I'm standing beside myself calmly watching a woman who is not satisfied until it's lying in shreds and scraps on the floor. My thoughts are crystal clear and unbidden. In the Old Testament it says of people who hear bad news that they rent their clothes. I never believed it. Now I'm doing it. I gather the rags up and tip them in the wastepaper basket, take a jacket off the hook in the hall and pick up my car keys. I sit on the bottom step of the staircase for about 20 minutes. Aidan is no longer moving around and I assume he's asleep. My mind is empty, my breathing shallow. I can't stop trembling and my teeth chatter. When I hear Richard drive up I know exactly what to do. The moment I see his silhouette in the glass door I fling it open and push past him. He guesses at once. I jump in the driver's seat and turn into the road fast and fearlessly.

21

ZURICH

'I'm here,' I explain, 'because no drugs can persuade my heart to behave. And I don't want to die just yet. In three years' time I'll be as old as when my mother had her first stroke'.

The light from a large window overlooking Ladbroke Square in Notting Hill falls on the speaker, a slim, elegant, pale woman, an American-born analyst who trained at the Jung Institute in Zurich

'You've come not a moment too soon. You tell me the tests show that your heartbeat is arrhythmic. I'm telling you that it's trying to beat to someone else's rhythm, trying to harmonise at all costs. At this moment you're literally 'beside yourself'. You must find your own rhythm. Our bodies give us messages when all else fails. They might call us hysterics or mad but it's our unconscious trying to reach us. You've got to listen. You can't go on like this'.

We settle into low curvy chairs in black leather and I talk for a long time.

'You've been betrayed by your father, your mother and your husband. If you try to make yourself a more sincere and compassionate person than you really are—by putting on the costume of someone else—you'll fail. You have to face your own blackness and hardness,' her voice is passionate, 'Will you listen to your rage?'

What rage? I don't do rage. It's not well-bred. I don't even do anger. Anger's one of the Seven Deadly Sins. Once on a boring train journey I tried to draw them all: Sloth with a broken shoulder strap, Gluttony with his belly propped up by broken promises, Pride wobbling on her high heels talking to herself, Envy with shades because he couldn't stand the glare of things he lusted after, Avarice tripping up over her possessions . . . . but I couldn't manage Anger.

As if she can read my thoughts she says, 'Your rage is curled inside you. It's a wild cat. Don't chase it out of the yard. Let it curl up in your lap and listen to its murmur'.

She's right of course. I am angry.

'I've been so very, very good. It's not as if I haven't had chances. The first time it happened I felt as if I'd won a lottery when I hadn't even bought a ticket. Someone had chosen me. But I thanked him kindly and talked fast until he'd had time to realise he'd come to the wrong address.

'Did you tell Richard?'

'Always. I couldn't wait . . . but he was never interested'.

It's nearly dark when I walk out into freaky weather. The snow which fell this morning was only half-thawed when a sharp frost froze everything as it lay: puddles are turned into flawless sheets of ice and footprints are outlined with crunchy ridges. I slither, grab the iron railing. A setting winter sun glitters behind the dark lacy trees in the Square.

At the tube station I queue for a ticket only to find that my handbag is unclasped and my purse stolen. An application form for a job in London is still there. I could find a tiny flat and go home to Bristol at the weekends. But the form has to be delivered by 7pm. I have no money to pay for the tube or bus or taxi. I try a reverse charges call to my therapist but by now she has another client and doesn't answer. I go back on the street and see two people slip and fall. I take tiny, tiny steps and edge my way along Hyde Park holding on to the railings, keeping my eyes on the ground like a very old crone. I reach the Westminster office with 5 minutes to spare.

The following week when I tell my analyst of the theft, she's enigmatic, 'You were ripe to be robbed. You were distraught when you left here. If you try to hold on to too much, something will be taken from you—job options, ideal marriage, perfect home, children, Tyna . . . What do you choose to let go?'

'What's the cost?'

'No, what do you give up?'

'I can only think of things I don't want to give up'.

'What are they?

'Competence'.

'You needn't'.

'Health'.

'You needn't. We're lucky, you and I. Our bodies give us messages when all else fails. You've come in time'.

'Then what must I give up?'

'Your self-image must go. You waited five years for him as his fiancée, then chose to play the game according to his rules. You have played at 'House' with daddy too long. Unless you look well in his eyes you don't look well. It could destroy you'.

I try to take this in.

'Remember that people with your particular birth wound spend their lives adapting, not daring to be rejected. If you look at people who are driven to leave the world a more comfortable place than they found it, a lot have been outcasts and orphans'.

So I'm doing good because I'm screwed up and feel bad. Two mothers and a blank space . . . do certain sorts of childhood predicate certain outcomes? Are my campaigning and lobbying just a need to make amends? Do I go around trying to control things outside myself because I'm living with chaos within? After the first shock I don't care. I can't afford to be choosy. If I had to wait for pure motives before I did anything, I know I'd have to wait a long time.

'I've been asked to write a book about that,' I try to move the conversation on to more comfortable ground, 'I've been writing for some time. My publisher is very keen on the idea and has paid me an advance. In fact it's called *Doing Good, Feeling Bad'* and it's about . . .'

She interrupts.

'And what about your heart? How do you see that?'

'My heart feels like a hooligan living inside me. It's caged, it threatens me, another slug of adrenalin is what it's asking for, another rush . . . .'

Once my therapist says, 'Have you ever been in love with someone since you got married?'

I pause. 'Yes, twice, some years apart'.

'What happened?'

'One taught me to drive a car, the other to paint with watercolours and look at clouds. We'd made marriage vows and didn't sniff around what might be. We managed by setting up a sort of Highway Code as to how far we could go. None of us could imagine picking up a cowpat of lies and excuses and snide remarks about our spouses'.

I feel hot with embarrassment. I sound so smug. I've made it sound so easy, but it was hard at the time. I'm relieved when my therapist stops talking about me and gets down to talking about my father. She comes up with a plan.

'You need to get to know the country he came from. And you need to be alone to do that. I have a colleague who's got a basement room in Zurich. Go for a couple of weeks. She'll hardly charge you anything'.

'What could I possibly learn about Roman?' I ask her,' I've no idea where he lived or grew up . . . only where his birth was registered'.

'You know enough. You don't know a word of German but now is the time to meet him at a deeper level than words. Go to the Rietberg Museum, it's on a hill above the lake in beautiful gardens. Sometimes you're so high up you look down over the tops of tall trees and feel you could fly. Go and look at the Swiss masks. Find the ones which are 'yours', the ones from the place your family came from.

Look into their eyes. Recently you've been seeing their faces in your dreams'.

'But', I hesitate, 'I don't know . . . I've got this book I'm writing. I've planned to use the summer vacation for that. I've been commissioned. I've got a deadline'.

'You can work in the Jung Institute Library. I'll give you a letter of introduction'.

At the end of the session as I walk to Notting Hill tube station I wonder if there's been a log jam in our marriage for some time. Perhaps Richard and I have both been standing on the side with long poles in the water trying to clear it. We could have fallen in. We could have drowned.

My basement room is in Witikon, a wooded suburb perched on a hill with wide views of Zurich. It has a window just below the level of the front garden so for two weeks I have no alternative but to look up the stems of the flowers at their bottoms where they hide their working parts and their scaffolding, so as to present a good face to the sun and the rain. I'm living on bread and pate and cheese and tomatoes, with an occasional hot meal at the Movenpick cafe at the train station.

Most days I catch the bus to the city and then hop on the steamer which zigzags across the lake to the Jung Institute at Kusnacht. Stepping out of the blazing August sun into the house where Jung once lived is a shock. I walk past the huge wood-burning stoves which stand by cold and idle, stroke the cool blue, lemon and white tiles and try to decipher what terrible things Alexander the Great, Pharaoh and Emperor Charlemagne are doing to those they don't take to. The basement is so dark I feel I've walked into the unconscious. I imagine I'm not the first to think this, and wish I could be more original.

Being original is an issue. I was telling the truth when I said my publisher likes the idea for the book I'm trying to write. He likes my paradox: why are women so 'good' yet feel so 'bad'? It's mostly men not women who cause real trouble: they're more likely to start wars, become dictators or terrorists, desert their children, get violent and alcoholic, end up in prison. Let's have some statistics, my publisher said. Well a baby boy born in one district of Bristol is 15 times more likely as a teenager to be convicted of a crime than a baby girl born at the same time in the next street of an adjoining area. Hardly fair on the baby boy. Of course it's true that men usually have more chances in life. Meanwhile women are 'good' in that they keep out of trouble and sign up for the care of the young, the sick and the elderly. Even more important they hand over to men a scarce resource—time—by doing essential jobs for them like cleaning, cooking and clerical work. Yet often they feel 'bad' and sit in rows in doctors' surgeries, benefits offices and advice centres because they're more likely to be wrestling with poverty, depression, illness and self-harm.

But my writing is not going well. I'm sitting alone one day in the Institute Library making notes about women's bodies. A timid knock at the door and a group of visitors from Japan peer round the door. They have little English but I gather they'd like to take a photograph of me studying.

The picture may well circulate as a study of a serious scholar of the life and works of Jung. I know I am a fraud. I haven't the words to write the book either. Increasingly I don't want to write about women as if they were always victims, or the only victims, nor do I believe what the nuns implied about women's moral superiority. What we have in common is the need to take in our stride our unpredictable monthly rhythms; and the emptying and filling and emptying again of childbirth and lactation. What's the effect of all this? Does that give us a bonus: skills in handling transition and managing relationships? Does that make us more (or less) interested and skilful in control and mastery? It's too confusing.

I must tell my publisher that I haven't the time to research it well enough in a world which is changing so fast. Which is true. I try hard but *Doing Good, Feeling Bad* is never finished. And I feel I'm falling apart. I've begun to bulldoze a highway through my past where all the stories I've constructed so far are tumbling down.

I know I must take a day off and tackle those masks in the Rietberg Museum. I start in the basement—I'm in no hurry—and meet a spectacular exhibition of Chinese porcelain starting from the 16th century, which bathes my eyes in colour. It's hard to leave. I go back upstairs and shuffle from floor to floor looking for masks. My legs feel as heavy as lead. I stand at the foot of each flight of stairs and stare up as if I faced a mountain. I find no signs of masks anywhere and feel relieved, but dutifully walk downstairs to ask at the desk. The mask section is at the top of the building and closed to the public, I'm told, but no trouble.

'We'll go up in the lift and I'll unlock the display and you can stay for as long as you like'.

She leaves me standing alone in the centre of a room surrounded by glass cases crammed with faces frozen in varying degrees of surprise and horror: masks of women and men and animals draped with scraps of fabric, twine, animal pelts and what looks like human hair. All the eyes are black, empty holes but the faces are fascinating: what looks like a cheery inn keeper has a smile I would run from: a horse with wonky eyes has a mouth turned downwards in bitter disappointment and a woman with beautifully carved eyebrows is snarling, her curled lips about to spit venom.

Louisienne Howald of Bern City Archives has told me, 'We Swiss all have a place of origin, the place from where the family has its citizenship and is not necessarily the place of birth . . . Your family branch has its origins in the canton of Solothun'. I can't find Solothun on any label but eventually make a tenuous link. Lötschental is in the Bernese Alps, and Roman was born in Bern so that's good enough for me. I like the sound of Lotschental, an area settled in Roman times but largely cut off from the world until the 20th century. The notice nearby say it's famous for its unique local custom involving the so-called Tschäggättä, when scary figures wearing furs and carved wooden masks walk the streets during carnival 'tossing soot at their unsuspecting victims'. I fail to see how any of their victims can possibly be unsuspecting if they see something like this mask coming at them. The tiny empty eyes peer out from beneath hair made of scraps of gingery, white and brown animal skins. The wide open mouth displays 24 teeth, each one far too long and pointed to be capable of anything pleasant. I spend time trying to empathise with the monster but it's beyond me. A local prior in 1860 lamented the difficulties of enforcing a ban on 'the terrible misuse of the so-called Tschäggättä'. I'd love to know what he meant by 'misuse'.

I walk part of the way back along the lake. It's always changing—from mother-of-pearl to milky grey, aqua then indigo, inky blue, then black. It can hide under a misty rain but today it stabs my eyes with prickly sunbeams glancing off the waves. Is it a sign I'm getting cataracts?

Back in my room I lie on my bed and try to read James Joyce, because he used to live in Zurich and died here in 1951. It's not the best of reasons for choosing a book. Every day the temperature has been in the 80s but now there's a storm worse than any that used to frighten me in Lowestoft and make me plead with Tyna to come into my bed. The lightning is end-to-end and the thunder sounds as if there's an air raid overhead. Some trees look as if they'll snap in the wind. Nothing makes sense and I'm very tired. I slip to my knees on the floor and start to cry. I imagine walking onto the lake because it's made of semi-liquid green marble. How appropriate it would be to die in Switzerland, in the night perhaps, just slip away. Then they'd have to take notice of me and put my name in their records because I'd have a Swiss death certificate.

No harm would be done. I'm matter out of place. I shouldn't have been born. Unblemished flesh would grow again where an excrescence had been, leaving a little scar for a time, then nothing. The universe would get back on its axis. While I'm thinking this I'm despising myself for giving space to a grotesque infantile fantasy of my importance, but no matter how much I glare at it, the fantasy won't subside. I get up, open a bottle of cheap wine but it's so nasty I pour it straight down my washbasin. Outside it's quiet again. I pick up a P G Wodehouse paperback and turn to page one: 'The summer day was drawing to a close and dusk had fallen on Blandings Castle'. I spend the night in Blandings Castle where nothing can ever alarm or hurt me.

When I wake in the morning everything looks better. I catch the bus to the Swiss National Folk Museum, which is like plunging into a cheerful family attic. It has a kindly woman attendant with whom I've had several conversations without words during my stay. I weave my way through the same galleries each time: French saints gossiping in the corner, a silent barking dog, a rearing arthritic horse and a Spanish martyr taking forever to die. My first stop is a tiny picture of the Annunciation. The background is gold leaf—only the flesh, the robes, the angels' wings and the prie-dieu are painted. For most of the last 600 years it's inspired monks in their cells to pray but at times it's found its way to the castles of rich women and men. Perhaps they used it as a talisman like a mobile phone and packed it in their luggage when setting off on a pious pilgrimage.

I wonder what the monks thought of this picture? At the top the white dove of the Holy Spirit looks like a hat blown off the head of a benign God the Father. The unborn Christ is a secret curled up in Mary's womb. But what I've never seen in any other Annunciation—and why I love this one so much—is the look in Mary's face when she sees the angel. Here's a woman who's minding her own business having a quiet read, with two more volumes to go tucked inside her prie-dieu. Then this happens. Life is never going to be the same again. But there's a smile on her face. Those books, that angel, have opened her mind to possibilities she would never have imagined. Her future looks distinctly interesting. I'm beginning to think that, despite last night, most of the time mine does too.

When it's time to go home I pack a messy scrap book. Over the fortnight I've been breaking off bits of Switzerland. Like a child I've collected bus tickets, free hand-outs from galleries, logos from paper napkins, menus, maps, postcards, timetables and the side of a Birchermuesli packet.

I take it to show my analyst: 'They're precious because they were sold or given to me by real living, breathing Swiss men and women'.

'Are you ready to meet any of your relatives yet?'

'I think not'.

22

ENGELBERG

Tyna's as cheerful as ever when I break the news that I'm moving to London. I have a new job at Church House, Westminster, and have bought a tiny flat in Paddington to live in during the week. Richard will follow later when he finds a vacancy as a priest in central London.

'My friend Aidan will keep an eye on me,' she says, giving him a hug. Aidan chooses to stay in Bristol to finish his A levels

The previous summer Richard and I had booked our first winter holiday, in Engelberg, a train journey away from Solothun. Richard asks if he can still come. Love is not love which alters when it alteration finds—and I want a companion by my side when I walk into the shadow of my father. I say 'Yes, yes'.

Tyna doesn't ask why we've chosen Switzerland for a holiday. I send her some postcards: *Today we went cross country skiing and I didn't fall down too often but I'm very stiff. Tonight we're going by horse-drawn sleigh to a fondue party and disco. The temperature was –25C (the coldest for*

100 years). I love the socks and leg warmers you knitted for me. x x x

Bigga was right about snow and sun in Switzerland. Gusts of wind blow snow crystals from the trees in tiny rainbows. Richard, despite icicles on his beard, is graceful and poised. He picks up cross-country skiing easily. He'd been an expert young dancer in the days of Victor Sylvester and His Ballroom Orchestra, whereas I can hardly keep upright. When eventually I'm up to it, we set off along slender paths through silent woods and crimpling snow. Cunning machines have sliced two narrow parallel tracks, firm indentations in the snow, and the knack is to keep one ski in each. To overtake you temporarily step aside into the rough snow and get back on to the track as quickly as possible. Overtaking is not a problem I'll ever be troubled with. I envy local women, older than me and with trustworthy thighs like hams, who speed by and vanish round the next curve. Could I have been one of them?

At Ende der Welt (The End of the World) we prop our skis against the outside walls of the inn, among children's sledges, fur wraps and toboggans, as if thieving hadn't been invented. We move out of freezing cold air into a warmth which hugs you like a friend. Goulash is followed by black spicy cake and a glass of hot gluhwein. If God wants to have black spicy cake on the menu in heaven, he'll have to import it from Engelberg. I'm dizzy with excitement and deeply in love with my father's country. It can do no wrong.

The good news about cross country skiing is that every scrap of attention goes on staying upright and there isn't a single brain cell left to think of anything dismal, such as an appointment with a cardiac consultant at St Thomas' Hospital waiting for me when I get back. My new London doctor listened when I told him that for years my heart and I have had an uneasy relationship and that therapy hasn't helped. It feels like a bird trapped by a fowler's snare, beating its wings against my ribs. I lie in bed at night and think, 'If the snare breaks the bird will fly away and I shall die'. I imagine Richard knocking on the door of a neighbour who doesn't like me, but she's a nurse and she'll look after me until an ambulance wakes up the street before taking me to St Thomas' Hospital nearby and I wonder if I'll die and does it matter? My GP's reassuring, but thinks it's worth getting someone to check it out.

Back in Engelberg we take the 8.33am train to Lucerne, then on to Olten and Solothun. At the Town Hall I explain that we've come from England and would be pleased to have some information about one Roman Strub and here is his date of birth. Staff who speak German, French and Italian are two-a-penny, but that's no help to us. Within a few minutes an English-speaker is found.

'If you would be so kind as to come back after lunch, we will have some information for you'.

My stomach tightens as I think of what I might discover in the next hour or two. In the cafe I sip coffee. Richard's igloo of chocolate and ice cream, with caramel sauce inside, is a step too far. When we go back to the Town Hall an official, kind and courteous, hands over the counter five sheaves of foolscap paper. They are called Familienschein, family certificates, one each for my father, my grandfather, my great grandfather, my grandfather's brother and one of my half-brothers. On each is typed their place of origin, their birth, marriages, deaths, and their children. There is no charge.

No mention of me, of course, but the friendly official who gives me the photocopies says, 'Are you his daughter?'

'Yes, I am'.

Richard says as we walk out onto the street, 'That's the first time I've heard anyone call you a 'daughter'.

'That's because no one has'.

'And he said it in public too'.

On the way back we slip into the Jesuit church of St Franz Xavier which stands by the edge of Lake Lucerne. Richard can't stand its baroque, overblown architecture and statuary, so soon walks out to watch the paddle steamers ply backwards and forwards. I stay for a while rejoicing in an interior which is as strange and as other as the names of the people inside my handbag. I sit in a pew and peek at my treasure. I'm in the company of Klara, Lukas, Karolina, Viktor, August, Ludwig, Aloisia, Yardena, Jurg, some of whom must certainly be alive. The names sound crunchy and unfamiliar. There are a few typed notes in German, unreadable except for one which looks as though one of my half-brothers has settled in Canada. There are no addresses, past or present. No means of contact. Excellent. I'm glad they're trapped in paper. I can't yet cope with thinking of them as real human beings.

Back at the hotel Richard and I spread the papers out on a table. Now I know the names of my paternal grandparents—Emil and Anna Louise. I work out the sums. Roman, my father, would have been just four years old when his mother died. A year after her death, his father married her younger sister, Bertha, aged 20. So Roman and his sister Eva must have been brought up by their step-mother, who was also their aunt. Richard points to the entry showing there was one child of the new marriage.

'She was born 15 years later. She could still be alive. You wouldn't want to trace anyone, would you?' Richard sounds nervous, 'It would be such a shock for them . . . some of your half-brothers and sisters must be in their sixties by now, upright Swiss citizens, no doubt. The last thing they'd want to find out was that their father had had an affair resulting in a child.'

'No, I don't want to contact them. But what I'd like more than anything else in the world is to be in the same room. Just to see them. I don't want to be introduced. But I wouldn't be able to take my eyes off them'.

Back in England my consultant at St Thomas' turns out to be a man with whom I enjoyed a demure tea party or two when we were both keen members of the Cambridge University Christian Union. Grace used to be there too as my trusty Christian friend—and chaperone? I'd have married him on the spot given half the chance, but he didn't ask. Now he doesn't recognise me, but calls me 'ma'am', as he does all his women patients. I find it soothing, a flicker from a bygone age of courtesy and calm. I daren't risk extinguishing it by mentioning events he'd have forgotten years ago. He diagnoses mitral leaflet prolapse.

'Which is nothing to worry about,' he says, 'post mortems sometimes reveal that old ladies in their 80s and even 90s have had the condition for years and it did them no harm'.

But he also mentioned something called paroxysmal atrial fibrillation which is not quite so jolly. The snag is that it increases the risk of a stroke. I don't like that word 'stroke'. It's two-faced: sometimes it caresses you but at other times it kills. He prescribes digitalis. I know it's a derivative of the foxglove, a lovely flower which lines the Cornish lane leading from our tent to Treen, our secret beach, where we've camped year after year. Sounds good.

Now I know when Roman died, I could get his death certificate. It feels all wrong to be chasing after a corpse, or a pile of ashes, but I send away for it anyway. It tells me where he died—St George's Hospital, London—and gives his home address at the time.

3, Salem Road is in Bayswater, not a part of London I know. On the way there I walk past Queensway Skating Rink and remember Bigga saying that 'Uncle Ro' had designed it. I stop outside and watch a young, confident, noisy, athletic crowd of many colours go through the doors. I wonder if Bigga ever came here?

I go round the corner into Salem Road. Number 3 is just a facade. In its prime it would have been my favourite sort of town house, terraced with three narrow storeys, a gate and path leading to a door between two small bay windows. I ring the bell of the building contractors' next door who tell me they own it, it's full of dry rot and they use the back of it as a builders' yard. I cross to the pavement opposite and turn to face the shell of the building. My father must have walked down that path and opened the door. He could have looked out of those windows to see if it was raining. I turn back to Queensway Station and go down onto the platform. My father could have stood on this very spot nearly forty years ago. I take out the death certificate and read it again.

I realise for the first time that if a man has died, he must once have been alive. Several trains come and go.

Now I have a real man as my father, I can wonder what he was like. Aunt Amy's sons would have been teenagers when I turned up at Clapham as a baby. Do they remember anything?

> '*Yes*', comes the reply in a six-page letter written on blue lined note paper, '*Aunt Gertie and Aunt Doris were great favourites of ours: seaside visits, Christmas, a new cricket bat just when I needed it*'. Then he continues: '. . . *your mother first met (Roman) at the Foreman's Mutual Society Dinner and Dance to which she had been taken by Father. When I finished my apprenticeship I wanted to broaden my work experience and join W.H.Allen's . . . Your mother gave me a letter addressed to the person*

who interviewed me . . . He agreed to give me a position in the Diesel Drawing office . . . (Roman) was the Chief Designer . . . he was a great help to me in my career.'

I'm glad he was a great help to someone. I read on:

'He was a very tall man and big built—in fact he used to blunder round the office like an elephant, but a crowd from the office used to go with him skating on the river at Bedford and there he was as graceful as a fairy'.

Obviously that particular balancing gene escaped me. I've always mistrusted anything which separates me from the good earth: roller skates, bikes, ice skates, horses, flying . . .

'When war was declared he vanished . . . We all assumed he'd been interned because he was Swiss German and I told Father that's where he was. He made no comment. In the winter of 1940/41 I had to visit a captured Italian boat in Liverpool docks to examine the diesel engines. Walking round the end of the main engines whom should I meet but Mr Strub. We had quite a chat about the old days when we both worked at Allen's. I never saw him again. When I told Father about the meeting he said, 'Yes, I didn't correct you when

> *you said he was interned, but I know he's working for the British Admiralty on secret missions'.*

I want to say to my father in a calm reasonable voice—but I never shall say anything to him in any voice—'You got bored with us all, didn't you? Did the outbreak of war come in handy? Did you spy for us? Perhaps as a marine engineer with many languages you grilled the crew of captive ships to unpick enemy technology. Perhaps you were a war hero and your records are in secret files somewhere in England. But you're not a hero to me. You're a man who released a new child into the world and ran away, as if I were a grenade which might explode and damage you'.

Years later I'm walking across Hyde Park with a friend, a doctor, who has just received some very bad news. We sit in silence on the grass looking across Marble Arch at the Lanesborough Hotel glowing in the sun. On an impulse I suggest we take tea there. Suddenly all the pedestrian crossing lights are green and we're at a very grand Reception desk being told that the Tea Room is unfortunately fully booked. A fashion show hosted by a famous magazine has guests at every table.

I take pains to look devastated. 'Alas,' I say, 'My father died here during the war when it was St George's Hospital. I've made a special journey with my friend . . .'.

'One moment please . . .'.

A table for two is found.

'What did your father die of?' my friend asks. I know the answer by heart. 'The death certificate said 'heart failure, coronary thrombosis and atheroma of the coronary artery'. He was 56 years old'.

'And you never knew him?'

'No, I'm trying to imagine him in a room upstairs, his four children gathered round his bed saying their good-byes. I'd have been seven at the time. I don't suppose he gave me a thought'.

But I soon lose interest. To be honest what's going on around us is gripping. A silent stream of beautiful women snake their way between our tables, slim, untouchable, not of this world, resurrected time and again in different wondrous clothes. You knew that if they walked around in their skeletons they would be lithe and graceful.

'Look at the arms,' my friend whispers as several girls glide past. I can see nothing. 'Notice the cuts—self harm,' she says with a dermatologist's eye for messages from the skin.

After tea we walk back to Hyde Park, crossing Marble Arch again. The pedestrian lights this time are their usual red, apart from a tiny green interlude which you have to prepare for by standing tip toe on the kerb. There's a crowd pressing close and I'm directly behind a young woman with piebald hair which springs out of her head jet black—and black it is at the ends—but in between its blonde. Her black bunches are beautiful starbursts, cut, glued and sculpted to within an inch of their life and her whole head is a work of art, but I'm close enough to see what her best friends probably don't tell her: a bright pink scalp angrily trying to grow wistful, thinning hair which is slowly giving up the ghost.

Oh why do she and I try to be loved for what we are not, instead of for what we are?

23

HAMMERSMITH

'Why didn't you come back to see me earlier when you felt so ill?' the consultant asks not unreasonably, 'Digoxin doesn't agree with some patients'.

'I didn't want to make a fuss'.

He doesn't understand. The nuns were our example: they licked their bodies into shape, hair invisible inside a coif, breasts flattened. We prided ourselves on ignoring the trivial pursuits of our bodies: yawns, laughter, tears, period pains, headache, toothache. By the time I'd left school I could hide all the riff raff of daily life and that evening when I broke my leg at Newnham I could easily convert it into a 'sprain' to lug it to Addenbrooke's Hospital by myself.

The consultant prescribes various other potions but those missing healthy beats still elude me. I'm scared. And ashamed of being scared. Eventually my GP suggests a second opinion.

'At Charing Cross Hospital one of the cardiac specialists is trying an unorthodox approach called Sleep Therapy, instead of drugs or surgical intervention. It might do the trick'.

The hospital is nowhere near Charing Cross but is in Hammersmith, the place where I was possibly misbegotten and certainly born. Bits of the hospital are in the wars, patched up and waiting like patients to be made better. Today a lift is broken and roped off. I climb the stairs and wait. It's a building with eyes and ears because somewhere there's a file with my name on the outside, while inside are X rays, graphs and numbers. I rehearse words in my head: will the doctor say, 'Go away, you are a neurotic middle aged woman, self-obsessed and hypochondriac. Stop wasting my time'. Or he might say 'I'm sorry to have to tell you that your heart is fatally flawed. You have a few months at the most. There is nothing we can do for you'. In other words, will he say, 'You're lying' or 'You're dying'? And which is the more embarrassing?

I'll probably apologise in either case.

I sit outside the clinic feeling like a transparent doll with all my insides showing. I've thought a lot about the outside, though. I never wear patterned clothes and usually restrict myself to two colours. It used to be black and a jewel colour: brilliant turquoise or sapphire blue or emerald green. I've noticed that lately it's even more pared down and I wear black with grey and silver. I've just bought some new ear rings—two tiny strings of pearls, each inside a small engraved pewter bell.

A comic version of my name ricochets down the corridor and there I am, sitting opposite the Registrar who has stepped straight off a Mills and Boon cover—bronzed, smiling, flanked by two dazzling women who later become 'my' nurse and 'my' occupational therapist. The black nurse has her hair drawn tightly back in slender plaits over a head so beautiful it's crying out to be sculpted or painted. The white nurse has a halo of tight curls the colour of sand. All three are robed in white. Together they remind me of an altar piece, a triptych.

'What would you like to tell me about yourself?' asks the Registrar.

I relax. I am on safe ground here. This is just what I say to students whose work is sinking or a man in the dock waiting to be sentenced or to strangers at the vicarage door wanting money. I've heard so many tales over the years and felt sad, angry, amused, bored, desperate, amazed . . . I say nothing.

'Where would you like to start?' he tries again.

I feel a jet of anger inside my throat. I don't want eyes and ears and hands spying on me. I imagine slipping out, down the silent escalator (the one which is working) into the street, down, down into the Underground. I remember seeing a bunch of cold, limp, pink tulips on sale at the hospital kiosk, sheathed in transparent paper. I don't want to be unwrapped and placed in a hospital ward for a few days and then discarded.

I babble, 'I have a husband and three children and many close friends. I have one of the most interesting jobs any woman can imagine. I have lots of excellent colleagues and at the moment I'm busy with a book I've been commissioned to write. I'm always in demand . . .' He waits, then persists.

'You were checked out by a cardiac unit at St Thomas. Did they tell you to relax more?'

'Yes, but I can't'.

'Tell me what that feels like. When you're working, for example'.

'The busier I am the better it is'.

'And when you relax?'

'Something crushes my throat so that I gulp down great chunks of air . . .'

'Can you give me an example?'

'Last week I was at the Royal Festival Hall trying to listen to Cleo Lane and Johnny Dankworth but my heart was beating so loud I could hardly hear them. I just wanted to get out but I couldn't bear the thought of people looking at me if I made my way along the aisle'.

'When is it at its worst?'

'Bedtime. Years ago I used to shiver and quake when I went to bed. Sometimes my teeth would chatter. Now I'm calm on the outside but my heart shivers instead. And the pillow is a kind of sounding board, making my heart thump out its beat'.

'Does it frighten you?'

'Not now. It happens so often and always passes'.

I can hear a prim, cold woman talking.

Silence.

'That's not really true. When I close my office door on Fridays, I think I'll never see it again because I'll be dead by Monday'. I tell him I've spent a lot of my life in fear and I don't know why and that is what frightens me most of all.

'How well do you sleep?'

'In bits and pieces. The night's like a sheet of perforated stamps, hours get torn off at random'.

'You're very tired. It's as if you're colour-blind to normal tiredness because you've ignored it for so long. We'll do a few routine tests, then I look forward to seeing you in about half an hour when I'll introduce you to my colleague who runs this clinic'.

By now I'm used to blood tests and ECGs. I know my veins are deeply buried and hard to find and it's better not to mention this beforehand because it makes some nurses nervous. This time sticky red liquid runs cheerfully into phial after phial. Part of me is relieved that I'm in good hands and part of me sees every cell as a traitor which will tell secrets about my body to experts in a language I do not understand.

'Congratulations, you've taken the most important step by admitting you have a problem,' says the consultant half an hour later in a voice which sounds as if he's really pleased to see me, 'Your heart is using the only language it knows'.

'I don't understand'.

'You hyperventilate, you breathe fast from your shoulders, not your belly. You flush out too much carbon dioxide and poison your blood. I'm going to change all that'

'But how?'

'SABRES', he says triumphantly. 'SLEEP, AWARENESS, BREATHING, REST, EXERCISE, SELF-ESTEEM. Cylla here will teach you to breathe properly and balance rest and exercise but first I'm going to put you to sleep. Sleep Therapy isn't a cure. It's a bit like putting a splint to protect a broken leg while it heals. Your heart will find its own rhythm again when you're rested. You can start the treatment from home, then come in for a few days when we've got a bed free.'

'But I'm due at a conference in Canada next week'.

'Get your secretary to cancel it. Adrenalin is an expensive fuel to run your life on. We talk of a heart-stopping moment—and believe me sometimes it is. Trust me and in six months' time you will be a new person, full of life and energy'.

As the registrar walks part of the way with me to the hospital pharmacy he puts his arm round my shoulders.

Downstairs in our basement bedroom with a glass of diet lemonade, I strip and put on a white mock Victorian nightdress with a high frilly collar which Richard gave me years ago. My clothes are usually thrown on a chair but this time I fold them. I think of the folded grave clothes of Jesus at his tomb. And Lazarus who rose from the dead. I tip out on the duvet my first dose of 10mg Diazepam and 10mg Promethazine which are supposed to induce quality sleep from which I can easily be roused, not heavy drugged sleep. I am a life-long pill-abstainer but I swallow them.

Each day is the same. I sleep all morning, Richard brings lunch and tablets, more sleep, supper and tablets, I sit in a chair in the evening. Newspapers, radio, TV, anything which might bring bad news is banished. I go back to bed at 10 o'clock. By day three I feel distant, light headed. When I wake the bedroom walls look soft and smooth as fondant icing. I raise a mug of coffee to my lips as in a slow motion film. My pulse rate is a lovely lowly 59. On day four I play Scrabble with Richard in the evening and he wins. By day five my life is a mess, a wasteland, Richard a fiend, no one is to be trusted. Tears come with great chunks of breath, straight from my belly, and my rib cage aches. I try to read but slap the book shut when I see that I've used one of my doodles as a bookmark.

I lie back on the pillow and close my eyes. I'm in an airless room with cream walls and the floor is covered in dark brown lino. It's shiny, glossy, clean, smelling of Ronuk polish and pock-marked with indentations where furniture once stood. It's empty. Absolutely empty. I notice a fuchsia coloured sweet wrapper of cellophane paper in the corner.

Then a tiny ball of screwed up silver paper nearby. I kneel on the lino, picking them up and carefully smoothing them on the floor, a silver square and a fuchsia oblong. My nail catches the frail thin foil and tears a hole. I pick the fragment up and look through the hole. I can see myself, young, moving easily down the steep garden path of an Italian villa. I'm wearing a sun dress in broad red and white stripes. Now I'm in a jade and turquoise jacket skiing in Engelberg, skin tanned and healthy. I'm in Russell Park by the Ouse in Bedford singing a nursery rhyme to two imaginary laughing grandchildren on the swings. I'm floating on my back, weightless, looking up at an azure sky without blemish. My white belly has a row of creamy brown smudges like pearl buttons down the front where the Mediterranean sun can reach between the fastenings of a swimsuit that opens like a corset.

Now I'm back in the empty brown room with its slippery polished floor and not a speck of dust. There's a damp patch not far away. I dip my finger in and smell the liquid. Urine. Someone has been here. I know it's a small child, trapped and frightened. So afraid of disgrace she disgraces herself.

I open my eyes. I start to get dressed, I want to catch an overnight train to Penzance, arrive at first light and walk through the empty rainy streets to book in at a hotel on the sea front. Instead Richard brings Ovaltine and massages my feet.

A week later I'm admitted to a cardiac ward which looks like a monster space capsule, each patient threaded to machinery with wires and monitors and masks. We decide not to worry Tyna about my little difficulty. The first thing

Richard tells me when he visits me is that he's climbed all fourteen flights of stairs to get to my floor. I hate him, I burst into tears.

One afternoon I wake and try to move my arm. It's paralysed. I try to lift my foot from the sheet but it's rigid. I've had a stroke. I'm dying. I mustn't make a fuss. When I can, I slowly turn on my side and ease my legs over the edge of the bed. I sit still as a statue. A nurse sees me through a crack in the curtains. She puts her arm round me.

'I dreamt I was my mother having a stroke. It really happened when I was 16. In my dream I was sitting on her settee and I could feel a tiny hole in the bristly grey moquette of the arm . . . perhaps a cigarette burn, which got bigger, and sawdust was running out all over my feet and ankles. I couldn't stop it'.

'I'll make you a nice cup of tea. Cylla and I have two beds to make and then if you like we could come and give you a massage'.

Over the next few weeks I meet occupational therapists who teach me deep breathing, hypnotherapists to help me sleep, dance therapists who get me to move.

One plain straightforward psychotherapist says 'Your hold on life is slippery. It says in your notes that you were depressed after you had your first baby. Have they got this right?'

'Yes, and I was rescued by my god-mother Tyna'.

'Did you talk to her about your depression?'

'I didn't want to worry her, but I was really protecting myself . . . Naming things out loud makes them more real'.

'What else didn't you talk about?'

'The lies she told me. And what she hadn't said. What if Bigga had tried to get rid of me? Or that she begged Roman on bended knee to marry her? Perhaps my two mothers tried to blackmail him? I felt as though Tyna and I were a couple of duellists, pistols at the ready, each afraid to hurt the other, yet neither could walk away'.

'Were you depressed during pregnancy?'

'No, it was the happiest time of my life. I'd got what I wanted: a husband and a home and a baby. I adored her. When things went wrong the psychiatrist traced it back to my mother. It was all her fault, he said. I began to think of my parents' absences and illnesses as my winding sheet . . .' What a stupid thing to say. She'll think I'm a drama queen and she'll be right.

'We see things differently now', she says calmly, 'Think back to what it was like in Scunthorpe. You were a young woman with a good degree in a strange town with no money of your own, few books, no car, no driving licence, no career, no control over housing, no pension. As well as that you were an orphan with no grandparents or brothers and sisters, no family support at all. You might have had every reason for feeling trapped and panicky'.

Six weeks later, rested and refreshed, I go back to the work I love and try to breathe and sleep according to the rules. From now on I'm someone with a coronary history and a management problem, not someone with a capricious and progressive disease.

The following year I wake up one morning and pull on a pair of white panties. In the evening I notice a pinprick of blood. I know something about this. I've read about it. At ladies' hairdressers if you have thick hair you sit under the hair dryer for hours turning scarlet and your consolation prize is a heap of out-of-date ladies' magazines on your lap. Each has a Problem Page with a cheery portrait of a kindly woman with an innocuous name. I've gathered that blood in the wrong place is always likely to be bad news.

I check in with the doctor and tests show there's a cell or two which might one day be slightly dodgy. I resent this. My womb has always been a best friend. Three big bouncing babies each started the very month of asking. Each time it had been brilliant at expelling its precious cargo intact, without tearing or splitting me. Not a single stitch. Then, job done, it snapped back into place and hey presto I had a waist again. And now this. My feminist friends warn against a hysterectomy. Perhaps it's a male medical conspiracy against women. But I will need an investigation every six months. I love my work and don't want regular interruptions. I take up the hysterectomy option and am back in my garden dictating to Jacqui my PA within a week. When I turn up for the three week check-up the consultant is subdued.

'Endometrial cancer,' he says 'which we really didn't think was there. The good news is that it has only penetrated a third of the womb's lining. Because we discovered it so early, it's contained inside the womb. No further treatment is appropriate and you have an 80% chance of living five years'.

'And after that?' I ask, though I'm not sure I want to know.

'You have the same chances as everyone else of your age and sex'.

All I can think is 'If I'd chosen black panties that morning I'd probably be carrying my own death around inside my womb'.

Outside the hospital it's pouring and Richard stops to give a lift to a couple standing at a bus stop with a young child. They're from Sri Lanka and conversation about the weather and the traffic flows gently between the four of us, but inside my head I'm back in Zurich. Outside the Kunsthaus, in the courtyard, I saw a dozen life-size figures made of sticks and charred papier mache—a crowd scattering in terror with one figure at the edge seized and buggered. I'd been so moved I'd written to Claire about it, 'I didn't have time to check but I think it's a protest against what's going on in South Africa.

A protest. That's the word. I know what it means to be a protester. But can you have a protester inside you? Not one, but two. Can my womb be protesting? And my heart? The organs of sex and love. How many more bits of me have to gang up in order to make me listen? I haven't time to wait and find out. Perhaps the letters and papers from Aunt Amy will tell me what I need to know. I might even start by talking to Tyna.

But I've left that too late.

24

WHITCHURCH

Tyna and I are at Bon Cottage with a cup of tea, a green baize cloth on the table, a hand of canasta and an ace at the top of the discard pile—what more could either of us want? The M4 from London to Bristol regularly ends up at the card table. If we're not playing cards, I watch her crochet brightly coloured squares made from woolly jumpers friends bring her from jumble sales. She hates sewing so she sits and talks while I stitch the squares together to make blankets for refugees.

She's telling me again the story of climbing the pear tree to tie the bell under Ethel's wedding bedstead. I'm hardly listening. I remember 'Aunt Ethel' because we used to visit her thatched cottage when I was a child. What, I wonder, would happen if I knocked on Aunt Ethel's door now? She'd invite me in and pour tea into cups made of egg-shell china and give me a slice of home-made Victoria sponge filled with home-made raspberry jam. And I'd ask her, 'Did you know Gertie was going to have a baby? What did Doris say about it? You were there at the time, weighing it all up.

What did you think was going on? In particular how did Doris and my father get on together?'

She'd say, 'We all wondered about that'.

Of course the cottage is now in ruins and Ethel died long ago.

Five days later she's admitted to hospital. We drive down to Bristol and as soon as we arrive we get the playing cards out. The good news is that Tyna is dealt two aces, a joker and four sevens. With a hand like that she spreads her cards in triumph over the white plastic tray which lies across her frail legs and together she and I have no difficulty in winning the game against Richard and Aidan. Of course she's the scorer. She's been adding up in her head all her life: in a draper's shop where ribbons cost a penny-three-farthings a yard; at the local bookies when she's calculated her winnings on sixpence each way; and as the fastest member of the darts' team at The Windsor Castle to work out what score's needed to win.

Richard gathers up the cards, shuffles them and begins to deal the next hand. Then something strange happens. Tina announces our scores for the previous hand and they're wrong, not just by a small error but bizarrely wrong. We draw closer to the bed, pretending not to notice, just as we'd lied to her about our reason for driving down to Bristol to visit her without warning. Instinctively we all begin to speak at once, giving her time to right herself, like a canoe which almost capsizes.

She's getting tired and we prop her up against her pillows. She's white as the sheets on her bed, and for a moment struggles to breathe. Susannah starts to cry.

'Cheer up', says Tyna and calls a nurse over to pull back the covers so that Susannah can see the great clumsy furry boots she's having to wear in bed, 'I bet you want a pair of these don't you?'

Someone brings Tyna a copy of the Daily Mirror so she asks Richard for his pen.

'I'll just check my Bingo results', she says.

She and I have our routine patter ready. Every time I say, 'Waste of your money, Tyna. You'll only be disappointed again,' to which she replies, 'You won't be saying that, my girl, when I win a million and you can have . . .'. She finishes the sentence with whatever I've been longing for that week, a house in Tuscany or a Mary Quant original. She always has the last word, 'Never mind, better luck next week'.

But this time when she's checked her results she throws the Mirror to the end of the bed without a word.

The next day, Saturday, she seems a little better and on Sunday morning when I arrive the nurse in charge asks me to bring her some day clothes. I'm surprised as Tyna has been too tired to change into them for several months but I don't question her decision. I drive back to Bon Cottage and return to the hospital to find a physiotherapist pummelling Tina's frail back to try and find space for some air. The treatment looks so cruel I can hardly bear to look but surely they know best. The last time I see Tyna she's sitting upright in a stiff chair in a day room, a little surprised but uncomplaining. I kiss good bye because I have to get up at 5am the next morning to speak at a diocesan conference in Carlisle tomorrow.

By the time we get home to London Tyna is dead. I weep in Richard's arms because she died alone. Why ever did I leave her? Why did I put work first?

He says, 'I think she might have preferred to die alone. Sometimes when I've been with the dying it's as if they choose the moment. She'd have hated to be a nuisance'. He strokes my hair, 'Dying was something important she needed to do by herself rather than put us to any trouble'. I try to believe him. I'm still trying to believe him.

The next morning I drive to Bristol, not to Cumbria. When I sign the form to acknowledge that I've been given Tyna's belongings, I notice her purse is empty. Someone—a visitor? a medic? a cleaner?—has taken the two £10 notes she'd asked me to put there 'in case of emergency'.

As I drive away I write an imaginary poster in the air and pin it up on an imaginary wall in the ward.

'To Whom It May Concern: if you took Tyna's money you might like to know that she would have gladly given it to you if you needed it. She was very poor all her life, but a more generous person never lived. People said of her that she would part with her last penny, and that's what you made sure she did'.

Back home to Bon Cottage which is colder and quieter. She's not here to say 'take your shoes off, get on the settee, you look like death warmed up, here's a cup of tea, drink it while it's hot, I'll stroke your feet'.

Aidan comes with me to the funeral parlour where Tyna is dressed in a white satin gown with a frilly collar which distresses me, but I think she might have liked it. Her hair is far too neatly coiffured, as if she'd just got back from the hairdressers. Her finger with the crinkly nail lies still. Neither of us has seen a dead body before and we're not sure of the etiquette. As we stand there looking on, I can only think of all the knitting patterns, rules of arcane card games, phrases, memories of dead friends, saucy jokes, catch phrases, stored in her head that have gone forever. As someone said, an old person is a library in flames.

We go back to Bon Cottage and Aidan finds a large wooden box under Tyna's bed. In it he crams the contents of her sideboard drawer while I pull out of her wardrobe dresses to take to Oxfam. I can almost hear her say, 'That will do somebody a good turn. Crimplene's built to last'. Perhaps even now one of her indestructible frocks is hanging on a rack with a surprising price tag in the retro shop *What the Butler Wore* in Lower Marsh, a market street where I shop most days in London. Sometimes I look through the window to see if I can recognise one of her fabrics.

Aidan has found the black photo album she showed me as a child. Inside is a press cutting of Kipling's poem *If (*which Tyna's father had made her learn by heart) and a romantic birthday card from a Lowestoft suitor, an elderly widower whose ardour and ownership of a row of houses failed to move Tyna when she was widowed. She told him she wanted to be free. Inside an autograph album given to her in 1927 is a pen drawing dated April 1942 of a man and woman staring longingly at each other across the page. The man is in army uniform, letter in his hand, and must be Jack. In the centre is a neat house and garden. The letter from Jack which Tyna showed me on the beach all those years ago was written in the same year, 1942. She'd have been a mere 38 then, Jack a little younger. They married in 1947. Why did they sacrifice five years of happiness and possibly the chance of children? Was it loyalty to Bigga? Or was I in the way?

When Aidan lifts the lining paper at the bottom he finds a single sheet of paper hidden beneath: a list of snippets from the in-tray at the office where she briefly worked during the war.

> *Mrs B has no clothes and has not had any for a year. The clergy have been visiting her.*
>
> *Please find out if my husband is dead as the man I am now living with won't eat or do anything until he is sure.*
>
> *Please send my money at once as I have fallen into errors with my landlord.*
>
> *I am glad to say my husband reported missing is now dead*
>
> *Milk is wanted for my baby as its father is unable to supply it*
>
> *In answer to your letter I have given birth to a little boy weighing 10 lbs, is this satisfactory?*

And below that, a mystery solved. A press cutting from *The Bedford Record* dated August 1929. One evening at about 9pm four teenagers were walking home along the Embankment where the stone balustrade skirts the bank of the Ouse. One of them was Annie Maund, Tyna's 13 year old step sister, walking abreast with Stanley who was pushing his bicycle. Charles and Sylvia were on the pathway. A car drove up from behind.

At the time the driver said: 'I was driving my car when I met another car with bright headlights. There was drizzling rain at the time. I couldn't see a thing and I ran into some people walking on the road and two have been taken to hospital. I was driving at 10-15 mph'.

'Why didn't you pull up if you were dazzled?' Annie's father asked him at the inquest.

'I saw no reason to do so. I didn't know there was anyone on the road'.

'Why didn't you sound your horn? Why was there no warning?'

'There was no time'.

A witness on the spot described how he 'saw the boy I now know to be Stanley under the car, his head near the pavement. I lifted him out first, then I saw Annie under the engine. Two or three people rushed up and we lifted up the car to release her'.

A juryman asked, 'If there'd been such strong headlights, why didn't they show up the children in the road?' No one seemed able to answer.

Annie died of a fracture at the base of her skull. After a brief retirement a verdict of accidental death was recorded and the Coroner sent his sympathy to Annie's father and his family. So that's how Tyna's father lost not one daughter, but two. Tyna had said she'd been thrown out of the family home by a wicked step-mother and now I think I know why. Judging from the date, I imagine that his wife, no doubt crazed with grief at the loss of her only child, turned on Tyna. And Bigga invited her to live in the family home at Clapham.

As a 77-year-old childless widow, Tyna had come to Bristol knowing no one except us. But she'd never been short of friends and at her funeral they fill the church. One of them put her arm round me, 'Don't be sad. If Tyna were here she'd be saying, 'At 84 I've had a good innings, haven't I?'

Aidan also found my baptismal card slipped inside Tyna's album. It has a picture of a man in a brown suit leaning piously ever the font. Did I have a man in a brown suit—or any man in a suit of any colour—at my christening? I ring the secretary of the Church of the Holy Innocents, Hammersmith, but the Parish Register names parents only, not god parents. The Vicar at the time recorded my mother as Jean Inskip. Why Jean? Was it what Roman called her? Perhaps he was there. Perhaps that day I had two real live parents of the sort nuns wrote letters to. Three weeks later on my birth certificate she'll be Gertrude Maund, transformed by a fictional marriage to poor old fictional Herbert Inskip. By then he'll be recorded as dead as a doornail anyway.

It must have taken courage for Tyna and Bigga to tell such a barefaced lie to a vicar, but it would have been as unthinkable for them to leave a baby unbaptised as to leave her unfed. My baptism must have been a bit like an elopement: you have to go somewhere secret to get the secret deed done. I expect he listened patiently to what would not have been the first fairy story he'd heard from people standing on the vicarage doorstep. Perhaps it was a rehearsal for the story Sister Madeleine heard when I went to school.

One Easter Sunday morning I set off for the Church of the Holy Innocents. I don't like the name. It's a reminder of the Bible story where King Herod slaughters babies and young children, wiping them out of his life just because one of them might get in his way. At first I stand outside pretending to read the noticeboard. A congregation of strangers of all ages and many tongues stream through the door. Inside there's music and singing, bells and incense. One day Tyna and Bigga must have walked through this porch with me in their arms. It was December so Bigga would have been wearing her musquash coat. Now fifty years later the church is dark, with a huge Easter candle standing like a fat chimney in front of the pews as the sole light. Tapers dip into its single flame and light is spread from person to person as we touch each other's small hand-held candles until the whole church is lit up. At the Offertory procession an iced cake shaped like an open Bible is taken up to the altar to celebrate the recent Confirmation of some young people. Did I have an iced christening cake, with or without candles? But who would have come to the party? Aunt Amy and the rest of Clapham knew nothing and my mothers could hardly have made many London friends in less than a year.

When the service is over the children hunt for small Easter eggs hidden in the church and everyone is invited to breakfast. We troop across the road to the wooden pavilion in Ravenscourt Park for sparkling wine and croissants, orange juice and Danish pastries. Then I slip back into the church and stand by the font. Once Bigga was here, as once Roman stood on the platform of Bayswater tube station.

Bigga, it's time you and I had a conversation.

25

EVERY KIND OF COCKTAIL

Dear Bigga,

Although I haven't wanted to hear your voice, I made sure that I kept some of your words.

In the palm of my hand is your tiny notebook, no larger than a credit card. Maroon cover, ragged at the edges, with a wavy watermark which catches the light. Each page has pale green lines which you ignore as you dip your nib into navy blue ink. No fountain pens, no biros, no felt tips. You look as though you're in a hurry—just a few words from time to time in a large, emphatic hand, smudged and cramped. It's half empty. 709 words. I counted every one of them.

Where did you keep it all those years? Particularly when you had to sell up and live with your sister Amy. You wouldn't have liked her to see it. Any day you could have destroyed it but I'm glad you let it live on. Your illness meant that your life slipped away slowly, imperceptibly, while I was still young, and still so angry with you. I like to think you wanted me to see it one day.

I've got another photo of you too, probably taken in the 1930s, about the time you wrote the diary. Here you're a woman in authority, centre stage, dressed in black with a rope of what look like pearls round your neck. You're smiling, relaxed and confident, anchored in a crowd of girls who worked for you at Marion and Foulger's. Is that Tyna standing on the extreme right? There's no one I can ask.

And then 1935 comes bowling along and everything changes. You start writing in January, a few days after your 38th birthday. As I flick through, what first strikes me is the fun you had that year: dances each week, the 'flicks', birthday parties, whist drives, teas and suppers. Then there're country pubs at the weekend—*The Cock* at Pavenham, *The Star* at Clapham and *The Red Lion* at Stevington. You'd have cycled there I imagine, or walked—only the boss's son Georgie, and Harold the taxi man, had a car and could take you for drives in the country. And you loved London too, going regularly '*up to Town*', to the theatre, sightseeing, shopping (once bringing back your musquash coat), coming home '*on the Midnight*', which I presume was the last train. You never seem to be alone. Tyna's hardly mentioned, although you're both living in the Clapham family cottage, but making guest appearances are Kitty, Florence, Rowley, Kath, Eric, Ethel, Winnie, Phillip, Norman, Freda and many more, as well as your beloved nieces and nephews. You seem so very happy.

Here's the first surprise. The year starts with a marriage proposal:

> **February 20** ***Went to Shire Hall Whist Drive. Mr Gould begged me to marry him.***

No mention of what you said to him but a month later it's

> **March 20** ***Promised to go to tea with Mr Gould on Sunday***

After that he disappears without trace.

Then there's Geoff:

> **January 22** ***Just had a row with Geoff. I wouldn't go to the Corn Exchange.***

January 26 ***Up to Town . . . Geoff met the midnight train. I was not alone.***

That's the last we hear of him too. When you stepped off the train with someone else, Geoff knew it was too late.

January 25 ***W.H.Allen's Dance. He was not there.***

'He' is an absent presence, something you'll get used to.

February 15 ***Allen's dance—best one this season—he was there.***

They would have been mortified to find that your boyfriend was an adulterous husband and father.

Now you see him, now you don't. Unlike everyone else in your diary he doesn't have a name, though here comes his initial.

> **February 16** ***Went out for first time with R . . . . felt very guilty***

From now that magic initial is on almost every page of your diary. Why the guilt? Because you knew that 'R' was not only married but had a family. Bedford is a small town and some of our Inskip relations worked where he worked, W.H.Allen's. They would have been mortified to find that your boyfriend was an adulterous husband and father.

I want to imagine what he looked like when he met you, so I made this collage from a photograph of him taken around that time. It comes from a book published in 1995 describing him as 'a remarkable young Swiss engineer' who, having graduated in Zurich and Berlin, joined the staff of W.H.Allen's Queen's Engineering Works at Bedford in the 1920s. The book shows him as a man with a confident stride powering along an embankment. I've changed that. I've reduced him to the size of a cigarette card and stuck him down striding across a holiday snap I took of the Jungfrau. I'm glad my rough cut-out suggests that he's wrapped in a transparent film, impervious to touch. And I'm not at all sure he should feel as confident as he looks. I notice his feet don't touch the ground.

Anyhow your affair is beginning in earnest. After a day in London, you know he's the one for you.

> **March 16** ***Saw the Tower, then went to Wyndhams to see Sweet Aloes. I am in love.***

When he asks you to go away with him for Easter you say, '*I was very undecided about it*'. I'm not surprised. But you say 'yes' and go to Wood Cottage, near Oldham, a cottage I can't trace.

> **Easter Saturday** ***Bought O at Huddersfield, R bought me flowers and fruit, took me to the pictures. We saw 'Mrs Wiggs of The Cabbage Patch'.***

The 'O' is a double circle, drawn rather than written, and suggests he bought you a ring. It must have been the gold signet ring which you wore day and night on the fourth finger of your right hand. You never mentioned where it came from and I never asked. After you died I took it straight to a jeweller's in Cambridge and sold it for 10 shillings. Even now I wouldn't want it back because it was the wrong ring on the wrong finger and it said to the world I didn't have a father.

I wondered what film the two of you would choose and looked up *Mrs Wiggs of the Cabbage Patch* in my Radio Times' Film Guide. It's the story of the poverty-stricken but always cheerful Pauline Lord and her five children, whose father has disappeared without trace. I'd love to know whose idea it was to see it and what you both made of the plot, sitting side by side in a dark cinema. You might have known about Roman's four children in Bedford. I wonder if any of them asked where he'd disappeared to that Easter.

> **Easter Sunday** ***Went to church and a walk over the moor.***

I can understand why it was important for you to go to church at Easter. You never missed. Did 'R' go too? Did anyone confess any sins?

> **June 26** ***Went to Stevington. R sang all the way home.***

Stevington is a few miles from Clapham and I assume you're in 'R's car. I wonder what he sang. Was it in English or German or French or Italian? Is it true, as George Steiner said, that anyone fluent in several tongues 'seduces, possesses, remembers differently . . . that the love and lechery of the polygot differs from that of the monoglot, faithful to one language'? Did you have lots of lovers? Did you compare? Did you sing along with him? I don't remember hearing you sing, except in church. I think that both you and I are pretty useless at it.

There's another visit to Wood Cottage a few months later.

> **August 5** ***Went to watch sunset over the moor***
>
> **August 6** ***We went up the glens and bathed in the evening . . . we had a lovely time with every kind of cocktail.***
>
> **August 7** ***Very sad. . . . Ro drove me to Bilstone and then went on to the bungalow.***

'The bungalow' must mean he went back to his family at the The Foc's'le, Snettisham. At Bilstone you'd have caught the train back to Bedford. Alone. You say you're sad. I'm not surprised. Had you thought about the future? Did you expect him to leave his family and marry you? I doubt it, because anxiety creeps into your diary from now on, seven months into the affair, What you can't know is that in two or three years' time you'll be at The Foc's'le yourself—with his sixth child in your arms.

But by the following day you don't sound too heart-broken . . .

> **August 8** ***Played tennis at Market Harborough Vicarage.,***

Three weeks later you have a double concern, first about R's health and then about whether or not he is a liar.

> **August 29** ***R ill. I am worried.***

> **Sept 6th** ***Letter from R. I do not know if I shall end our friendship.***

So it's 'friendship' now, no longer 'I am in love'. I've searched out that letter. This is what he wrote:

> *You met me last night on my first outing for about the last fortnight. I haven't had very good luck since my spell in bed, as I fell and smashed my knee and hand and also I feel not too well, got sick repeatedly, probably liver . . . my son is safely back from India . . . my sister's wedding is in Switzerland on October 3 and I shall probably go there. Yesterday and two days before I drove to Clapham Road after 5.30pm but could not find you.*

> *Please Jean do not be angry with me because I did not write before, but I am not and have not been feeling too well and I don't want to present myself when I am feeling miserable. Now I have marching orders to go to Liverpool and I don't feel a bit like travelling . . . drop me a line here at the works'.*

It sounds as if you and he met unexpectedly in Bedford. Perhaps he'd told you he was too ill to see you or that he was working away? Something makes you doubt him and you must have spoken your mind. His need to write a conciliatory letter the following day suggests more than a lovers' gentle tiff. Were you very angry? The next entry shows how serious it was:

> **September 19** ***Have nearly decided to end it all by this time. Nothing seems straight forward with R. Then I saw him up Linden Road. He explains. I believe him.***

That was close! If you hadn't believed him, there'd have been no baby. The final entry reads simply

> **October** ***Went to live at 12 Spencer Road.***

That was a flat you shared with Tyna.

Let's pretend I'm interviewing you. Once I did a series for HarlechTV on changing family patterns, so I'm going to imagine I'm back in the studio and you're sitting opposite me, wearing the same black crepe dress you wear in your Marion and Foulger picture, with a string of artificial pearls. I always start off very positive, assuming you're nervous and need reassurance.

'Welcome to *Women Only* here at HTV. We're going to be talking about your very happy and eventful year in 1935. You've been promoted to a senior executive position, something which not many women can aspire to. At your firm's Annual Dinner in March, 'the Governor' chose you to make the main speech. You have a giddy social life in Bedford and up in Town. And now you have an exotic lover who travels all over Europe'.

Then the questions come tumbling out. 'What did Roman see in you? You were educated at the village school, have been nowhere, seen nothing and lived in one house all your life, as English as your surname in the Doomsday book. You weren't even some bright young thing to be swept off your feet. What did you get out of it? Did your blood stand to attention every time you glimpsed him? Was having a baby a way of having part of him? If you wanted a child and felt time was ticking by, why not settle for Mr Gould? I rather like the sound of him, formal, reserved, dependable. Why risk secrecy and shame with someone else's husband? A man without a conscience. And how come you conceived when the affair had been going on for over a year? You may have had plenty of practice at 'being careful'. What did Roman say when you told him you were going to have his baby? There wasn't a National Health Service in 1936 so I'd like to know, did he offer you money towards your hospital expenses with something thrown in for a nappy or two and a tin of Cow and Gate baby milk powder? If so did you accept it?'

I try to calm down. Let's look at the facts. I've no evidence of any money changing hands but I still have the stubs of a blue book of National Savings Certificates for an account opened in my name in 1938, which may have been a gift from him or may have been what you and Tyna had saved. 24 certificates worth 15 shillings each, a total of £18. Given that that was the year when the rental for the *The Foc's'le* was £5 5 shillings a week (which I assume 'R' never collected), £18 doesn't sound much but it must have helped. I know we cashed the certificates in gradually over the years because my signature replaced yours after I was seven, when the law judged children old enough to sign for themselves. Perhaps it helped towards my school uniform.

There's something else I'd like to ask: did my father ever lay his hands on me? Did he ever visit you in hospital and hold me in his arms, for example? Did we ever touch skin on skin? Perhaps men didn't cradle babies in those days. He couldn't have come to see you often or questions would have been asked. I imagine you told the nurses at Hammersmith Hospital 'Her father died'. I don't think they'd have been fooled but that would have kept them quiet. I have to tell you that now I know who 'R' is and that he died in 1944 in Westminster. I'd have been seven then. That fits in with my memory of you telling me one day 'Uncle Ro is dead'. How did you find out? Because Bedford is a small town where news travels? What you may not have known is that he and his wife had divorced three years earlier and that he'd married a much younger woman in Scotland 10 days after the divorce. He'd clearly lost interest in you and me long ago. I'm sorry to put it so bluntly.

There's something else I don't understand. How did you decide whether or not to keep me? Would I have been adopted if I'd been a boy? If I owe my life to carelessness, perhaps my birth plunged you into a lifetime of lies and the fear of being found out. Your life was blighted by mine. Did the worry and financial responsibility of bringing up a child by yourself make a stroke more likely? In other words, did you die early because of me?

All I can hear is silence.

So that's all I know about how 1935 was for Tyna and Bigga, except for one postcard 'R' sent Bigga in July. He posted it in Ostend, and it's a reproduction of a painting in romantic style of two ships on a glassy blue sea, with a clear sky and a hint of a rosy horizon. On the right sailing towards us is the S.S. Prinses Astrid, part of the Ostend/Dover ferry line. I later discovered a dramatic account of that ship's afterlife in Stan Hough's story of active service during WW2, but even here it's making its presence felt, a black iron ship looking strong, determined, and unstoppable.

The sailing ship on the left with slender masts and many sun-tinted creamy sails is altogether more dreamy and fragile. It's dependent on the elements and built to adapt to whatever conditions it encounters. It's probably painted not from life but from the artist's imagination because commercial ships dependent entirely on sail were not being used any more in

1935. Anyhow it's a pretty picture of two ships sailing past each other, caught at a moment when they are closest.

Back in Cambridge days I read Tolstoy's *Resurrection* and was strangely moved by a tale of passion between unequal citizens, a Prince and a maidservant who, now pregnant, was abandoned by her careless, but not evil, lover. Katusha is the frail vessel in this picture. So were you. But the Russian Prince, and Roman—each at the helm of a powerful steamship—sail straight on.

What I also found among your papers was this letter:

London County Council, Public Health Department
Hammersmith Hospital, Du Cane Road
Shepherd's Bush W12
October 26 1936
Number 16401

Dear Sir or Madam,

I beg to inform you that Gertrude Inskip in E ward gave birth to a female child at 5.45pm on Monday

Yours faithfully
E H Sargent (Steward)

What the form doesn't say is that it was nearly followed by your death certificate—a Caesarean section was just in time to save both our lives.

26

PLEASE JEAN DO NOT BE ANGRY WITH ME

The postcard of the liner and the sailing ship is the first Roman sent to Bigga, or at least the first one she kept. Was I waiting for Tyna to die before I dared read the rest? She used to say 'What the eye doesn't see, the heart doesn't grieve over', and maybe she was right. If I'd traced a Strub while Tyna was alive, I would have had to keep it a secret from her. We'd had enough of secrets, she and I. Now she's beyond being worried by anything I do. I'm free to read what he wrote and interrogate this man who couldn't resist women, who wasted his seed and then wove a web of lies around them. It's time to turn his apparent carelessness and self-interest into something easier to live with.

The first card I pick up he wrote from the 1937 Paris Exposition Internationale, designed to show what 53 nations from three continents could produce in the way of art and technology when they really try. Modesty didn't get much of a look-in. The official guide promised that 'In a few hours you will have completed a world tour'.

The postmark on the card is September. I imagine a sunny day and can see him trailing round the huge site wearing immaculate black patent leather shoes and silk socks wrapped around hot and bilious feet. Maybe he was in Paris eyeing the enemy munitions, thinking of the role he might play if there was war. What's going on Berlin, for example, where he'd once been at university? In two months' time there'll be swastikas on the stamps of the cards he'll send to my mothers from Munich. Suppose he wanders into the Spanish Pavilion. Perhaps he'd heard the story of how German bombers appeared in the skies over the Basque city of Guernica and razed it to the ground. Perhaps he's standing in silence in front of Picasso's long thin Guernica painting where bones crack and break and the crushed bodies of horses and humans are jumbled together in the mud and slime of a world gone mad. I now know he did secret work for the British War Office.

But he was also the man who sang in the car, sharing theatres and fun with his mistress. Maybe he invited her to the exhibition? If he did perhaps she'd choose new shoes, have her beautiful hair styled and buy the latest makeup for her first trip abroad. What if they had a meal afterwards? He could have written about it in a secret diary. I like to imagine it might have read something like this . . .

> *. . . I ran my hand over the thick white damask table cloth, smooth and soft, until my fingertips touched hers. Her nails and lips were scarlet, perfectly etched, a pen and ink drawing.*

> *Her cream rouge was a soft, deep pink with a hint of fuchsia—Leichner's 'American Beauty', I should say. She was wearing black, of course, but not a piercing, punishing black. The feather from her hat with a curved brim stroked her cheek from time to time but she didn't seem to notice. I longed to tenderly brush it away and touch her beautiful hair. Round her throat was the necklace of hammered silver panels each the size of a tiny postage stamp. And the matching bracelet I gave her. The silver and scarlet danced on the black stage . . .*

He didn't invite her of course. He sent her a postcard instead. Only the jewellery is real—Bigga gave it to me without saying where it came from but I can guess. It's Claire's and Susannah's now.

I turn the card over and the fantasy disappears:

> *I am just returning after a strenuous time but I had two hours at this Exhibition which is beautiful. See you again soon. Yours, R*

He sounds like a good-natured friend of the family, not the father of an unclaimed 10 month old. Which makes it even harder to read his cards. They're so chatty, so effortlessly innocent. It makes me feel I'm eavesdropping. These words were not written for my eyes. When I was growing up Tyna used to say 'People who eavesdrop never hear well of themselves'. I had every reason to believe her. But one sheet of paper I can read with a clear conscience because it has my name on it.

It's crisp and thin and rustles like tissue. It's been folded into seven columns, then three times across to make 21 boxes. Inside each box are girls' names in every letter of the alphabet except X and Q. So once upon a time—after he knew he'd got a girl but before my name was registered—he cared enough to draw up this list. Unless of course he wasted time making two lists, one of which he screwed up and threw in the bin when I was born. The writing matches the postcards exactly, except for 'Juliana' which Bigga wrote not once but three times, but no one listened. Why Juliana? I think Bigga must have been enjoying a current celebrity story. A few weeks before I was born a royal engagement had been announced between Princess Juliana of the Netherlands and His Serene Highness Prince Bernhard of Lippe-Biesterfeld, a suave young man with a dashing lifestyle. The young Princess had fallen deeply in love with him when they met at the Winter Olympics in Bavaria, and Europe loved a fairy story with a real Princess in it.

The first thing I notice are my granddaughters' names—Charlotte (Lottie's there too) and Beatrice—together with my daughters' names, Claire and (Susannah) Rose. I love the fact that Richard and I together with my parents and our children simply dipped our arms into a pool of tried and trusted beautiful European names.

But there in the list is the name of a daughter he already had. How dare he? Was it his favourite name? Or did Bigga suggest it and he could hardly say, 'No, I'm sorry, we can't have that because I've one of those already'. Or did he really want two daughters with the same name? I thought of this when I read Annie Proulx's short story *Family Man.* Fred is an 84-year-old in a retirement home still tormented by a secret he glimpsed at his beloved father's funeral 70 years earlier. Over decades he pieced together the truth: like me, his father had not one but several secret families and he had saved himself trouble by calling all the boys Ray or Roger and the girls Daisy or Irene. Could Roman want to do the same?

That's enough for one night.

But I keep going back to the papers. They're my relics, my inheritance. One evening I read every postcard and letter mechanically, determined not to get tangled up in the meaning. *Glassworks* by Phillip Glass ripples and throbs in my head. Most of the correspondence is addressed to 'Jean' which is clearly what he calls Bigga. I couldn't understand why he changed her name until I cross referenced with my Familienschein papers to find that Roman had a younger sister called Gertrud who died as an infant. Perhaps he grew up in a household which talked of 'our poor dear Gertrud' or where the word must never to be mentioned? Or did he give each lover a new name?

All his letters are in pencil. Was he afraid of making an indelible mark? Nothing is dated but I can trace the order as some cards have a legible postmark, some need a magnifying glass, and only a few are indecipherable. I start to transcribe the text, but make mistakes. I'm not up to it. Was I there when my mothers picked the cards up from the doormat after the postman had been? Were they excited? Disappointed? Angry? What did they say to each other? I fold the letters and place everything in a small black file. That will calm them down. In there they look like school homework, the postcards' pretty faces trapped inside clear plastic.

I start afresh another day looking for a theme. The first thing I notice is that Roman is forever about to be ill, already ill or has just finished being ill. Accounts of his ailments are always linked with broken promises to visit or write. I'm alarmed. Forget broken hearts, broken vows, lies and secrecy. They're all very sad but it was a long time ago. What do Roman's illnesses say about my genetic inheritance? Am I going to die as young as he did?

> *I have suffered a lot from acute pains in the head and yesterday the congestion became serious and I had to be transferred in a hurry to the above Nursing Home. I shall probably have an operation on the head to relieve the constant terrific pressure . . . So don't think hard of me if I could not come lately. All the best to the three of you,*

I don't know what 'congestion' means here but clearly it's something you could do without. Another time he writes

> *I shall have to go quietly for a time because congestion of the brain is not to be trifled with, and apoplexy of which my father died when only 3 years older than I am now.*

I don't like this talk of apoplexy and dead fathers. I go to the file and pull out the Familienschein documents. What's the news there? How old was my grandfather Emil when he died? 51. And his brother? 57. What about Urs Viktor, my great-grandfather? 35. What about the women, my Swiss grandmother and her ancestors? Nothing. The town hall official who gave me seven pages of family history didn't think I'd be interested in the women. I lean back in my chair. I've had a week in a cardiac ward already. I've had cancer of the womb. Two brushes with death is two too many.

I need to outwit my body in case it has any more plans to see me off. But perhaps these early deaths have nothing to do with me? These men might have fallen headfirst down a mountain or been run over by a train or been tossed by one of their cows. Or was it something they ate? I can see generations of Swiss ancestors tucking into creamy cheeses, butter and milk from local Alpine herds the colour of caramel and honey; mouth-watering steaks with crispy crackling; fat, glistening, spicy sausages; probably followed by a wedge of Schokoladekuchen or Sachertorte. Maybe all of us Strubs share a rogue gene which fails to transport cholesterol to a safe disposal unit, the liver, because it's too stupid to recognize an enemy when it's staring it in the face. It may have been Urs' and Emil's and Roman's good fortune to live a life free from worry about cholesterol and calories. They didn't have to make their lives a guilty misery by walking past bookshop windows stuffed with titles like *The Cabbage Soup Diet*, the *I Can Make You Slim Diet*, the *Fat Flash Plan*, even *The No-Diet Diet*. The downside of living in the nineteenth century, though, was that their medical advisers, unlike mine, could not prescribe statins and aspirin which work faithfully and patiently night and day to clear the channels.

Do I believe this? I feel as though I'm gnawing away at these documents for a scrap of comfort but so far my belly is empty.

The next thing I notice is that if he's not ill, he's working too hard. He's '*rushed*', '*cooped up*', has had '*an exceedingly strenuous time with nothing but work and worry*' Another time he's '*been flying to catch night train; very bumpy with night and rain; not so good time*'.

But what he does outside working hours doesn't help:

> *My doctor found my blood pressure so high that he ordered me instantly to go to the nursing home. There is a constant stream of visitors who are allowed in only for a short time in my darkened room . . . By the way, I got the train with 10 minutes to spare that night, it left 12.20am.*

Which must have been after a flying visit to his Hammersmith lover.

Another time . . .

> *Just a line in a hurry for some nurses to take to the post. The nursing home is overflowing and they want me to go to convalescence as I am better now. Can I come to you? I must have absolute rest,*

> *early to bed, but otherwise no fuss. I could come tomorrow but would wire first. If not convenient wire here . . . don't be shy if you can't have me, tell me, In haste, R*

If Bigga and Tyna said 'Yes', where on earth did he tell his wife and family that he'd gone? And which bed did he sleep in to get 'absolute rest'?

When I pick up the next card—a golden and pink Jungfrau in the setting sun—and see what he's written on the back, I don't believe a word. He starts off in the usual way . . . *I have been laid up almost all the time* . . . but then goes on to complain about the weather and the view. But I recognize the view and I'm beginning to recognize the hum of his whining voice. I'm sorry he's ill but he's staying in Wengen, near where we've camped as a family in the Lauterbrunnen valley. I've seen the Jungfrau summer and winter, in snow storms and thunderstorms and when clouds lay waste the whole mountain range. There isn't a day when you can't catch glimpses of unutterable beauty: pink shadows at dawn, pine trees negotiating their way into view through the mist, quick, random, teasing shafts of brilliant sun light like a Martin Creed installation

It's the same story on the back of a card from Whitepoint Cobh, County Cork, He's out '*sailing every day amongst the fishing villages of the South Coast of the Irish Free state . . . and food is wholly vegetarian . . . the mackerel I catch myself. People ever so kind and helpful*'. But don't let anyone think he's enjoying himself, he's only there, he reminds us, 'because (his) doctor said so . . .'.

In Adelboden he says *'I have had an extremely strenuous time lately . . . I have just been sent off for a few days' recuperating holyday (sic) I am here in and out of the Wely Mountain . . . but the amount of snow is horrific, the level going up to halfway up the bottom storey'.* Did ever a man have such a run of bad luck on his holidays?

He keeps seeing himself as a victim. He's at the beck and call of his job; he's ill; he fails to write or call but it's never his fault. And what is Bigga doing all this time? While his cards show that he's free to travel all over Europe, to holiday in beautiful places and to dip in and out of the relationship, his child's mother is left holding the baby.

It's at this point that I check to see if he mentions me. There is a baby there but it's not me, his new daughter, he's interested in.

'My new niece is a sweet little thing with straight curls'. Why doesn't he call me 'a sweet little thing', with or without straight curls? She's '*already talking nicely*'. Does he know if I'm talking nicely? Does he know anything about me at all? I pause. Am I mad? This baby is a real person, and isn't it about time I stopped being jealous of a nameless Swiss woman of my age who doesn't even know I exist. I'm angry with myself and accidentally sweep some cards off the table. I pick them up and do a scan. Quick. Where does he mention me? On one card he asks, *How are you and Doris and Rosebud?* On another he says he hopes to see '*your*

Precious soon'. Hang on. Shouldn't it be 'our Precious'? With his experience he could hardly believe in virgin births.

Calm down, I tell myself. His cards are trying to say 'I'm here,' and 'I'm busy,' and 'I'm thinking of you'. And 'No texting, no email and I don't have time to write letters but I've taken the trouble to choose your cards and buy your stamps and find a post box. I couldn't put anything long and complicated and private on a postcard because it could be read by anyone including the postman'. Perhaps he said nice things to Bigga and Tyna about me even if he never wrote them down. But I don't believe a word I'm saying. Instead I hear, 'Well, you were born and I'm your father but other people have a much better claim on my time and my money. Don't expect anything from me. I'm busy with my affairs, you understand, and you really must learn to fend for yourself'.

I pick up another postcard to Tyna from Adelboden and I search for one of those Hammersmith studio photos of me as a baby, make a copy and cut out a silhouette. I stick myself centre stage on the card. Years later I used it on the front of a birthday party invitation. Some of my guests saw a warmly-wrapped little girl in pink angora snuggling into the hollow of a cosy hillside; for others she was an infant abandoned, possibly slipping down an icy mountain into the frosty lips of a black lake.

The next morning I'm calmer. I pick out a set of six unstamped and undated cards from Liverpool. On the back of each there is either one word or two. I imagine they were sent one at a time in a tantalizing sequence. I spread them out in a line: the River Mersey; the Liver, Cunard and Dock Offices; Exchange Flags; the Town Hall; St Georges Hall; lastly a traffic jam of immaculate vintage cars packed inside the Junction Chamber of the Mersey Tunnel. When I turn them over there's a message there:

Do/ you/remember?/Back/ on Tuesday/ Your R,

An urgent pithy message. Are his ardour and impatience inflamed by all this marvellous engineering and architectural achievement? And what's so special that Jean should remember Liverpool? She mentions weekends away with 'R' in her diary, but Liverpool? I go back to the black file and read the early correspondence carefully. There it is: *marching orders to go to Liverpool* and *I don't feel a bit like travelling*. It's in a letter he wrote in their early courtship days around the time when he had been pleading 'Please Jean do not be angry with me' at the moment when Bigga was thinking about splitting up. Did he book another train ticket and whisk her away to Liverpool? It sounds as if it was an encounter worth remembering.

I rummage around to find out if he sends any other cards in sequence. There's only one, a yacht on the Limmat in Zurich. *I wish you a very . . .* is scrawled across the card. It's posted on Boxing Day 1936 in Bern where I presume Roman's spending Christmas with his Swiss 'clan', for it's the town where he was born. It sounds as if the next card would continue . . . *Happy New Year* but it's missing. But this New Year greeting is going to the mother of his new-born baby (well, eight weeks old). Bigga is spending Christmas at Clapham hiding her recent near-death experience and I am left with strangers in a Hammersmith basement. Couldn't he have sent something a little more tender?

Over supper that night a glass or two of Pimms' is called for. Richard and I speculate about what happened to Roman, once a bewildered four-year-old whose mother had died. What were Swiss mourning customs in the late nineteenth century? Was he allowed to talk about her and to cry? As a magistrate I'd read enough social workers' reports on the effect of death in a family to know how things can go terribly wrong. Some grownups can't bear their own pain, let alone that of their children: 'Forget about it . . . don't keep on about it . . . you dare mention her name again and I'll knock you into the middle of next week!' How can I be angry with a man who was motherless so young?

I leave till last the most puzzling letter of all. Roman sent it to Bigga when she was in hospital after my birth.

> *My dear Jean,*
>
> *I have had an eventful half week all over the country and haven't finished yet, but dear old Doris looked after me like a brick. We were always talking about you and that Rosebud and how beautiful and perfect she was. Doris is straining herself to the utmost. If you don't mind I am going to suggest to you that you only have her every other day. It's too severe for her to do the shop and the house and come out every night. Thursday night I made her go to bed about 10pm. She felt all the better for it next morning. Last night I was very late myself. Thinking of you and Rosebud,*
> *Your R.*

What's happening? Why, for a start, does Doris need an advocate to plead her cause? Why didn't she say, 'Look, Gertie, it's a lot to do—the house, the shop and catching the bus to come and see you every night, you wouldn't mind if I gave it a miss tomorrow night, would you? I could do with a bit of a rest'. And how did Roman make her go to bed about 10pm? How did 'dear old Doris' look after him 'like a brick'? How did he know she felt all the better in the morning? We had no phone. Did 47 Raynham Road have a spare bedroom?

At this point I notice something else. He's been sending cards to the wrong women. Both get a card from Koln but while Tyna gets an etching of a castle ruin at the spa town of Bad Godesberg with 'all the best from a German beer house' on the back, Bigga gets the beer-garden card. Just a man in a hurry? Or how far were Tyna and Bigga interchangeable? He writes to both, he sends them identical birthday telegrams. If Tyna, like Bigga, had kept a diary for 1935 what would it have said about Roman?

I have a picture of Tyna at that time which my cousin Lance Inskip gave me while I was writing this chapter: a woman in a porch, one foot half out of the frame, like the girl in the Hopper painting. She's outside our shop, *The Corner Handy Stores*, on the spot where a few years later the shrapnel nearly killed me. I go back and look at my cache of cards and letters. By the time this photograph was taken Tyna's receiving more communications from Roman than Bigga. She's even acting as a go between for the two of them.

> *'Very many thanks for Jean's letter. I'm afraid I will be belated with my promised Christmas visit, but I can tell you it hasn't been my doing.*

Why didn't 'Jean' send it herself? And why does Doris get a *Good Wishes For the New Year* card in 1939 with a picture of a golden bed chamber by Cuvillies and a congratulatory birthday telegram in March? There's no sign that my mother received anything. Or did she tear it up and throw it away?

Roman, one of the last cards you send is from The Royal Station Hotel, Newcastle. You are not at your happiest. You say you'd rather be in Hammersmith. Once again I'm not sure I believe you. Hammersmith has lost its charm by this time. You've finished with these places and people. Although I've listed and classified what you wrote about this minor episode in your life I understand very little. I am a tourist gawping at your private world.

The black plastic file of papers begins to reproach me. I relent, unfold each letter and document, gather up the cards and carefully place each in its own envelope, making sure they're in chronological order. Roman's pencil marks, which have held out for half a century, deserve a little protection in their declining years.

But there's something missing. It's Bigga's diary, so small it's easy to mislay. I slip that into an envelope too and clip it in at the front, because she it is who tells the story of how it all began. I close the file and the two of them lie together between the covers.

27

GABRIELLE

A half-century of silence, but things are about to change. I'm at The Footstool, a restaurant in the 17C underground crypt of St John's Church, Smith Square, a close neighbour to Church House, Westminster where I work. I've said I'll be wearing a long purple coat. I get there 30 minutes early, order a sherry and sit shivering with excitement. My eyes don't leave the door. The women coming in are mostly younger than me, and with colleagues. Gabrielle, my half-sister, has a rural address and I picture her as an elegant woman in her garden, with a wide-brimmed straw hat and a trug on her arm trailing salmon pink geranium plants. I wonder what newspapers she reads? *The Times* or *The Independent*, I'd guess. She'll speak lots of languages no doubt, and will have travelled a lot. Does she have a house in Switzerland? A large chalet with wrap-around balconies where flowers always bloom—except when snow climbs up the bottom storey. Perhaps she has children?

I'm so lucky to have found her; I'm ready to be discovered, like a shell on the beach picked up before the tide comes in. It could easily have been too late. Nowadays if you want a Swiss Familienschein you have to prove you're a direct descendent by producing a passport or immigration papers. I would be turned away empty-handed, but in the late 1980s when we caught the train from Engelberg Richard and I were just in time

Since then I've been searching on and off for years. The Familienschein said I had two half-brothers, but one emigrated to Canada as a young man so he's lost. I've two half-sisters but I can count them out too because they'll have married and changed their names. My only hope was my remaining older Strub brother, now in his 70s. He could be dead or alive, married or single, with or without children and living anywhere in the world. Not much to be going on with.

Recently I've been spending hours in the General Record Office at Somerset House. Eventually I find a death certificate which fits his initials. I have a problem. His will would give me a name and an address. But what right have I to presume to get a copy of his will? My principled Aunt Amy had nothing but contempt for legislation which allows wills to be published so that strangers can pry and peephole into things they have no right to see. But I might find the names of his nearest and dearest: my sister-in-law, if I have one, and any nephews and nieces. I send away for a copy and discover that years ago he'd been living in a Lincolnshire village when we were eight miles away in Scunthorpe.

As soon as I have a free weekend I drive to that village and park the car across the road from the Old Rectory. I stand in the rain, my hand on the car bonnet to keep in touch with something solid. No sounds, not even traffic. No one goes in or out of the house. Through a wrought iron arched gate I can glimpse a garden behind the house and I try to imagine him there once upon a time, planting a wisteria or setting out shallots in tidy rows. Or perhaps he needed a gardener? Did his wife grow dahlias and fill antique vases with their blowsy colours? A woman in dark jeans and a white shirt peers back through the grille. I take a quick, guilty photograph of the house and jump into the car. At the local over half a pint of shandy I ask did anyone know anything about the Strub family?

'Mr Strub? Yes, he was an engineer. Died some years ago, I believe. His widow sold up and moved to another village. I don't know where she went. Do you know, Betty?'

'Somewhere in Lincolnshire, I heard'.

That's that. I can hardly knock on all the doors in Lincolnshire.

Back home I console myself by looking up the Inskips in the Bedford Archive office. One day I notice shelves stacked with a copy of every telephone directory in Britain. I pull out the one for Lincolnshire and there is an address of a married woman with initials which match my brother's. His widow, I presume. I can't believe I didn't think of this earlier.

What am I to do? I'll write on rather grand headed notepaper suggesting I'm an academic genealogist researching the Strub family. I'll hint that I'm trustworthy by throwing in for good measure the fact that I'm the wife of a man who was a local Lincolnshire vicar for 10 years in the 1960s. That can't be bad.

A month later comes the reply:

> *. . . I have no information to give you re my late father-in-law Roman Emil Strub.*

I've found my sister-in-law—and lost her.

Two weeks later I receive another letter. It's folded in four and written on thick cream paper, long and slim. A delicate, slender nib and clear, bold writing. Three sentences cover the page.

> *Dear Madam,*
>
> *Mrs Strub passed on to me, as one of R.E. Strub's daughters, your letter to her mentioning your interest in our family tree.*
>
> *Perhaps you would tell me why you wish to trace our family tree? Are you connected to us in some way?*

'Are you connected to us in some way?'

'Are you connected . . . ?'

'Are you . . . ?'

Yes, all my life I've wanted to be connected. I've been waiting for this moment. If I say, yes, yes, I am connected, I'm your very own half-sister, will you let me come in? Are you going to open your door a tiny chink? But I'm puzzled.

Why didn't you believe I was just a researcher? How did you guess there was something unsaid in my letter?

I spend a weekend filling up a wastepaper basket with drafts of how I might reply, finally settling on:

> *. . . yes, I am related to the Strub family. My knowledge is limited to some letters and photographs dating from the 1930s, some Familienschein from Trimbach/Solothun and a few other sources . . . I have refrained from contacting the Strub family in the past because I was unwilling to refer to the delicate circumstances surrounding my birth. But now half a century has elapsed.*
>
> *I have every reason to believe you are my half-sister. Like most people who never knew their father I would like to know more about him, and I wonder if you would help me either by correspondence or by meeting?*
>
> *My office is at Church House next to Westminster Abbey. If you come to London from time to time, could we perhaps meet for lunch? Alternatively, if you prefer not to meet, may I ask you to correspond with me once or twice so that I can learn a little about my family? If however you prefer me not to contact you again, I will of course respect your wishes, Yours sincerely*

Her reply is on similar paper with the same bold hand. It's full of characteristic warmth. It begins

> *Dear Yvonne,*
>
> *Life is full of surprises! Roman did make a lot of trouble I must say . . .*

This is the woman who is going to walk into *The Footstool* and into my life.

She'll change everything of course. A living breathing (half) sister will wipe out my favourite fantasy in which I have the power. For years I've imagined being at a party where I'm standing hidden in an alcove or behind the aspidistra, a glass in my hand, watching a woman in animated conversation with a group of friends. Always a woman. My years with *Little Women* mean that I'm better prepared for sisters than brothers. Would I walk over and interrupt with a dazzling remark? Or slip silent and unnoticed into the group? Both are unthinkable. I only want to stand apart and look at my imaginary sister and think of how her hand, now holding a glass, might once have tucked itself into Roman's hand when she was learning to walk, or how she might have grasped his hand as he lay dying. Perhaps as a little girl she might have stretched out her arms—now bare, elegant and with an opal bracelet round her slim wrist—and run towards him to be scooped up and twizzled round. I want to hear her voice too and think, 'That's my sister talking'. The fantasy is attractive because I know something she doesn't know. I'm the one who knows I have a sister, she doesn't. As long as I'm silent that's how it will stay. If I went up to her and said 'I'm your sister,' she could say, 'No, I have a sister already, thank you', and turn away.

But now I'm ready to take the risk.

An elegant woman does indeed come down the stone staircase into the crypt, steps through the archway wearing distinctive, colourful clothes, and comes straight towards me. I stand and we exchange a kiss on both cheeks.

'It's like seeing myself when I was younger,' she says as she settles down. 'I must have been about 12 when you were born'.

I have no recollection of what we ate or drank. I cannot take my eyes away from the woman across the table wearing a robe rather than a dress, of natural fabrics in russets and browns, with a flash of peacock green. I may never see her again. She wears a hat which reminds me of those jaunty pill boxes of the 40s except that instead of being made of, say, navy blue petersham with a cunning little veil over one eye, it's the colour of sable and made of a soft, luxurious fabric.

'My sister-in-law, Faith, thought you were a Mormon or a Jehovah's Witness when she got your letter—that's why she didn't want to have anything to do with you'.

I study her handsome face, her dark eyes which miss nothing, the smile on her lips, the way she lifts her head to one side as if in self-mockery. Of all the faces I've ever seen hers is the one I've been looking for. Yes, I think, yes, I love your confidence, your style. How amazing that I'm related to someone like you. I want to be like you when I'm grown up . . .

'You'll like our sister-in-law,' she pulls me back into the present, 'Brilliant gardener and lovely sense of style'.

She must have been talking on the phone about me—'our sister-in-law', words I never thought I'd have any use for. Ouch, I've missed fifty years of family life: Christmas cards, birthday gifts, holidays, births, illnesses, marriages, deaths, fallings out and fallings in. She tells me that our elder brother died 12 years ago. Our younger brother who lives in America is very poorly. But I grow to love my other sister, Clemency, a remarkable Seventy Something, witty, profound, tender, once matron at Burrswood, a Christian hospital and healing centre in Kent, which offers help—but doesn't promise a 'cure' dealt out at random by a bargaining God. She's one of the few people who knew Dorothy Kerrin, Burrswood's founder (and adopter of sundry children). She often sits with the dying. I secretly hope that she'll be around when I die.

My sister thanks the waiter who is pouring out a glass of wine, then suddenly turns to say 'Our father was born in Bern'. I'm speechless. All my life 'Our Father' has been followed by 'which art in heaven, hallowed by Thy name . . .' as surely as night follows day. I want to giggle. But what else can she call him? There must have been a family name for him which is not for me to know because it springs from earlier times in which I have no place.

'And you have another brother too. He's the child of Roman's second wife but when she was widowed she took him to Canada where she remarried. He'd be about six years younger than you. I doubt if he's still a Strub. I heard he took his stepfather's name. Could be anywhere in the world. I've never met him'.

When I ordered my sherry that morning, I had been an only child for half a century. By the time we got to the coffee, I am the fifth of six siblings.

My sister is a generous gatekeeper. When our older brother visits England for the last time she thinks up a cunning plan. His ill health means that it would be unkind to trouble him with news that he has a new sister. Richard and I will be introduced as friends who happen to be passing on the M4. We arrive on a glorious summer day and find Gabrielle's house empty. Everyone is in the grounds so Richard goes out through the back of the house to search for them. The hall is spacious with a tiled floor, intriguing carpets, and a wide staircase to the right. It's cool and peaceful after the glare of the sun and I'm glad of a moment by myself. Suddenly the double doors at the front of the house open and sunlight floods in. A tall handsome man in his seventies is framed there for a moment, sees me, and strides across the hall. He throws his arms round me and holds me tight.

He holds me tight as if I were precious. I feel the warmth of his body and lay my head on his shoulder. He says, 'This afternoon we have three sisters in the house'. I shiver. Later when I tell Gabrielle the three sisters story she is matter of fact. She has three little granddaughters playing in the grounds. But why did he hug me so warmly and why did he mention three sisters to me? I want to think he knew.

We join the others for tea. I'd been told that he'd been friends for thirty years with Max Bill the artist and architect and owned several of his paintings and sculptures. And he knew Buckmaster Fuller, man of ideas. I imagine his house as one where you'd find a coffee cup standing on a van der Post letter. But his illness means it's too late for conversation.

What is it like to be the newcomer?

I want them to know I'm worth knowing. We take Gabrielle and her husband to Lambeth Palace to a supper party arranged by our closest friends, Bishop John Yates and his wife Jean. My new relatives are taken on a tour, as they are first-time visitors to the Palace. After supper we set up a projector and show holiday slides of the Yates and the Craigs, ten of us altogether: tents destroyed by Cornish gales, Richard tumbling into a Welsh canal and our narrow boat. wedged on an iron mattress in the middle of the Trent and Mersey canal during a drought, being rescued by friendly men from a nearby steelworks. We also play silly family games like *Matthew, Mark, Luke and John*. Another time our good friends at Westminster Abbey, Freda and the late Paul Bates, invite us for dinner at their stylish and witty home in Dean's Yard. And when my first book is launched—*Learning For Life*—I make sure invitations go out to my family and am delighted when Gabrielle and one of my nephews join us.

Do I mention the Inskips? They've been around since the Doomsday Book, mainly working the land as labourers or yeomen, their wives and sisters listed as housekeepers, domestics and lace makers—scratching a living no doubt, dosing their children with laudanum, poaching, paying taxes, starving, getting conscripted, getting by. The Inskips I feel closest to are the religious and disputatious lot. When they fell out with the local minister they moved on to a neighbouring village and started another chapel more to their liking. My favourite is John Inskip, a follower of John Bunyan, the author of *Pilgrim's Progress*, the first international best-seller written by someone from the working class. Alas Mr Inskip got thrown out for being drunk, but was later forgiven and welcomed back.

One branch escaped to Bristol. Lady Inskip and I sometimes sat together as magistrates. Drawing seemed to sharpen her concentration: while two oriental motorists argued for hours as to which one had caused a crash when each car was stationary, she had time to sketch a pair of camels at loggerheads, which I'd would have loved to frame. But it never seemed quite the moment to introduce myself as a bastard relative. On the other hand there was Sir Thomas Inskip, Tory Lord Chief Justice in the 30s, a man of many sterling qualities which did not include welcoming reform, including desperately-needed changes in the Church of England. I have his picture as one of 50 Notable Members of Parliament. It's from a set of cigarette cards.

28

THE STRUB SEVEN

'Our father had another daughter before you were born,' Gabrielle says one day out of the blue. We're walking through the grounds admiring sheets of bluebells, 'When you wrote to me I didn't believe for a minute that you were a disinterested researcher. That's why I asked if you were connected to us'.

So I'm not special—just another one of Roman's litter of unwanted young. In fact that makes seven of us children so far and I'm catapulted straight into *Little Women,* being the youngest of four sisters.

'Who is she?'

'She's called Rose Marie and her mother was a girl who worked at W H Allen's, like Roman. Her family threw her out—I think she went away to an aunt to have the baby. It all happened about 10 years before you were born'.

'What happened next?'

'Some Swiss cousins of ours adopted her when she was about six months old. She lives in Geneva'.

I hardly like to ask how she knows all about this. Has she met Rose Marie? Might I too meet her one day?

As if reading my thoughts, 'She came over to England about fifteen years ago with her teenage daughter and introduced herself to us. Rose Marie adored her adoptive parents—she said they were her real father and mother'.

'I can't understand why so many women were attracted to him. He looked like Adolf Hitler if his record card at the Embassy is anything to go by'.

'But it's not'.

Gabrielle lends me a copy of this photograph, taken in 1911, the year Roman married his first wife, Gabrielle's mother. Delete the moustache and that well-behaved hair parting and it could be my son Aidan looking out of the page.

I have a copy made but when I send the original back it gets lost in the post. Not only does my sister forgive me but she invites me to lunch in her London house. When I arrive she announces, 'I'm so busy in London I get two men to do my cooking'. I find it perfectly possible to believe her. She has a way of talking about things and people as though you will naturally understand who or what she's referring to. I find it enchanting because she's acting as if I were in the know as a family member, that the story is continuing and that I'm part of it. But I'm also anxious. She leaves gaps I might fall into and I might make a fool of myself. All my life I've had a pressing need to understand a new situation as quickly as possible. I only know she's joking when she tells me their names are Mr Marks and Mr Spencer.

'Gabrielle, why did Roman go from woman to woman? What sort of family did he grow up in?'

'Anna Louise, his mother—our grandmother—died in her twenties when he was four. Perhaps complications to do with another pregnancy. Or TB or something infectious we could cure nowadays. On her deathbed she made her husband promise that he would marry her younger sister Bertha. Bertha was 19 at the time and they married a year later'.

So perhaps Roman, like me, could remember two 'mothers'. Maybe Bigga and Tyna reminded him of them, and it was part of their attraction.

Gabrielle continues, 'Perhaps it was a love match. Or he may have thought it was best for the children to be brought up by someone they knew. On the other hand having a wife was very convenient for a mån who was in demand all over Europe

'But what was Bertha like as a stepmother?'

'She didn't have much time for that. She enjoyed the life which came with being the wife of a celebrity. Roman was a brilliant engineer. He was the one who designed a railway which could snake up to the top of the Jungfrau. He blew up some bits of mountain for the trains to flash in and out of a giant worm's tunnel part of the way. They built a village camp up the mountain and horses took cartloads of macaroni and potatoes, fifty thousand cigars, meat and coffee, a litre of wine a day for workmen from all over Europe. Most important he designed a cog system which meant the wheels gripped the track, whether or not it was the right kind of snow. It meant you could access ski slopes and glaciers all the year. You could say he invented the winter season. You must go to the Transport Museum in Lucerne to find out more.'

'But what about the children?'

'They were largely brought up by the household staff. There's the story of a spoilt Christmas when Roman had longed for a super-fast sleigh which would skim over ice and snow and he'd be the envy of all his friends. Instead when he unwrapped the parcel he found a beautifully carved and decorated sleigh with a tinkling bell and a little seat at the back for Eva his sister who was two years younger. He lay on the floor and howled and raged'.

At this distance I'm sympathetic to everyone: Roman and his sister Eva, two motherless little children; Anna

Maria, their tragically dead young mother, and even Bertha, the second wife, who may have watched her sister die as a result of pregnancy or childbirth and could be forgiven for not wanting much to do with motherhood. It was fifteen years before she gave birth to her first and only child.

When Richard and I next go to Switzerland for cross country skiing I wonder if there's a chance that we might be able to meet Rose Marie. Gabrielle is doubtful but says she'll ring her.

She's right to be cautious. Rose Marie is not at all sure she wants to meet me when she learns that I live in Lambeth, which, she feels, is on the wrong side of the river Thames. And I'm only the daughter of one of Roman's other mistresses. But my sisters must have given me a good reference. When Richard and I are next in Engelberg, Rose Marie rings to say she'd like to meet me alone at Bern station at the Movenpick restaurant, neutral ground, Bern being halfway between Engelberg and Geneva, where she lives.

'On Sunday in the huge monastery where we go to church there are rows of couples in furs and brown hats, like beetles or moths. They have eyes which do not see strangers and I feel frightened'. When I wrote this in my journal I was feeling jittery about meeting Rose Marie on Monday.

The day starts easily, not in the monastery but with Epiphany Mass in a chapel with flowing curved walls hewn out of the mountain. I can't understand a word three handsome young priests from New York are saying, except 'Drei König' (Three Kings) but the ceremony comforts me.

A large Christmas tree by the altar is decked with twinkling transparent baubles and 15 live white candles. The candles die out one by one, the last one hanging on until it flickers out with the Blessing at the end of the service.

It hurts to get up from kneeling at the altar rail. Yesterday while skiing I fell over three times, once crashing into Richard so we both slid along for several yards with him in my lap. But a mild thaw in the afternoon made the snow slightly slower, so at last I got the knack—bend knees, lean forward, never mind if you look ridiculous, off you go. I came home exhilarated. Worth the pain.

At the Movenpick restaurant Rose Marie and I recognise each other from the clothes we've described. She's sitting at a table with her back to the wall, light flooding in from the window opposite. There's not a trace of family resemblance. She's slightly built, blue eyes, fair hair and fair skin, an English rose, utterly unlike my pale and sallow face. She wears soft pastel colours and fabrics. Her elegant handbag is small but perfectly formed.

Words come tumbling out, without hesitation or repetition. It sounds like a story she's told many times before. I try to catch and hold every precious syllable. Again I've no idea what we eat or drink.

'My mother worked at my father's factory in Bedford. I don't call her my mother. She means nothing to me'.

'So you haven't tried to trace her family?' I'm disappointed. I was hoping she'd always longed to find some English relations and that I could please her by offering to go back to Bedford and do some research. I could picture a happy reunion with half-brothers and sisters, nephews and nieces, all saying (between sobs) how they'd wondered what had happened to her and longed for this day.

'Of course not. All I know is that my mother's brothers threatened Roman when they found that she was pregnant and her family threw her out'.

'Do you know what happened next?'

'An aunt took her in and when I was six months old, my mother handed me over to Roman. For ever'.

I wonder what the mother felt. She'd called the baby June, Gabrielle had said, after the month in which she was born, but in Switzerland June vanished and was replaced by Rose Marie. Did she think of her daughter that first Christmas, exiled in a foreign land?

'Roman made her promise that she'd never ever try to see—or even contact—him or me. A promise she kept'.

'So you've no connection with Bedford? But your mother might have married and you'd have blood relations . . . half-brothers and sisters . . . I could find out'.

'There's nothing there for me. I went to Bedford once and it was raining. I looked around and got straight back on the train. No, my real mother and father were the couple who adopted me'.

'They were Roman's relatives, weren't they?'

'Second cousins, Von Arx was our name. They were in their 50s and childless. My father was Professor of Music—or was it Mathematics—at Winterthur. I had a wonderful childhood: skating on the lake, musical soirées at the house, tobogganing, horse-drawn sleigh rides through the woods.'

Contrast and compare. She was brought up by a musical family in a lakeside villa in Switzerland. Probably with a library stuffed full of books. There's a wonderful Museum and Art Gallery at Winterthur too, set in the house and grounds of the couple who founded it. The furniture's still there, and I'd visited it. It was nearly empty. I'd walked through the rooms pretending for a few minutes that I was the daughter of the house. I had no idea that years earlier my own sister may have visited as a family friend.

Meanwhile, I was brought up over a corner shop by two single parents who on weekdays never stopped working. Glenn Miller playing '*In the Mood*' on the wireless was Tyna's idea of music, while Bigga preferred '*Begin the Beguine*' and '*Blue Danube*'. Nobody had time to read. The magazine *Picture Post* was my idea of art. It isn't fair! I suddenly feel chilled. Resentment sours my mouth. This isn't going to work out.

'And when did you leave home?'I ask, wanting to know if Swiss girls like her went to university. Or, if they went to work, what did they do?

'When I was seventeen my father died, and then my mother. I knew that my father Roman had died a year earlier'.

'What do you feel about Roman?' I want some sympathy from her. Here we are, two fatherless little girls. I'd also like some ripe words from both of us castigating this reckless, cold man.

'I'd always been told he was my father. And when he visited me—I was about six—I liked him very much.'

More gnashing of teeth. She's actually seen him! He'd been nice to her. She knew she had a real father and had probably been told a sad story of how he couldn't bring her up and so and so on . . . Let's talk about something else:

'And how did you learn to speak English so perfectly?'

'I spent a year at Durham as au pair to a professor's family. But everyone wanted to try out their German on me. It was hard to get anyone to speak English so I spent boring hours walking round parks giving German conversation lessons. Then, both my parents died.

I wanted to interrupt, 'What did you do now that you're an orphan. Surely you tried to trace your real mother?'

She continued, 'I decided I wanted to see a bit of the world. I went to Kenya as an au pair to a high born Swiss family. In Kenya I worked for six months with no day off—well I had time off but there was nowhere to go, no car, no friends, no fun, nothing. Then I got invited to a ball and got pregnant by a charming German'.

Our plates are cleared. Her fingers stroke the unopened laminated menu card now lying on the table. 'No desert for me, I think I'll have a coffee. And you?'

'Coffee, too'.

'I was very young. I was alone in Kenya, no one cared what happened to me.'

I can see what she means. First her birth mother handed her over and Roman faded away. Then both her adoptive parents died.

'So I married him. I had the Swiss possessions I'd inherited shipped across: silver cutlery, china, linen, carpets, furniture. He set about spending my money, speculating, making ridiculous purchases of land for development which came to nothing. And within a year he was bringing his girl-friends home. Then he disappeared with the rest of my money and possessions'.

'What did you do?'

'I came back to Switzerland with my two year old daughter'.

'And then?'

'What could I do? I had no money, no training.'

Another mother abandoned with a little girl.

'How could we live? Well, I found a job in a bookshop in Geneva and I found some foster parents for my daughter in Winterthur. I went to visit my daughter as often as I could, but it wasn't very often'. She stops. So here's another little girl without her birth mother and father. I wait.

'I fetched her back when I had another daughter. I'd married an Italian I met when I was working at a night club on Capri. So then we were a proper family'.

'How old was your first daughter then?'

'About ten. My second husband—he was Italian—always had some grand plan. At first I followed him around: Italy, Germany, France, Switzerland . . . eleven jobs in 10 years'. She pauses and strokes her smooth grey hair, held back by an Alice band, and I get a glimpse of a pretty fun-loving party girl. I'd like to put my hand out across the table and touch hers but I think she might not like that.

'I had a third daughter. When she was born my husband was away on business but his brothers and sisters all gathered round my bed pretending to be my friends and they lied and they lied. For five days they said that the baby was ill and they wouldn't let me see her. I kept pleading and crying. When I found out she'd already been buried, I never forgave them'.

She has told this story many times but telling brings no relief. Her voice is as sharp with pain as from a fresh wound. I don't want to hear any more about the past.

'Do your daughters live in Geneva?'

'Yes, one's nearby'.

So I have two nieces and they have an unknown aunt. Will we ever meet? What sort of impression am I making on Rose Marie? She sounds as if she has high standards and most people fall short. I'm not sure I'll come up to scratch.

We kiss on both cheeks and part, she agreeing to send me some photographs. That's a breakthrough. My other relatives are very private people, not given to photographing each other and singularly lacking in any impulse to ask someone else to do it for them.

I slump into a corner seat on the train back to Lucerne. I don't want any more surprises. I've been listening to a story which spans continents, decades, husbands, children, lies, deaths, fortunes won and lost. I can't help noticing that by his lifestyle our father cancelled out us two little bastards and moved on. I wish I could have put my arm round her. I don't think she cries much and nor do I.

The train draws in to a station and I notice an advert on a platform for Nestlés milk. Did baby June (or was she by then Rose Marie?) drink it on her voyage to Switzerland in 1927? In museums I've seen feeding bottles of those days, shaped like fat bananas with a rubber teat at both ends to make cleaning with a wire brush easier. I cannot see Roman—or any man of that time—feeding a baby or struggling with safety pins and nappies. A nurse perhaps? Did he travel First Class and she and the baby Third? Perhaps she was Swiss herself, someone from his household staff who could be trusted with such precious and secret cargo. And how secret was it? Surely his children didn't know of their little sister but perhaps Roman's wife made the arrangements? Perhaps she was used to accommodating her husband's way of life. Lots of wives did in those days. Indeed some do today, judging from the conversations I have overheard in the Ladies' Changing Rooms in various Westminster Fitness Centres. She may have known when she posted the postcard to Mrs Maund at the Snettisham bungalow that this was another little escapade which need not upset the family.

At Lucerne I can't find the platform for the train to Engelberg and the whole of Rose Marie's breathless story blows out of my mind. I'm a child again, terrified at the prospect of being in the wrong place, getting on the wrong train and rushing round Switzerland tongue-tied, without a valid ticket and the words to explain what's wrong. The Swiss are strict about the law. Will I go to prison?

When I find the right train I calm down. I let the facts sink in. These pictures tell the story. Within about a decade Roman had three little girls, each born to a different mother. His daughter Gabrielle by his first wife is on the left, probably in the family garden, then in the centre is Rose Marie in Winterthur in about 1928 and I'm on the right in a Hammersmith studio in 1939. It's taken fifty years for us to discover each other's existence and the three of us never meet together, as Rose Marie's health is beginning to fade by the time I contact her.

Another train stops and the platforms are crowded with skiers. Why can't I ski beautifully? Why do I keep falling? I bet all Roman's children except me learnt to ski. Down mountains. Huge ones. Very fast. Pigeons strut on the station canopy, their wings folded like hands behind their backs, secure and sure footed. It's a year when skiers wear silky padded clothes the colour of ball gowns: white slashed with lime and olive green, purple and yellow subdued by black, copper laced with indigo. One man just below my train window wears five colours—raspberry, plum, maroon and grape—and is close enough for me to read an inky blue design label on his collar. His face looks bony and workmanlike as though carved out of wood. The finishing touches are a moustache, blue eyes and a halo of cigarette smoke. The Swiss are not a handsome race, I decide. What am I doing in Switzerland anyway? I don't belong. What if Bertie Maxie, whom Bigga loved and had promised to wed, had not died? What if Bigga had married him—or Mr Gould—both solid Bedford citizens? I'd have been a Bedford girl, measuring out my life in coffee spoons, a good cook, serving meals which look beautiful, interested in little nothings, going to church, then one day to hospital and getting bad news.

In bed that night I feel tattered and raw. Richard sleeping beside me has listened patiently but I'm still full of words. I put my ear phones on and stretch towards my transistor in the dark, navigating towards the red light. I silently press the stud in slow motion so as not to disturb Richard's sleep. There's only perishing 15th century Polish music. I have nothing against Polish music—or the 15th century for that matter—but this is not the moment. I slide silently out of bed, drop down on all fours and creep towards the suitcase under the bed. I open the zip, which makes a snarling noise in the dark, to get my hand through a crack onto a bottle of sleeping tablets. On the way back to bed I glimpse Engelberg, the Angel Mountain, as I've never seen it. I stand in the moonlight watching a ring of light fluffy clouds chasing each other round the peak like angels holding hands. Its beauty is mesmerising. The crackle of words inside my head fades away. The here and now steps daintily into the hotel bedroom. After all, I'm alive and well. Tomorrow a fresh day will lie open before me. The cold creeps up from my bare feet but I slide inch by inch back into bed and wrap myself carefully round Richard without waking him. No need for a bottle of any sort.

The next day I try cross country skiing again. This time I can't do it and stand still in the silence. I'm too old to ski, to take risks. The shadows of the trees stretch and shrivel on the snow like slow balloons. I can hear the slither and squelch of toboggans down to the valley and the crackle of rapid water against green bricks of ice in the stream. I can't move. I fear tumbling onto hard baked ice and hitting the rocks until my bones crack, I fear falling softly into pillows of snow by the side of the path, stranded upside down like a tortoise, legs waving in the air. I look down at my body. I've abandoned the mint-green Asda padded suit I first wore when I came to Engelberg. Instead I've heaped layer upon layer to keep out the cold: scarlet, emerald, black. I look up and glimpse a mountain peak between the trees the moment it catches the sun and glows ripe as a peach. I'd like to greet the sun naked.

I visited Rose Marie several years after that, usually in Geneva, and met her delightful daughters and granddaughter. I never felt able to ask how she came to marry a man who brought his girl-friends home. One of the lovely things she did every time I stayed with her was to draw for me a deep,

deep bath so that I stepped straight into a luxurious chunk of sweet smelling water. No one had done that for me before. Rose Marie's younger daughter was vulnerable but no one knew how to protect her. I first met her two weeks after her boyfriend had died of a drug overdose She sat in her mother's flat, thin almost to the point of transparency, leafing through Vogue fashion magazines, ready when she saw me with a lovely smile and a gift of chocolates. She died in her early thirties of pneumonia. Rose Marie was adamant that there should be no funeral ceremony and that a visit from me would not be welcome.

When I heard of Rose Marie's own death I printed on glowing golden paper this picture of her, a Twenty Something posing beside Lake Geneva, taken during her ten years as a single women, while her older daughter was in Winterthur. On the back it says 'August 1953, Nautique, Geneva'. 1953 was the year when Bigga had her first stroke and the month when I was minding the shop and waiting for my O Level results. 'Nautique' is the SNG, the Société Nautique de Genéve, a sailing club whose regatta got world-wide attention when Alinghi, the team from land-locked Switzerland, won the America's Cup in 2004.

I hung this photograph in our hall among my collection *The Quick and the Dead* which consists of 70 off-beat family photographs spanning six generations: Inskips, Craigs. Harveys and Strubs. Rose Marie's photograph is in a wide, matt, aluminium frame. She stands there, confident, one arm akimbo, wonderful legs on show, wearing a striped tunic. It must be navy. I imagine a breeze ruffling her fair curls. She knows we're looking at her but she's not bothering to look at us.

I'm standing at the kitchen table watching Bigga stir something sticky in a big mixing bowl. Tyna has finished the washing and is in the shop serving a customer.

'You have to make a wish while you're stirring,' says Bigga and closes her eyes. Then she gives me the wooden spoon and waits. I close my eyes and wish that Patricia Muggleton would be my Best Friend and play with me in the playground tomorrow. I hand the spoon back. She dips her hand into a Bisto gravy packet and sprinkles brown powder into the pudding.

'Why are you doing that?'

'To make it nice and dark and rich-looking'. She grates some carrot into the bowl.

'Why are you doing that?'

'Because it makes it moist and it makes it bigger. I'm not sure I've got enough pudding to go round'. She divides the mixture between two small white bowls, then wraps each with a square of white cotton I've helped to tear from an old sheet.

'Do you want to lick the bowl out?'

'No,'

'What do you say?'

'No thank you'.

That evening the puddings are boiled to within an inch of their lives in the scullery, making rivulets of water run down the cream distempered walls. In the morning Tyna wraps them carefully in crisp brown paper and a lattice of string. We take them to the post office at the end of Whitbread Avenue. One is going to Uncle Louis and Aunt Margaret but when I ask where the other is going Tyna says, 'Never you mind'.

Why do I think the parcel was for Roman? Because Bigga sent home-made Christmas puddings to very special friends she wasn't going to see over the festivities. She, who never did any cooking, made this one exception every year. I've no idea what it was like (we only ate Aunt Amy's) but war is a great leveller: any cook was glad of any ingredients she could get and with a shop Bigga could probably rustle up more than most. She produced a gift which was personal, perishable, impractical, slightly comic and edible. This is what happened next.

In December 1942 a Mr Rob Stewart writes to Bigga from The Union Bank of Scotland, Cardonald Branch, Glasgow:

> *It is some time since I saw (Mr Strub) but he appeared to be in the best of health . . .* (he) *has now received your parcel per messenger and I trust you will hear from him soon.*

The following May he writes again:

> *I regret I am unable to give you Mr Strub's address. All I know is that he is now in London. He left Glasgow about February last and has now no connection with us here.*

What the banker may or may not know, and what Bigga certainly doesn't know when she received the second letter is that Roman is by now married to his second wife and that she will give birth to Roman's seventh child, his fourth son, in the next fortnight.

'Hi, sis! I'm your brother Adrian'.

Courtesy of the internet he contacts me in 2001—my younger brother. We invite him and Jo his wife to come over from Canada to stay with us for a month. Nothing prepares us for the man—huge in more senses than one—who comes through the swing doors at Heathrow. His luggage includes a complete set of Elvis Presley clothes. I'm not exactly sure what karaoke is but I'm about to find out. Can I find a karaoke pub? Nothing much on the internet but then Adrian sees a notice outside The Lambeth Walk pub a couple of streets away. Jo and I dress up in our jazziest and the four of us walk round one Thursday evening. There are unwritten rules about turns but Adrian knows his way around. Is this what it feels like to go to a church service for the first time? I sit sipping a glass of wine and imagine him as a young man, how I would get up and dance and he would hold me tight and twirl me round. My high heels would fly into the air and so too would my 50s circular crimson skirt showing layers of stiff net petticoats underneath. Adrian has the X factor. Later he sends me a picture of him being mobbed by fans in front of an audience of 5,000 at the 3rd Annual Penticton Pacific Northwest Elvis Festival in 2004.

All four of us go to Grundelwald for a week. Adrian's a practical man and when it comes to Swiss scenery, he can take it or leave it. It's engineering which excites him and brings out the camera: a tiered garden teetering on a precipice, railway tracks and bridges, chalets being built at an altitude and angle normal people would run a mile from. Any passing stained glass gets scrutinised too, because Adrian has a workshop and gets commissions for Elvis memorial buildings.

On the day when we take the train up the Jungfrau he walks through the carriages saying, 'My grandfather built this railway,' which is met with the calm, inscrutable smiles of fellow-passengers, mostly Japanese. Richard and I keep our distance. At the terminus Adrian and I jump over the track and kneel to examine the up-to-date version of the Strub cog rail system which caused such a sensation. We hop about and crisscross the track as if we were children playing with our own train set.

Back home Gabrielle, my gate-keeper sister, and her husband organise a family luncheon party at the Court Restaurant in the British Museum and 28 of us sit down together. Roman is the absent presence. He's the only person who met all the four mothers and seven children he left behind when he died. Mistress's daughters should not be flashy, so I end up dowdy, with no make-up and only a silvery pink necklace by my favourite designer Virginia le Bailly to redeem the situation. I'm on my best behaviour, afraid of being snuffed out, finished before I've started. I feel that my sudden appearance fully fledged and well stocked up with personal history must be a disturbance. We call it a Family Reunion but it's not, because you can't re-unite people who've never been united. We have no shared history to draw on, nor did we choose each other. The ground we stand on is goodwill. Aidan's wife Sara—who understands my need to reconstruct a family because of her own background—takes portrait photographs of everyone, but there's no call for a group photo. If we are a family tree, we're a Christmas tree with no needles. Sap has flowed through and shaped the branches but there has been no chance to deck it with the greenery of history and family bonds. My new relatives have many languages but I'm tongue-tied; they've travelled widely but I'm mostly land-locked; they have land and money, I haven't. It's far too late to patch and weave together a common history and trajectory but I love the richness of our friendship. When my elder sister Clemency was buried in the village churchyard, close family members threw flowers into her grave. Gabrielle's daughter saw me at the edge of the crowd, gently took my elbow, led me and my two small grandsons to the grave and gave us an armful of flowers so that we could join in.

Adrian was 13 months old when he was taken to Canada. Two stepfathers later he knew little or nothing of his birth father Roman. He told me how he had a vasectomy shortly after marrying Jo, then a young divorcée with five small children. He set about bringing up Jo's children as his own. Now he and Jo are surrounded in Kittemat by a vast clan to which great-grandchildren are being added as I speak. Roman, the man who was a trifle careless in his attitude to the children he begot, has a son who delights to love and care for someone else's.

29

JUNGFRAU
by Aidan Harvey Craig

Five of us climb aboard the Jungfrau Express: my wife, my two young daughters, me—and my claustrophobia. We settle comfortably at the back of the train in upholstered bottle-green fold-down seats, near plenty of space for my daughter's buggy. Why are we here? Because my great grand-father Emil Strub made this railway possible by designing a cog railway system which didn't know the meaning of 'the wrong sort of snow'. Because my mother bought us the tickets. She's recently got interested in Emil. Perhaps she wants facts about the journey to include in her life-story. Can I bring a missing jigsaw bit back home for her?

As we pull away, I check: how do I connect with the past. It's a tough call. I'm not used to looking out of my train window and seeing the tail end of a glacier. It's smooth, it's taken on the ashen grey of the rock around it and looks like huge folds of leather. Emil would have thought nothing of it, seeing it every day.

Suddenly the glacier's gone. We're in a tunnel of rough-hewn rock and you can see the marks of the ice picks as sharp as if the workmen had just gone off duty for a smoke. It takes a few minutes before I notice that my claustrophobia has moved up into my carriage, is squashed uncomfortably onto my seat and is whispering that this is no mere tunnel. This is it. We're inside a f**king mountain for the next god-knows-how-long. My claustrophobia takes delight in reminding me that, should I have a heart attack at this moment, I'm approximately 2500 km from the altitude at which most paramedics operate and countless *millions* of tons of rock away from the daylight they prefer to work in. My claustrophobia then casually points out that worrying about how *utterly inconvenient* it would be to have a heart attack at this point makes it more likely. Having silently drawn this spiral of terror my claustrophobia has little to do. He's sitting back, reading a magazine, legs crossed, glancing across now and then to satisfy himself that I'm fuelling my own panic, then returning to his article about the fragility of human existence.

To keep myself sane, I have to latch on to something. There's a young woman down the carriage, early twenties I'd say, looks Germanic. She's attractive in a masculine way, but more importantly she looks robust—healthy. She's talking and smiling at the person opposite her whom I can't see. Then I glance at the plasma screens—something about the early climbers of the Jungfrau, black-and-white stills of men with moustaches and leather trousers and ice picks. I can't help it—my eye is drawn to the rough-hewn rock just outside the window—both windows—all of the windows. This rock—which, until Emil Strub and his gangs of men got at it, had not seen the light of day for around 10 million years—stares at me. I stare back.

Suddenly we halt beside three incongruously chic neon adverts attached to the rock walls. We're in a station and we make our way off the train into a cavern which leads to the edge of the mountain. Everyone is moving quickly. We all jostle to get a view out of a series of Perspex windows. It's cold and the lack of oxygen means that carrying my daughter makes me dizzy. As I drop her down on the floor, having had our share of looking at snow and rock, I turn to see someone running back to the train. The train stops for a set time and will not wait. People running inside tunnels of rock—it's a scene from some disaster movie that I can't quite place.

Cut to me walking on snow—this is August, in bright sunshine—with an icy wind whipping through me. I have my two-year-old daughter in my arms, one hand holding the back of her head, her face buried in my shoulder. Believe me when I say she's clinging to me—we're talking 'dear life'. My claustrophobia won't come out here and now I'm not afraid. I look down on a glacier, the width of a huge river, bigger than the Thames. It's on its own mystical journey, always setting off, always promising adventures never dreamed of, hardly moving, never arriving. And because it looks like a river but is utterly unlike a river, its immense stillness and silence crush the babble of thoughts in my head.

My daughter clutches me tighter as I trudge further out onto the snow. We're experiencing conditions which climbers encounter when they're at the top of a mountain. But we've cut out all the planning, the exhaustion and the elation. The whole mountain has been forced to conspire in this theme-park idea, giving idiots like me and this constant stream of tourists the experiences you used to get after years of practice and physical endurance. I'd like to ask Emil 'Is this why you did it?' When Emil and his workers were blasting through the rock, spending whole winters in a temporary village on the mountain, was it really so I could take a digital picture of me and my family standing by the Swiss flag out here? I don't think so.

The cliché about climbers is that they climb mountains 'because they are there'. It should read 'because they are there and I am here, and I wonder if I'm brave enough, clever enough, tough enough, resourceful enough . . . Perhaps this mountain will finally settle the question for me.'

It's time to leave. My claustrophobia is waiting for me at the platform. The queue is five deep, those at the front squashed up against the barriers. My claustrophobia strains his neck to look across the expanse of people in the queue, then feigns concern as he points out, as if to himself, that we can't escape, that we won't get a train back for some considerable time. We take our place at the back, and almost at once an official appears and takes us right past the front of the queue. He gestures to us to wait on our own by the tracks, ready to get on first when the train arrives. It seems like a miracle. We look at Emil's cogs, in the middle of the tracks, which made all this possible. Had he singled us out because our party incudes two of Emil Strub's Great Great Granddaughters? Alas, it's her buggy he's noticed.

There's a moment of confusion. We end up running to get to the buggy-friendly compartment at the far end of the train and, in our hurry, my eldest daughter trips on the Strub cog-rack system and has a nasty fall. In the train I wipe oil from her hands and comfort her tears away. My connection to Emil makes me feel special but it's has also caused its fair share of pain.

The train snakes through the Jungfrau back to common sense. People used to think dragons and hobgoblins haunted the Alps, but painters and poets saw it as Sublime. Zurich brides used to insist on a clause in their marriage contract entitling them to an annual trip for their health's sake. Mountaineers saw a chance to dice with death while the rich cheered when they saw a new playground. Climatologists were just as excited when they built laboratories. Perhaps it's a vast mirror—so solid we can throw all of ourselves at it in order to see what comes back at us. I wonder if my mother is scaling her own mountain, only instead of blasting through rock she is using words to blast through the unspeakable parts of her past, wondering if she's brave enough, clever enough, tough enough, resourceful enough.

30

FREQUENTLY ASKED QUESTIONS

Were They Lesbians?

Are You Betraying Your Mothers' Secrets?

Who Needs Fathers Anyway?

Who Needs Families?

Parents Aren't The Whole Story, Are They?

How Much Do You Really Remember
And How Much Are You Making Up?

Is It Ever Right To Keep Silence In A Family?

Is The Past Good For You?

What Good Did A Therapist Ever Do For Anybody?

You're An Anthropologist.
Why Haven't You Written Like One?

What Is It Like Discovering Late In Life
That Half Of You Comes From Another Country?

WERE THEY LESBIANS?

This is the first thing question everyone asks. I didn't expect that. I was prepared for 'What did you miss by not having a man around?' or 'How did you feel about boys as you grew up?' or even 'I expect that means you value friends very highly'. Instead it's always a bed they have their eye on. People want to poke under the blankets and between the sheets with torches and inflamed imaginations. The phrase 'they slept together' used to be a coy way of talking about sex, nothing to do with sleep. I should have been prepared. I had to face it publicly one day. I'd written a couple of articles in *The Guardian* and *The Mail*, and when an invitation to go on *The Richard and Judy Show* came, I saw a chance to say how every child should be wanted, and live secure in the knowledge of where she came from.

As I was writing this I thought I'd see what I'd said that morning in the Manchester TV studio. I search for the video of the recording. When I find it I can't make the machine work until I take the back off the remote and find a yellowish caterpillar of crumbling chemicals which once was a battery. When that's been scraped out and replaced, a woman appears on the screen with a cloud of pre Raphaelite (but black, not burning gold) curls specially installed for the occasion by an expensive hairdresser. I'm wearing a black skirt, and a black Yarrell jacket edged with discreet triangles and squares in apple green, a yolky yellow, red and the fierce purple of a Lenten vestment. My Yarrell top is in the same colours, pure Abstract Expressionism with rushed strokes of paint splashed over a crisp chiffon. It's fortunate that I'm sitting in an arm chair of quiet and quilted grey. In the background, behind a glazed screen, people come and go.

The first shock is that we appear to be talking about two people called Teena and Greeta. I'd forgotten that this was my amateur attempt to disguise their identity. Richard sits one side of me, Judy the other looking demure inside a stunning pink jacket. When I turn from one to the other I move my head quickly, trying to keep up, and my ear rings—tiny acrylic squares of red and yellow—spin beneath my ears like crazed insects.

'So you were brought up by two women who lived together,' Judy says, 'in those days a lot of women did, didn't they, there wasn't necessarily anything remotely sexual about that, men had been killed in the war'. I agree and she continues describing how they'd upped and moved to London and came back saying that together they'd adopted this little baby. I sit nodding and agreeing with every word. We race through my life history and the only surprise was 'So you married the first man you met?' which is true, but I'd never put it so bluntly. I briefly wonder what Richard will make of it.

She continues and yes, they did indeed share a bed but so did most people. Even strangers. I think of our wartime lodgers who came, usually in pairs, some on secret work at Bletchley Park. Each time two complete strangers of the same sex climbed into our spare double bed and slept side by side for the duration. Sometimes men, sometimes women—not both at the same time of course.

She hesitates for a second. Out of the blue it's 'Were they lesbians?'

All the things I'd like to say flash past: 'both fell in love with men, Tyna got married and Bigga had a child'; 'they thought sex was rather amusing but their jokes always included one of one and one of the other'; 'they wouldn't have known the word . . .' But none of this will do. I'm vanquished before I start. No one who hadn't been on 24 hour surveillance for their 17 years together can say categorically what happened between them. And that would include having the stamina to be in their bedroom for more than 6,000 shared nights. But if I protest too much it'll sound as if I think there's something wrong with being a lesbian. I mustn't do that.

'I don't know,' my voice trails away, 'I'm pretty sure they weren't . . . I don't think it matters'. I wish I'd added, 'What's wrong with friendship?'

Judy was right to ask that question and she did it gracefully. It was a programme with the knack of understanding what everyone wants to know and of asking as simply as possible. But I feel angry with the world. After the broadcast I was especially sad to receive a letter from Esmé, the woman who arrived at our house during the Blitz to take shelter with us, bringing her baby son wrapped in blankets and splinters of glass. She loved Bigga. I have a photograph of her as a child, taken long before I was born, her hand in Bigga's at the Clapham Village Show, wearing a panama hat with a blue and silver convent school band just like the one I would wear 20 years later. Now she must be in her eighties and my equivocal answer has distressed her.

As it did several other people. 'Did you know Gertie got engaged but her fiancé died? She was heart-broken,' a friend wrote. Others were protective of Tyna: 'And what about Doris? She married when she was in her 40s. Why should you assume she didn't want to fall in love and marry when she was a young woman? You can't possibly imagine what it was like for a country to have to wait decades to raise another crop of young men to marry the brides of England. Those who should have led your mothers down the aisle were rotting in the fields of mainland Europe'.

There is a famous painting by Henri de Toulouse-Lautrec called *The Bed* which challenges our twenty-first century obsession: sex. The two people he's painted side by side, snuggled deep into pillows and masses of heavy bedding, are somewhere safe, just drifting off. They are sharing a bed for a non-sexual reason: sleep. Which is what most of us do for most of the time we are in bed.

The much-mourned art critic Tom Lubbock wrote brilliantly of this picture: he said that in the past artists had painted some ordinary things like having meals or washing or combing their hair, but when they painted beds they usually had sex—and trouble—in mind. It's likely to be the Bible story of a voluptuous Potiphar's wife trying to seduce a nervous Joseph, or a passing god surprising lovers when they rather hoped he hadn't noticed. If you do see an image of a bed without sexual intent, you'll probably find a solitary figure wanly dying or just plain dead. But in this picture it's different. The artist is asking us to look again at something so tender and personal and mundane that we pass it by.

I think Toulouse Lautrec's painting *The Bed* is about two things every bit as basic as sex, two things you can't live without, two things much less talked about, probably because you can't make money out of them: sleep and friendship.

ARE YOU BETRAYING YOUR MOTHER'S SECRETS?

When I first put together a collage of words and images for my own family, I asked myself that question. I decided that as long as I showed the limited options available to them at the time, they wouldn't be demeaned by my story.

When the possibility of publication came I asked myself again how would they react? Differently. Bigga would enter into the spirit of the thing and enjoy her 15 minutes of fame, coming a century after she was born. And I can imagine Tyna coming out of a press interview at a launch: 'How did it go?' I'd ask. Already she'd have put what she'd said behind her, because the interviewer she'd just met was more important. She'd say 'Oh, he (or she) was such a lovely person, his partner left, you know, and now he takes his little girl horse riding every fortnight and he wants to go on holiday with her . . .' and away we'd go with a brief life history and a sympathetic grasp of the current dilemmas.

What interests me now is the way that our secret—illegitimacy—has been rebranded. In the 1930s it was something so terrible it could cause violence. When Rose Marie's mother became pregnant and was driven out of her home, her brothers went round to Roman's house, and a cup of Earl Grey tea on the lawn was not on their mind. The sinful baby was born secretly at an aunt's house, then given away. Fifty years later this had turned into a sexy story on which I could dine out. Now 'two mothers' is yesterday's story, one of many patterns of co-operative parenting. But shame, like fame, doesn't give up. It slides on its belly seeking whom it may devour. Now we agonise over other things: our body shape or goods and services we can't afford and may not much like, but other people might envy us if we had them.

WHO NEEDS FATHERS ANYWAY?

Even one excluded father casts a long shadow. Out go a whole batch of uncles, aunts, cousins, in laws and grandparents, plus a cargo of genetic data, which now for the first time ever is useful. The fact that some fathers are not up to the job is neither here nor there. To marginalise men is no more morally sustainable than to exclude a different race.

Many single mothers-by-choice have reminded me how much their child benefits from still having a male relative around: a grandfather. But fatherless children will have no generation above to fill the gap for their own children. It can only get worse. We are fast using up a non-sustainable resource: our national capital of stable older couples.

More and more children have a blank space on their birth certificate where their father's name should be, and something like a third of fathers lose contact with their children after a divorce. By giving up fathers are we punching holes in our social structure every bit as lethal in the long run as those ozone holes we didn't use to worry about? What happens to the world if fathers as well as glaciers melt away?

WHO NEEDS FAMILIES?

It is a truth universally acknowledged that a new born baby enters the world as the Ultimate No Mate, who will die within hours without help. Each child is a one-off product individually crafted, demanding intensive care over a long period, with rapidly changing needs. It cannot flourish without some adults—whether or not connected by blood—who will put its interests first and stay with it even when it's tempting to wander off to pastures new.

I believe that there are dozens of ways of making a family, but the inclusive family—with both sexes and other generations around—has something special to offer. At the very least it has a chance of modelling how difference can live together.

But a union based on something as difficult as lifelong support and sexual fidelity doesn't come cheaply. Studies suggest that the glue is more likely to last if the adults make their promises to each other (and the child) in public. The great religions of the world have distinctive sets of rituals and sanctions designed to help, such as colourful naming and blessing ceremonies where the newcomer is welcomed by the wider community.

Parents have no control group to learn from, and no chance of scrapping the product and starting again. When we experiment with new ways of parenting we need to think carefully.

PARENTS AREN'T THE WHOLE STORY, ARE THEY?

Of course not. People outside can turn things round. A vicar's family, a G.P. and a history teacher did it for me.

Looking back I also see how fortunate I was to be cared for by three 'moral communities': a school, a church and a secular college, places where you had a chance of experiencing generosity, courage, confidence and capacity for friendship and love. You find such places everywhere, secular and religious, places where the young are welcome—the extended family, schools, choirs, clinics, clubs for sport, drama, languages, science; groups on politics, the environment and much, much more.

Later I had to renounce some of the things I'd learned—the fundamentalist teenager I became would have difficulty in understanding some aspects of the Christian faith I now have. Healthy families and institutions never stop asking questions and contain within themselves the seeds of change. It was the start of a lifelong journey for which I am deeply grateful.

HOW MUCH DO YOU REMEMBER AND HOW MUCH ARE YOU MAKING UP?

It's a tricky time to be making claims for memory, which is now a bit like a war zone. Research results keep blasting in and destroying what we thought we knew about it. Each time we revisit a memory it goes back into our brain changed, and we swear that the last account is the most accurate.

I based the story as far as possible on artefacts which testify to real events—certificates, letters, minutes, leaflets, cards etc. And a few journals. My writing about Cambridge is reliable, it was a time of introspection, as were my conversion, some therapy sessions and my fortnight alone at Zurich. At no other time have I written systematically. I always intend to keep a journal, I love stationery shops and stroke the satin pages of new notebooks and make resolutions, then after a few entries I lose heart. I never throw my failures away. My 'journals' consist mainly of hand-made fragments written while I'm inside the event, many on the backs of picture postcards bought at the time.

Having said that, I see a difference between 'truth' and 'accuracy'. I believe I'm telling the 'truth', the essence of what happened, because each incident has at its core a white hot emotion wrapped in a fragment of dialogue (or silence) which is still with me. When I can't be accurate about the details of a specific event I make a collage of place and words from memory. I believe we're all specialists in memory. (I don't register makes of cars, for example—all I see are different coloured boxes-on-wheels, some bigger than others). My 'specialism' is fabrics: I can still stroke my first party dress, feel the black fur of a muff I made for Claire when John Yates was consecrated Bishop. Inskip women were seamstresses and lace makers for generations.

But what about childhood conversations? Here I'm helped by Tyna's repetitious and colourful speech patterns. As a child my hands were never dirty, they were 'as black as Newgate's knocker.' Miscreants should be 'shot at dawn for a week.' If anyone walked down the street wearing something unusual Tyna would whisper, 'What sights you see when you haven't got your gun.' If I was being what in Scunthorpe we call 'mardy', Tyna would look at Richard and sweetly ask, 'Is she coming back that way?' We still use some of her juicier sayings.

The only time I have knowingly made something up is when I changed the sequence of events to make a less confusing story. And I've changed some names.

IS IT EVER RIGHT TO KEEP SILENCE IN A FAMILY?

Sometimes it is. When I was a tutor I had a weeping student in my room, a man in his 20s. His parents had just split up and his mother was re-writing history. She rubbished every family holiday, denying she'd enjoyed family celebrations or loved their pets. The student felt he had misread the past so badly, he could no longer trust himself to make sense of life in the here and now. All he could do was adapt and endure. I think the mother needed a new narrative to justify her actions. Some parents are so full of unresolved anger or grief or shame that they use the past to frighten and manipulate their children of all ages. I wish she could have left home without using words to lay waste everything around her.

But sometimes by maintaining silence you can unjustly prevent someone from learning what they need to know. I'd like to say to my mothers, 'What on earth did you think you were doing? Didn't you know that a lifelong silence can be every bit as bad as a lifelong curse?' It was as if the three of us had a stale cracked egg which we passed from one to the other. One wrong move and you might break open. Out would come the putrid smell of decay, matter which should have been dealt with years ago but was left to fester.

I grew up inside a house where lies were not told but left lying around for me to pick up. Swaddled in silence, like any child I did what I could. It was as if I learned not to act, only to watch how I acted, so that I became my own life-long minder.

IS THE PAST GOOD FOR YOU?

It's good for you if you don't use it to stitch up the future. Cicero knew a thing or two when he said *If you do not know where you have come from, you will always be a child,* meaning someone without ability to act fully in the world. Alas, more and more people have their roots cut off either by war and persecution or good intentions, recklessness and bloody-mindedness. There's a word for it: deracination. It's a life sentence.

But perhaps the past should carry a health warning. The fact is that some shocking things make little difference but a minor incident can have shocking repercussions. Adam Phillips points out that we've turned to a belief in trauma as an agent which changes our lives. It turns up when people lose faith in God and character, cause and effect. I think we're tempted to use it because it puts a story, if not a plan, back into modern lives.

Bigga and Tyna did not value the past. They were bent on wiping the slate clean. They tried to live with their eyes closed. Alas, for a time I cast myself as a victim, a role which did me no good whatsoever. Most dangerous of all, you can use the past to take revenge. If you do that, remember the proverb: 'He (and she) who plots revenge had better dig a double grave'.

WHAT GOOD DID A THERAPIST EVER DO FOR ANYBODY?

Like Amazon forests, the best therapists soak up the muck. Not many people do that. They believe nothing is wasted, even despair and depravity and pain. They act as clearing houses for old ideas. They value rival points of view existing inside a person as well as between people. Therapists know that no one has experienced the same changes and challenges as you have.

I went for help at moments of knowing change was inevitable, but not knowing where to find the resources to cope with it. I didn't go because I thought therapists knew a great deal more than I did about the big things of life like sex or death or religion, nor did I look for inspiration or consolation. I wanted a special kind of conversation and behaviour which had a protocol, with clear beginnings and endings. I chose each therapist on personal recommendation (apart from the NHS ones) rather than for the type of therapy practised, and made my own rules about how often we met. All that made me feel safe enough to take risks in living life in a new way.

Only one of my therapists was baleful. Each Tuesday evening when I was going to her group I would get out of the Tube and stand on the platform looking longingly across the rail to where I'd be standing in two hours' time ready to go home. But even she had a silver lining. One Tuesday she backed my impulse to go to Greece and I caught the plane to Athens on the Friday. Thus began a life-long passion for that country, especially Symi, an island we visit every year.

One of the people to whom this book is dedicated is Dr David Zigmond, the therapist I met through the cardiac episode and who was my virtual companion throughout the search for my parents. Now I see him rarely but he is still an important (absent) presence in my life.

Also, since childhood, women and men in church congregations and communities have brought me courage, healing and inspiration—but this question is not about them.

YOU'RE AN ANTHROPOLOGIST. WHY HAVEN'T YOU WRITTEN LIKE ONE?

Oh, I've been so sorely tempted to help the child along as she tells her story. For example in Chapter 7 I describe the Lowestoft street where Tyna lived with Jack, a long street of small semi-detached houses and a few bungalows with hardly a fridge or freezer between them. Trawler men came home from a stint at sea with large canvas bags of fish, far more than their families could eat. In the not-very-affluent 50s an elaborate system of gift exchange had developed: back and forth went fish, home grown fruit and vegetables, errands, hair dressing, dog walking, knitting patterns, child minding, loans of tools.

'Look, look,' I wanted to say, 'See how 'gifts' aren't allowed to become inert, to sit on the mantelpiece like a reproachful unreciprocated Christmas card. Everyone knew in Kimberley Road that gifts must always be on the move. Whatever's given is supposed to be given away again. It doesn't have to go back to the same person and needn't be comparable in the short term.' Then I'd be tempted to go on with, 'Now that reminds me of the sea-faring Tikopia who risked life and limb in gift exchange, crossing treacherous seas in their canoes—and some rural Irish communities where to settle up your bill with the grocer would be an insult. It's a way of keeping relationships open and sound . . .'

But I keep quiet. Such a switch would drown out the child's voice. But making the decision was a powerful reminder that the self that finds expression in autobiography is a fictive construct.

I also tried to make sure that, as in a TV Makeover show, I had a skip on the lawn into which I could tip at least some of my here's-how-to-make-the-world-a-better-place words . . . I doubt if even a charity shop would want them.

WHAT IS IT LIKE DISCOVERING LATE IN LIFE THAT HALF OF YOU COMES FROM ANOTHER COUNTRY?

Confusing. The first time we crossed the border to camp on the edge of Lake Thun, I got out of the car, put my foot down on Swiss soil and just managed not to kneel down and kiss the grass. The scenery, the silence, the efficiency were breath-taking. I fell in love with Switzerland. Its people could do no ill, its history was a brilliant tour de force. In 1991 I bought Tinguely's mad splashy poster celebrating 600 years of union and local democracy in a country which has to bind together four languages and two religions in a terrain blessed with impassable mountains and harsh winters. Can anyone beat that? She has bred philanthropists, theologians, psychologists, engineers, architects, artists and mathematicians who changed the world—though most had to move out of Switzerland to do so. And educationalists. Most city streets and squares are spiked with lofty statues of generals, admirals, law makers, kings and emperors. But outside Zurich station in *Bahnhofstrasse* is a tender, gentle statue of a man, Johann Heinrich Pestalozzi, caring for a young child.

Now I'm more measured. I see Switzerland as a rich aunt, beautiful, courteous, efficient, remote, eccentric and impervious to mockery. Although dozens of generations of ancestors went into my making, she cannot and never will acknowledge me. She occupies international space and moves round the world as smoothly as walking from the lounge to the dining room, soaking up languages and cultures as she goes. She also knows that the needs of her family will be amply covered. Like the air we breathe, there will always be more than enough to go round. Alas it's one of my less appealing habits to worry about the cost of everything from a bag of tomatoes to a paperback. My default position is not 'Do I want it?' but 'Can I do without it?' But Switzerland is not an aunt who will ever do me any favours: she cannot and never will acknowledge me. She lets me ramble around her beautiful estate freely, like any other tourist, provided I pay my way.

Acknowledgement

Warmest thanks to my son Aidan for writing the last chapter, and my son-in-law Cliff for handling the illustrations and designing the cover.

I also know that without Claire's encouragement over many years, Richard's patience, Nora's critique and the interest of Susannah, Sara and Chris I might not have persevered.

And without Dr David Zigmond my journey of discovery may not even have started.

5632917R00228

Printed in Great Britain
by Amazon.co.uk, Ltd.,
Marston Gate.